Marriage Made Simple
A Couples Course, Written by a Guy for Guys, with Guys in Mind

All rights reserved. Published in the United States
by Keys4 Life Publishing, Omaha, Nebraska.

Grateful acknowledgment is made to the following for permission
to reprint previously published material:
All Scripture quotations are from the New American Standard
Bible, Holman Publishers, La Habra, CA: Foundation Publications,
for the Lockman Foundation, (1971) unless otherwise stated.

Cover art and design by Lisa Hainline, Lions Gate Book Design
Library of Congress Cataloging-in-Publication Data
Johnson, James G.
Marriage Made Simple / James G. Johnson
ISBN 978-0-9853317-2-6
ISBN eBook 978-0-9853317-3-3
ISBN Study Guide 978-0-9853317-4-0
Marriage & Family. 2. Counseling, self-help, Christian living

www.drjamesgjohnson.org
www.drjamesgjohnson.org/marriagemadesimple
www.keys4-life.org

Printed in the United States of America

DEDICATED WITH MY HEART:

Cheryl

"My Beloved ... my friend"
Song of Solomon 5:16

Endorsements

"IF you have the courage to open and read this book, it will change you, and you will be forever grateful.

Marriage Made Simple flows from the pen of a man who has learned to overcome difficulties by facing life head-on. Dr. James Johnson lives and teaches a grace-oriented approach to marriage. He delivers what you need — hope to confront and overcome your marital challenges and to restore fractured relationships in every arena of your life. Jim's experience as a coach helps him relate to men. He'll direct and encourage you to obtain and practice important life skills. This book will reorient you and recharge your energy and passion for a fruitful marriage."

Dr. Wendell Nelson
Pastor of Counseling and Spiritual Formation,
Christ Community Church, Omaha, Nebraska
Board of Trustees, Crown College, Saint Bonifacius, Minnesota

"I HAVE read your book! Yeah! And I LOVE it! What I like best about the book is it's incredibly conversational, easy to read, and full of rich, deep stuff.

Dr. Johnson uses analogies and word pictures that make practical interactions so accessible. It is easy to grasp what he is conveying."

Julie Sibert
Wife, Mom, Therapist, National Author and Speaker
www.intimacyinmarriage.com

"I HAVE known Jim for several years. While I was a pastor at Faith Bible Church in Glendale, AZ, overseeing adult ministries, Jim was teaching some classes. I also referred people to Jim as a counselor.

Jim has a special heart and giftedness in helping people. I have seen his counseling heal the lives of individuals and marriages. I consider Jim a personal friend and am always uplifted when we have the opportunity to speak. He has a practical biblical approach to the situations of life and is a gifted leader and teacher.

If you are considering participating in an event that Jim is leading, I highly recommend your attendance. He has a way to transmit God's message that you will be able to understand and apply. If you have the opportunity to have Jim coach you personally, I believe your life will be changed for the better in ways you can't even imagine.

I fully support Jim in his ministry efforts. I believe he has a great impact for God's Kingdom with the people he serves. I welcome anyone to contact me if they would like to discuss further."

Joe Gee
Pastoral Leader and Counselor
623-205-6099
joegatfbcaz@gmail.com

"BIBLICALLY accurate, inspiring, challenging and authentic — that's Jim Johnson and the Ministry of Keys4. This seminar is not an event, this is an encounter that left us with not only changed lives and marriages, but also with the sweet fruit of a changed church. Jim is an authentic person commissioned by God who gets in underneath the Christian leader to lift up and add value and quality to every area of that church or ministry. It's like having lunch with a friend and the Holy Spirit is speaking right to you, seeing right through you, touching your very soul.

Steve and Debbie Davidson,
Senior Pastor and Seminar Participant

"DR. James G. Johnson walks you through the trials of marital communication, and presents a unique perspective on God's plan for marriage.

As you read *Marriage Made Simple*, you will learn new ways to "DETOX" your communication and bring your marriage to a new level of peace and joy. As you process the information within this book, you will be taken step by step through the five levels of communication that will move you from Clichés or small talk through Shop Talk to a level you may have never dreamed possible, Trust Talk. This is where you learn to speak your spouse's love language, and are able to share with each other from the heart.

I recommend this book to everyone, whether you are a seasoned communication expert, or a person looking to heighten his relationship and gain understanding of how to live a Marriage that is Made Simple."

Jeff and Angie Davis
Marriage Mentors

"MY husband and I took the *Marriage Made Simple* class through our church as part of our premarital counseling. We learned how to love and respect each other with God at the center. We use what we learned in the conference daily and it has greatly helped us to reduce the number of silly arguments we have. We are able to better understand each other and how and why we respond to things the way we do. We are so thankful to Jim Johnson and the *Marriage Made Simple* conference for helping our marriage start off right and continue the way God wants us to."

Shawn and Erica Fewell
Seminar Participants

"IF I could recommend only one marriage counselor, it would be DrJ. Jim has a genuine heart for couples struggling to make their marriage work. His passion for coming alongside to help is unmatched. He offers simple yet practical steps to enable couples to gain insight into how we are wired so differently then uses this insight as a gradual launching place to grace each other with renewed respect. His admonition to 'speak kind words' to each other is one of the things that continues to resonate with me and still convicts me daily.

Evi and Steve Fulford
Business Owners and Conference Participants

Acknowledgments

As I published my first book, *Grace: Orphans No More*, I quickly realized it wasn't about how smart I was but more about relying on others far more competent than me. The same holds true for *Marriage Made Simple*. Here is my opportunity to thank so many who made this happen.

Cheryl, you are my best friend and life companion. Unknowingly, unwittingly, perhaps unwillingly at times, most of this was grown in the laboratory of our own marriage. You have been my testing ground, my proving ground as well as my greatest encouragement. Thank you, sweetie. We prove together, this stuff really works. I love you with all my heart.

I also wish to appreciate my family — Brent, Jeremiah, Monica, Cory, Kristin and our littlest "Minion," grandson "Action Jaxon." He is one of my teachers as he unfolds so much about life through his eyes and wonderment — "I'm just fweee, Papa."

Cheryl and I are incredibly grateful to our administrative assistant, Sue (and her husband, George) DeCelle. Without the two of you, this project wouldn't have happened. You have kept me on course and clarified thoughts, ideas and principles countless times. Literally, I believe you may know this material better than I do.

I also appreciate our editor, Pauly (and her husband, Alan) Heller. You have taught me much about writing, letting me look over your shoulder at the sea of red corrections you make for me. Marriage counselors and mentors for 30-plus years in your own right, your thoughts, comments, encouragements and corrections have been priceless.

I would like to extend honors to John and Rhonda Riva. Without question or doubt, this book would not have happened without you. John, you especially never gave up. You have been such an amazing idea man, "techy" and "garage talk" friend.

In addition, many thanks are extended to those who carefully read or participated in the "raw" material: Shawn and Erica Fewell, Steve and Evi Fulford, Ramon and Angela Lago, Jeff and Angie Davis.

Thank you, Frank and Judy Gerald, for your incredible encouragement and support. Thank you, Rick and Kimberly Mumma, for your constant encouragement as well.

And to all of the 50 participants in the live recording of the original material, I cannot possibly compose enough "thank you" notes to share what you have meant to me. You gave up so much of your time to help produce the video series. To the class and pastors at Faith Bible Church, Cheryl and I extend our appreciation as well.

Finally, special honors and thanks to our dear friends Pastor Joe and Cheryl Gee. Joe, I know you well remember the afternoon of March 15, 2013, as Cheryl and I sat in your office. That day, this project was brainstormed and launched with your incredibly amazing support and wisdom. You are such an encouragement. Your vision was behind it all. Thank you for loving Cheryl and me.

Gratefully,

Dr. James G. "Jim" Johnson
Omaha, Nebraska
www.drjamesgjohnson.org

Foreword

I HAVE been counseling and coaching individuals and couples in crisis for more than 35 years. My wife, Pauly, and I have led couples communication workshops since 1984 and together co-authored *The Marital Mystery Tour* (AMFM Press) in 2008. We know what it's like to sit face-to-face with a couple sweating out a tough issue in the counseling office. And we know what it's like to stand in front of an audience hoping to connect with people in a marriage seminar.

We were both part of Dr. James Johnson's test audience when he was compiling the concepts and visual aids for his *Marriage Made Simple* conference. I saw and heard firsthand the straightforward and simple way Jim puts his ideas across.

Jim designed *Marriage Made Simple* (*MMS*) to speak specifically to men. He understands how much guys dislike sitting in long sessions talking about marriage in ways that make them feel undressed in front of all the other couples in an audience. He knows that men want books they read to be direct and to the point. And he understands how much a man wants to be a winner in his wife's eyes. So in *MMS*, he gives you practical tips and tools to help you live with your wife as a champion. As a man speaking to men (and their wives), he's put the cookies on a shelf we can reach. And he knows how much we like cookies.

And cars ... and mechanical things ... and sports ... and movies ... and peace and quiet ... and one concept at a time.

That is what you get in *Marriage Made Simple*. It's an easily digestible smorgasbord of ways to live with your wife, as Scripture says, in an "understanding way." Jim uses illustrations a man can relate to, whether the topic is sex, communication, identifying your feelings or just understanding your differences as a man and a woman. Jim "tells on himself," giving stories from his own life — he's spent a lot of time in his garage — and from his decades of counseling and coaching experience.

Dr. J will help you drive for a slam-dunk marriage. He speaks from his unique point of view as a counselor and a regular guy, in a way that refreshes and causes you to think about how you can make your marriage meaningful and exciting. I commend this book to you and your wife to read and talk about together, and so you can keep that "new car smell" for life.

Alan Heller, president
Walk & Talk Counseling
Phoenix, Arizona
www.walkandtalk.org
alan@walkandtalk.org

And The Last Word

Most of us know how difficult it is for a woman to let her husband have the last word, so I'm compelled by my membership in the sisterhood of wives to add my two cents to Alan's Foreword.

Here's the thing, ladies. Even though Jim has focused this book on husbands, he's not exactly letting us wives off the hook here. He gives us all, husbands and wives, plenty to mull over as we consider how his concepts apply to our marriage. Maybe he's using terms like "Bent Bearings" and "Barricades" and "Auto Shop," but he's still addressing our need to be good listeners and to understand how our husbands' minds work and to not press them into overload by flooding them with too much information at once.

You have a job to do, too, and part of it involves reading this book along with your husband and waiting as he processes the information he receives from it. Jim has done his best to keep his delivery of some heavy content light and fun for you and your guy. I know he'd like you to keep your discussions of the material in that same tone, even if your marriage is in need of a lot of repair.

Here's the thing: Alan and I are communication "experts." We've led hundreds of couples through the process of learning the same types of skills Jim presents in this book. We've heard from couples years later, "Thank you! We're still using those skills. They've helped us so much!"

Yet does that mean we have perfect communication or that we never argue? No, of course not! It just means that we know how and when to sit down together and talk things through to get resolution and to repair the damage we do to our relationship and to reaffirm our love for each other.

Which reminds me, be sure to read all the way through to Jim's material on unforgiveness and forgiveness. This is where we make or break our relationships. This is where we decide if we want to build our house on the sand or on the solid rock. And no matter how it feels in the moment, no matter what your guy has done, no matter how much it hurts, you hold the power to make your own life (and his) miserable or to allow the Lord to flood you with His healing grace.

Read the book. Jim will show you how to do it right ... together ... simply.

Pauly Heller, co-founder
Walk & Talk, Inc.
heller.pauly@gmail.com

CONTENTS

CONTENTS   12
Introduction   13
Chapter 1: Marriage 911   16
Chapter 2: Batteries and Chargers   33
Chapter 3: Good, Bad, and Ugly   50
Chapter 4: Aliens and Strangers   64
Chapter 5: Bent Bearings   82
Chapter 6: Barricades and Barriers   95
Chapter 7: Super Glue   109
Chapter 8: Auto Shop   125
Chapter 9: Luxury Ride   137
Chapter 10: New Car Smell   152
Chapter 11: Detox Your Talk   166
Chapter 12: Couple(d) Talk   179
Chapter 13: Road Rage — Managing Anger   190
Chapter 14: Destinations and Stoplights   202
Chapter 15: Mapping Compromise   210
Chapter 16: Rearview Mirrors — Forgiving   222
Appendix I: Choosing a Good Counselor   236
Appendix II: 1 Corinthians 13   237
Appendix III: Hearing the Voice of God   238
Appendix IV: Additional Couple(d) Talk   242
About the Author   243

INTRODUCTION

THE TITLE of this book is an oxymoron. Anyone who has been married more than a couple of minutes knows that there is nothing at all simple about marriage. My favorite verse in pre-marital counseling is 1 Corinthians 7:28: "let not many of you get married for in doing so you will have great trouble." In fact, marriage is not easy or simple; it can be very complex and cause many struggles. According to one well-known author, about 187 books and programs are available to couples who want to make their marriage better. With all that potential input, I think most people feel overwhelmed at the idea of fixing their marriage.

After watching my own failures then trying to help many others who struggle, I kept thinking there ought to be some basic, simple principles that can help couples succeed in marriage. From personal experience as a pastor, counselor, and life coach, and most importantly as a husband, I identified some basic, common ground rules that, if used well, could translate into marital success. Almost everything you will read has been worked through the fabric of Cheryl's and my marriage. In other words, I don't speak an inch beyond my own experience.

Using a word picture, marriage is like driving a car. Most of us learn to drive as teenagers. We drive from point A to point B, sometimes in short, local jaunts, sometimes cross-country. We have different cars, different roads, and different destinations. But every one of us obeys a set of certain rules to get us there safely.

One such obvious rule in the United States: Drive on the right-hand side of the road, because the left side is for oncoming traffic. Disregarding this simple rule has disastrous consequences. Violating rules — for example, running red lights or stopping at green lights — also not such good ideas.

Just as basic rules of the road apply to driving a car, so it is with maneuvering a marriage through the highways and back roads of life.

Marriage Made Simple addresses sixteen basic rules of the road that I believe bring success to every aspect of a marriage relationship.

First, guys, I wrote this for us. Very few marriage books are written for guys; most are aimed primarily toward women. We know from statistics that when it comes to greeting cards and marriage books, 85 percent are purchased by women. The prevailing theory is that ladies buy a book or card, set it by the remote (or toilet) and hope their husband reads it.

So I intentionally designed *Marriage Made Simple* to be for guys, written by a guy, with guys in mind. I think we men need to know the basics, how to make the engine work, so to speak. So I have tried to appeal to the "bro code" and write in a way that allows us guys to see the real issues.

In addition, most of us approach marriage with the general idea that it should come naturally. You recite your, "I do's," then you move on. I wish it were that easy.

But the truth of the matter is that human relationships are very complicated. Our spouses have a great need to hear "I do" often, hear it said differently and hear it said well. Marriage doesn't come naturally. In fact it is really pretty alien at times (see Chapter 4, "Aliens and Strangers"), but it doesn't have to be.

Finally, I learned over many years that the primary problem in marriage is not in our mind; it is in our heart. Meaning, I need to start with my relationship with God and allow Him to work through my marriage to teach me about Himself and my own selfishness. The greatest surprise to me was that even after all my academic degrees, training and experience, most of my marriage conflicts were about my selfishness. God was using my marriage to show me those areas I had not taken captive to the Lordship of Christ.

Throughout this book, I will be using a contrast model between the self-centered, self-focused mindset and the unselfish, committed-to-one-another mindset to help contrast the motives behind what we do. To this end, no other being has exemplified and modeled this unselfish mindset like Jesus Christ. It is to Him that we need to turn. He created us, He knows us intimately and He knows what we need to learn. I would go so far as to say, marriage is not so much about two people as it is a reflection of unconditional love. But that statement is not my original idea. The Apostle Paul said it after he taught the marriage course in Ephesians chapter 5, saying, "But the mystery is great for I am speaking of Christ and the Church."

Marriage is one of two primary relationships that teach us what real love looks like, and that involves learning "the mind of Christ."

Gratefully given to His Glory,

Dr. James G. Johnson
Executive Director, Keys4-Life Counseling
Omaha, Nebraska
September 2015

CHAPTER 1: MARRIAGE 911

"Be kind to each other, tenderhearted, forgiving one another, just as God through Christ has forgiven you."

—Ephesians 4:32

ONE day a woman, who was never one of the brightest bulbs on the tree if you get my drift, had a kitchen fire and in the emergency called 911. When the operator answered she said, "Help! I have a fire! Please send help!" The operator, trained in calmness, said, "Ma'am, let us know how to get there." The woman replied, "You have to come quickly! There is a fire in my kitchen."

"Ma'am, before we can respond we have to know how to get where you are." Now frantic, the woman yelled, "The fire is all over the stove! There is smoke everywhere!"

A bit frustrated, the operator said firmly, "Ma'am, you have to tell us how to get to you; how do we get to your home?"

To which the woman replied, "Well, duh! The big red truck!"

In marriage we all have those times when we so wish we could call for the big red truck.

Like all relationships, marriage has those pressure-building moments, when the heat is rising, when our chest is tight, when we feel empty inside, when we are so frustrated we're just done ... done talking, done listening, done, done and so done! Not only sick of the discussion but sick of arguing altogether. And our spouse seems to be enjoying the debate. So it builds.

There oughta be a button, a horn, a life jacket, or a can of "shut the fat up" that we could just open to make it all go away. Or, why can't there be at least a phone number to call for help? A marriage 911 dispatcher who'd answer and say the big red truck is coming; help is on the way. But sadly for thousands of those relationships, help never arrives. And many others stop thriving and just surrender to surviving.

Well, God in His wisdom actually did provide a marriage 911 button. My wife, Cheryl, and I accidentally discovered this secret while hiking one day. Actually most of the solutions in this book came from the context of Cheryl and I relating to each other. It was there in a very simple phrase when she said, "Why don't we just ...?"

Wait, I've gotten ahead of myself. Let's do some background work about guys and women.

Guys enter marriage with some very particular ideas. Do you think fairy tales are just for girls? Most guys' basic idea of marriage is something like a headline from *The Storybook Gazette*: "Hero Slays Dragon and Rescues Princess." The End. Men are goal-oriented. Kill the dragon; get the girl. So we're all about the relationship until we've solved it then off to the next task.

Women come to marriage with a completely different fairy tale in mind. They want their knight in shining armor to settle down for happily ever after. So conflict reigns from the outset. He enters the castle with one set of expectations and she brings along another. The knight in shining armor slays the dragon, he rescues the princess, and then he is off to do what the knight code says he should do. Slay another dragon! And if he has some sense of integrity — which we hope he does — it's not to get another princess, right?

Meanwhile, the newlywed Mrs. Knight, our princess, realizes her knight belches, farts, and leaves his shining armor scattered all over the bedroom floor. He drinks from the milk carton, doesn't wash his hands, and cradles his remote or video game like his long lost best friend.

Guys come to marriage thinking she'll never change and she does. Women come to marriage thinking she can change him and he doesn't.

So things begin to change, and happily ever after isn't happening so happily as male and female expectations begin to collide and seek resolution. The resentment of disappointed hopes begins to build. Then one day as he is playing his video game sipping his favorite drink, she steps from nowhere to deliver a boot to the back of his head.

Let's see if we can figure this out. Then we'll apply some "rules of the road" to keep us from head-on collisions.

First of all, men and women are so incredibly different that it is almost impossible for a "new driver" to understand the dynamics that go on between couples. Let's build that out.

Dr. James Dobson underscores these differences in his book *Bringing Up Boys*.[1] Did you know that all of us start out as girls? In the seventh week following conception, we boy embryos got washed in utero with testosterone, which changed us from having two X chromosomes (XX, like our female counterparts) to having XY. Now that would be good and fine except that in the process of that wash, the connecting links between the left and right brain became severed or damaged.

So, guys, this is what I tell my wife: "Honey, I'm brain damaged." It is not fair. How can I perform to her expectations with that kind of deficit?

One consequence for guys is linear, goal-oriented thought patterns. Men come with a sense that we're simply going to tie a knot and run down a string to tie another knot then move down the string. Men fix problems one at a time. Women, on the other hand, enter marriage with neural connections running everywhere. They multi-task. Instead of a simple knot-and-string sort of thing, female brains are like a spider web that goes from here to there, then way over there and back again. Women can drop back and reverse and pass and run and catch the ball while holding a conversation on a cell phone. We guys don't process those things as quickly as women do.

Meanwhile, we come with brain-damaged thoughts: "I don't think I can take this anymore; it's just too much." Men come to marriage dealing with life differently.

There's more. That testosterone wash also has other things for XY's. We find it hard to be in touch with our emotions. We don't really know what we are feeling. We don't think in terms of "how do I feel about that." We find it hard to separate feelings from the mix of everything else going on. We basically have three emotions: mad ... pumped ... sad ... and maybe hungry. Add — get this — not only is it hard for us to know WHAT we're feeling, it is also hard for us to verbally SHARE

---

[1] James C. Dobson, *Bringing Up Boys*, (Wheaton:Tyndale House, 2001).

those emotions when asked. It's hard to tell our wives how we feel, what we think, how we reason, what we understand in terms of how we feel about them. And guess what? Your wife is passionate about WHAT you're feeling. Because that tells her, she is important to you. She knows you don't share your feelings with just anyone.

So our wives ask, "What are you feeling?"

We shrug. "I don't know."

"What are you thinking?" they say.

"I'm not sure," we reply.

"Well, what is going on in your brain?"

"I just need be alone right now."

What I'm feeling and how to share that just takes some work. I have a hard time communicating the things that I am feeling, and I am a marriage professional!

OK, sorry, but it gets worse. When they talk, women use about 22,000 to 25,000 words every single day. Men come to the table with about 5,000 to 7,000. That means they can out-talk us 3 or 4 to 1. It's the thimble versus the wash bucket. In my job, I do a lot of listening and talking. So by the time I get home, I want to just sit there and stare straight ahead like the walking dead.

In the meantime, our wives have been dealing with whatever job, juggling with children in the home, or people outside the home — for Cheryl and me, it's a one-year-old grandson. My wife is ready to talk. She says stuff like, "How was your day? How are you doing? What are you thinking? Who did you talk to?" I am in "Overload Mode"! I can't take anymore! I am literally out of words! My thimble-sized talking allotment is over the top. I can't take it, and she still has a bucketful to say. This talking imbalance sets up some really rough feelings.

This is just the beginning of differences in marriage. There are more than 30 male/female differences, 16 personality types (175 combinations), love versus respect, five different love languages, givers versus takers, multiple communication styles, multiple differences in emotions, forgiveness issues, resentment building, original family impact, and differences in attachment, just to name a few. Add to these the real killer —

pride or selfishness — and it's like one person said to me, "Dude, this is messed up." And then couples believe they can work through all this without any help. They rely on resilience and hope. When those run out, they are done.

Now we are going to really jack it up. Enter "the insane game," which works like this: I say something to Cheryl stating an issue of importance to me with very little emotion. I'm considering the conversation to be a basic "level 1." But kind of like betting in poker, my wife hears what I say, and based on experience or present irritation I've given her, she thinks, "Huh, that's a little irritating. I'll see your 1 and raise you 1."

"Level 2" emotion begins. I know what she means, so I assume and see her 2 and raise it another 2. Now at "level 4," I reply with my unkind abrupt response, and she then raises me another 2 in her voice and body language.

We are at 6 and this baby starts to spin. Pretty soon a couple is raising 5 and 10 at a time and they are in a meltdown. Play the game several times and now we raise in multiples. Bam! Doors slam, people hurt, and a sinister voice says, "And thank you for playing our game."

Two broken people. She has been trying to connect, and I've been trying to figure out peace and quiet. And we have totally alienated each other. It's called polarizing. Marriage from the corners.

THE QUESTION IS NOT, WHY DO SO MANY MARRIAGES BREAK UP?

THE QUESTION REALLY IS, HOW DO THE GOOD ONES SURVIVE?

The Apostle Paul said it plainly, "But if you marry, you have not sinned ... yet such will have much trouble in this life."[2]

So here comes that first principle: **How to dial 911 immediately in all situations.** Remember my hike with Cheryl? God in His wisdom provided a marriage 911 button for us. It was there in a very simple phrase when she said, "You know what? We just need to be KIND to each other."

I thought, *Wow! She's right!* So we started walking and talking, being very intentional and specifically kind. We were taking care of each other. Even though we still hadn't resolved things, we just started being kind and it made a difference. It was so amazing what happened. I felt better about her and I felt better about me. The kindness stuck the rest of the day and into the week. We were being kind. And then something else happened. We found we were building a reserve of being kind rather than being harsh. We were building kindness upon kindness.

It's like this. Imagine you get distracted in your car. Before long you're on the shoulder and it's rough and then onto the bank which is rougher still. Pretty soon you're in the ditch and now it's really bouncing. Then you hit a major hole and everyone is being thrown about.

Similarly, when you fill your marriage with negative comments you both get distracted and the going starts getting bumpy or rough; you're upset and she's upset. The "car" is filled with bad feelings and resentment. As you start behaving kindly to each other, you start moving back to the smooth pavement. This doesn't happen instantly, but gradually you make your way back up the ditch. Things slowly feel better. As you continue moving out of the ditch, the positive takes over the negative; you begin to relax more, and the ride becomes more enjoyable.

Imagine a straight line like the track in a sliding windowpane. Picture the window sliding back and forth day by day. Call that window "short-term memory." You can fill that window with negative remembrances, angry thoughts, and bitterness. Dirt and stones fill the track, and the sliding door gets stuck. Your marriage also gets stuck and eventually will break. But you have the choice to clean out the track and fill it with posi-

---

[2] 1 Corinthians 7:28.

tive images, kind thoughts, patience, and forgiveness. Then over time the window slides smoothly again.

So no matter what intensity level you've reached in your conversation — maybe she is up at 20, or 15 or 6.2, or 7.8 on the Marital Richter Scale — you can "dial" marriage 911, and suddenly it will start dropping toward a 1.

How do you do that? It's a choice. You choose to want to be kind. You choose to be polite. You take the time to touch her heart rather than try to win your point. Marriage 911 is choosing to recolor the events in your sliding window with the tint of kindness.

Kindness Defined

Kindness is an action we do based on giving value to another. In the Bible, the word for kindness comes from the Greek word CHRESTOS meaning "fit for use, or measuring up." Basically it means, be polite. Kindness is a statement of importance, meaning or value. It says, "You are special to me, you are important to me, you matter."

When we value someone, we practice many things like:

* Not assuming the worst.
* Extending acceptance without precondition.
* Choosing to be loving whether or not we think the other person deserves it at the moment.
* Politely slowing down when we speak.
* Listening, without trying to "fix" the other person. Without interrupting, really hearing the heart. Looking into the other's eyes instead of away.
* Trusting another's motives without pre-deciding he or she is incorrect or wrong.
* Being sensitive to the other's feelings, and considerate of his or her hurts or issues.

Caring Words and Actions

We show kindness to our spouse through our words and our actions. I'm troubled by how often, once we get married, we guys stop being the polite person we were when we were dating. For instance, do you still open doors and hold chairs? Stand when your valued wife leaves the restaurant table?

We really set ourselves up during the dating process by being so polite, holding chairs, opening doors, using our best manners, doting. Then after a year or so of marriage things begin to change. Early on, if she coughs, we might say, "Oh, honey, are you OK? Can I get you a glass of water? Should I go to the pharmacy and get you something for that cough? Can I make you some soup?"

After five years, it's more like, "Sounds like you've got a cough. You better get up and get some water."

Ten years go by, and we're saying, "Hey, you should do something about that cough; you sound like a baby seal and I can't hear my show."

Eventually, we don't even respond at all. Kindness is more than being polite; it is actually communicating "You are valuable to me."

Here is a suggestion that has caused tears in some of my marriage coaching sessions. Gentlemen, get a calendar and mark your wife's menstrual cycle. She will run about 28 days. Count from the first day she starts to the first day she starts again. Do not count from when she starts to when she ends, too confusing. Ask her to help you, she doesn't mind. Picture this. She gains water as her body prepares to ovulate. She bloats like she could float a small boat. She cramps and she has headaches. She will lose a lot of blood and can be anemic. She can't go too far from the bathroom and lives in fear she might leak. Oh, but it gets better. On about day 13 or so, her hormones will go from kitty to tiger, from wanting to be cuddled to ripping your face off. Kindness gets it. Kindness marks the calendar and watches over his wife. We as men and women watch over each other. Kindness protects each other.

Listening

Listening is both an art and a skill. It's not talking over the other person. It requires willingness to hear what the other one is saying, to reflect (or repeat) back to your partner some of the things that he or she has said to you that may hurt or cause you to feel defensive. Reflecting back means that instead of answering with your own response, you say simply what you have heard the other person say.

It goes something like this: "What I heard you say to me just now was this...." There is a sense of teamwork, of both of you listening together, hearing the other person out, and being willing to not be thinking about your own argument in response. It's more than just waiting for the other person to stop talking so you can belt them with your one-two punch in reply. Instead, you have a sense of actively wanting to understand what the other person is saying, even if it hurts and you're "itchin' for a fight." Listening means "I sincerely want to hear what you are feeling about this. Talk to me, share with me, and help me know you better."

Do you want a key to this? Watch yourself. Are you looking at your spouse's eyes or just her face? Is she a person? Or just an object?

Body Language

Another telling factor in flushing out kindness is what we communicate non-verbally. Research since the early 1970s has clearly identified that our actual words (their literal meaning) account for 7 percent of the overall message we communicate.

Amazingly, 38 percent of our overall message is in tone and inflection, while a whopping 55 percent of the overall message is communicated through body language. Arms folded, legs turned away, rolling of eyes, squinting in reaction, all "speak" non-verbally. A big one here is acting bored, or not being attentive, playing with the remote, looking away; all communicate that the other person has little value. Learn to communicate value before you even say a word.

Not Fixing People before Hearing Their Hurt

"Fixing" is a common dynamic in marriage because we guys love to fix things. You have a problem; I need to fix you. We love having problems to solve. Nothing drives us nuts like the "DTR" discussion (Discuss the Relationship). WE CAN'T FIX IT. Remember linear sequential "just give me the facts" solutions. Often, wives just need to come and share with us the issues they are facing. Did you know that we guys are designed to be burden bearers? We bear burdens. We fix things. When we try to fix something and it doesn't work, it drives us nuts.

Imagine a wife dealing with a toddler's diapers, and man, he is packing a load; diarrhea stinky mess everywhere. She is feeling emotionally overwhelmed. All she wants is a little bit of help, maybe just a listening ear and some emotional support. She sits on the couch, sighs, and says to her husband, "You wouldn't believe the mess back there."

He starts to give her his "helpful" checklist: "Well, hon, you need to do this, you need to do that, and have you tried such-and-such?"

You know what, guys? She does not need you to tell her how to deal with diarrhea. What she needs is for you to just listen. Something that I learned in my own marriage is that Cheryl does not need me to fix her. She wants me to hear what she is saying.

Not Assuming the Worst

Assuming the worst is so much fun! We like to go to extremes in imagining our spouse's worst possible actions or motives. But for the health of your marriage, you need to expect the best! You need to remember that your spouse truly is a kindhearted person.

I like to ask my clients, "Would you trust your child to your spouse?" Inevitably they answer, "Absolutely, I would!"

I follow up with, "Is your spouse generally a good person, kindhearted with others?"

"Yes, absolutely, he/she is!"

So then, you need to assume that your spouse remains a good, kindhearted person with you as well, and not assume the worst of him or her. Basically, kindness or ascribing value to someone brings you back to the feelings you had when first dating each other. For me and my relationship with Cheryl, kindness has been the reminder to never stop dating my spouse.

Touching

Kindness is also revealed in touch. I have many years of experience in marriage counseling and working with people from all over the country. I've discovered that many people who have been married a few years start putting some physical distance between themselves. They express it in the way they touch and hold each other. Often at their first counseling appointments, a couple will start out sitting with their legs crossed, chairs facing away from each other.

Here's an example of a classic case: After going through several coun-seling sessions, this couple comes to me and they sit, stiff as mannequins, at least six feet apart. I think, "Are these two married? Do they even know each other?" I see so much anger, so much bitterness, so much striving.

So I say to the husband, "Why don't you just hold her hand for a second? Why don't you just touch her arm?"

I've watched men and women break down in tears because it has been so long since they felt a kind touch from their spouse. Like dry-baked hard earth that's been in desperate need of rain, they spring forth with all sorts of new life. Just on a touch. Learn to spend some time holding hands, touching, rubbing each other's shoulder, tickling and the stuff you used to do when you were dating. And guys, playful hitting by a girl is a good thing. You can tell when she is meaning to hurt or not. Basically never stop dating.

The Golden Nine

When you talk with an EMT or someone involved as an emergency medical provider, you might hear them mention "the golden nine." Sta-tistics have shown that reaching a person involved in an accident within the first nine minutes gives them the greatest percentage of chances for survival.

Marriage 911 — this is where we start. Stop assuming the worst. Start touching. Start treating your wife as if you're dating her every day. She's your most important relationship. Run to open the door for her. Pull out the chair for her. Take care of her. Rethink your relationship as husband and wife because she is your most important friendship.

Let's say you've been married 14 years. Your kids are growing, and in eight years you'll be "empty nesters." I don't think God intended you to feel stuck with each other for the rest of your lives. He wants you to de-velop a best-friend relationship. If you work on these principles for just a few months, you'll look forward to the kids leaving home, so you can have more time alone with your best friend.

A pastor once shared with me regretfully, "I never opened or closed the door for my wife in 35 years of marriage until this moment." Don't be like that. This process begins with saying, "OK, God, You created marriage. Show us the way we can live together, some principles we can apply to make it through."

Outward kindness is evidence of inward kindness. What causes that kindness? How can you be kind? It's so easy to say, "Just be kind; you just need to do this." But serious stuff comes up. We're talking about dog food, about towels, how to wrap the toilet paper, toothpaste caps. This goes on at our house. Where does that sense of kindness come from in those nit-picky discussions? Bottom line — start dating again.

Laughing

Simply put, learn to laugh. Laugh at yourself a lot. See yourself for all the dumb things you do and get over yourself. Laugh it off. Cheryl taught me this.

Memorize this verse:

"A joyful heart is good medicine, but a crushed spirit dries up the bones."[3]

Seriously, laugh as much as you can together. Build fun-filled memories. I was coaching one couple on the brink of quitting when the young man said, "I just want to live the next two weeks as if nothing was ever wrong ... let's just have fun together." They did. And they are a trophy now of God's grace. Go to a movie, tickle each other, tease (without some hidden agenda), have fun. Play cards or games with friends, ride bikes, take walks, count your blessings, be around happy people or people who make you feel happy, be more spontaneous just for fun, stop being defensive, release inhibitions.

I tell couples that 95 percent of the time Cheryl and I laugh and enjoy each other; the other 5 percent we will deal with problems. If it's beyond our ability to resolve together, we get a coach.

- **Laughter relaxes the whole body.** A good, hearty laugh relieves physical tension and stress, leaving your muscles relaxed for up to 45 minutes afterward.

---

[3] Proverbs 17:22 ESV.

- **Laughter boosts the immune system.** Laughter decreases stress hormones and increases immune cells and infection-fighting antibodies, thus improving your resistance to disease.

- **Laughter triggers the release of endorphins,** the body's natural feel-good chemicals. Endorphins promote an overall sense of well-being and can even temporarily relieve pain.

- **Laughter protects the heart.** Laughter improves the function of blood vessels and increases blood flow, which can help protect you against a heart attack and other cardiovascular problems.

- **Laughter dissolves distressing emotions.** You can't feel anxious, angry, or sad when you're laughing.

- **Laughter helps you relax and recharge.** It reduces stress and increases energy, enabling you to stay focused and accomplish more.

- **Humor shifts perspective**, allowing you to see situations in a more realistic, less threatening light. A humorous perspective creates psychological distance, which can help you avoid feeling overwhelmed.[4]

Appreciation

Beyond kindness is a final, even more powerful way to express value. It is saying the words "thank you." It's what we do when we receive a gift or benefit from someone's actions. Typically the greater the value of the gift, the greater the gratitude expressed. If I get a fifty-dollar gift card, I'm pretty thankful. If someone gave me a brand new car, you'd better know I'd be REALLY thankful. See the point?

Another form of appreciation is knowing your spouse is a gift from a loving God. As a wise and generous giver, God has entrusted you with your spouse. I learned that because I was not thankful, I didn't have a "gratitude attitude," and God couldn't work in my marriage with

---

[4] Melinda Smith, M.A., and Jeanne Segal, Ph.D., http://www.helpguide.org/articles/emotional-health/laughter-is-the-best-medicine.htm

my lousy attitude. Being thankful is a statement of how much I value someone.

Secondly, value is not just expressed to the divine Giver of the gift, but in human relationships, to the one who is my gift. I express great kindness when I begin and end my day saying thank you to my wife. In random moments I will turn to Cheryl (or my kids) and say, "I don't think I have told you recently how very thankful I am for you."

I have a friend who taught me a special lesson. When I ask him "How are you," he more often than not replies, "Grateful." Makes me smile. And reminds me that it's what we need to do daily. This will come up again, so start practicing kindness now by being thankful. You'll be amazed at the results.

Patience and the Guy Code

There is a second secret to a 911 call. Patience. The EMTs and the Fire Department both respond when we call for help. The EMTs bring emergency healing like Kindness. And the firemen pour water on the flames, which is just like Patience. Both of these concepts come straight from the Bible, which says, "Love is patient, love is kind...."[5] These are the first two characteristics of God's portrayal of the real deal when He describes loving someone else. Kindness is mentioned second; patience, first.

Patience is different from kindness. It comes from two Greek words: MAKROS (meaning long, distant, or far off) and THYMOS (meaning anger). So literally it means that love keeps anger far away. It means to intentionally keep a long fuse. To further understand, picture a dam with a large lake reservoir behind it. Frustration builds and then BOOM! The dam blows. The damages below multiply exponentially as the human death toll mounts. In this case, farms and villages and animals and people normally protected from the fury are washed away.

We need to develop a long fuse that takes lots of time to reach the explosive point. Such internal patience results in external kindness. Anger comes from stress, injury, our perceptions, built-up resentment, especially in marriage. Guys will sit down in my counseling office, and I

---

[5] 1 Corinthians 13:4.

ask, "What's going on? What's happening here?" Finally it comes out: "I am so resentful." Meaning the pressure in the lake has been building for some time.

Guys, we don't talk. Wives will tell their husbands, "I knew it! I asked if you were resentful, and you kept saying no!"

He thinks, "What am I supposed to do? I'm a guy, I have a code. I can't come out and tell you that I'm resentful. That's not what I do. I respect my wife so I don't talk."

We have the "man code": It's not OK for us to talk to our wives. We have to keep things bottled up inside, building a storm of pressure, just like that dam. Then something happens and we blow the dam. Months and years of resentment cascade down the riverbed, washing out those who, moments before, were protected by our control.

Safety On; Trigger Off

Anger starts with a trigger. Feelings and pressure build up on past unresolved resentments. Something further is said and we react, explode. Guys (and ladies, too), I learned in my military training, "Safety on; trigger off." That means, don't let the environment push your emotions. Resolve your issues and learn to see the triggers. Keep your safety on when you un-holster your weapon, and keep your finger off the trigger. Never allow your finger on the trigger until you have made the decision to fire, which we should NEVER need to do in our marriage.

When you feel yourself growing quietly resentful (according to the "bro code") make sure you talk to the Lord about what's going on inside. We'll discuss this in a later chapter. But for now, rely on the Lord to give you a longer fuse. And then be proactive. Many times a wife digs and digs because she wants you to connect with her. Drain off emotional reservoirs by talking with your wife, communicating with her. Yeah, it's tough at first, but keep the safety on. And don't react. Keep your finger off the trigger! And get a pastor or coach involved, someone who will work with you and your spouse. Do it early.

When it comes to these two 911 responders, I challenge you to work together.

Instead of falling apart, fall together!

Lean into each other. Instead of walking out or driving off, determine never to leave the property when you and your wife are angry. You don't need to. You might sit alone on a rock in a corner of the yard, but don't leave the property. That's security for her. She knows you're stretching her security, so CHOOSE, DECIDE NOT TO CLOSE DOWN. Don't do that rejection thing. Lean together; don't give up. (It's called dating again.)

Feelings

I hear people say, "I don't feel like I'm in love anymore." Or "I will always love you, I'm just not IN love with you." Here's a news flash. Here's where we guys especially need to become strong and provide a platform to stand on. We don't give up. We figure it (her) out.

MARRIAGE IS NOT ABOUT HOW YOU FEEL —

IT'S ABOUT THE PROMISE YOU MADE.

Yes, marriage is about "I'm not going to give up on you." Communication is important, but marriage is all about CONNECTION. So when you're disconnected, be the one who starts the process of bringing you back together. Step forward in loving action and the feelings of "in love" will follow. Feelings follow your faith.

You see yourselves falling apart. What do you do? You dial 911. You take the initiative. You start refilling the window track with kindness; pour in patience.

Are you the one with the greater maturity? Romans 2:4 says that the kindness of God leads you to repentance. Jesus was the kindness of almighty God leading you to see Him on the cross. His kindness, valuing you, started this whole thing. 1 John 4:19 says that we love because He first loved us. So instead of blaming your spouse, how about stepping to the side and dialing 911? Say, "Lord, let me see again what you did on the cross." Experience a fresh flow of grace; understand you can give that love away to others. Give to be kind and patient right now.

The big picture? The Bible says, "For this cause shall a man leave his mother and father, and will cleave as one." And the next verse blows me away: "This is a great mystery, but I'm speaking about Christ and the church."[6] What mystery? "I'm speaking of Christ and the church," Paul says. And — here's the most amazing thing — in marriage relationships, God built a reflection of the love of Christ for the church.

Marriage was designed to reflect Christ and the church, and His grace impacts our marriages. So remember to be kind, like Christ. Develop that sense of kindness toward your spouse again. Remember where you started in Christ, and go back there. Grace seeks someone else's best interest, not based on their characteristics or behaviors but based on your character. Your love for your wife is not based on her actions; it is based on who you are, your character.

Now, please understand, just like 911, this is an immediate first-responder posture. You can't constantly call 911 or rely on it for the long term. This is the beginning, the emergency call for help. Please learn to get a coach. Yeah, you have to pay for it, but your marriage is your most important relationship. It deserves to be guarded and protected. Maintain it. Remember:

WINNERS USE GOOD COACHES.[7]

Prayer:

Father God, help us to be the kind of people you want us to be, to see each other's value rather than be irritated or discouraging to each other. Open our eyes to see how we reflect Christ and the church. Help us understand that every relationship we have in our marriages and families is by divine design, a reflection of Your love. We commit ourselves to You and our marriages. Amen.

---

[6] Ephesians 5:31-32.

[7] See Appendix I "How to Choose a Good Advisor."

CHAPTER 2: BATTERIES AND CHARGERS

"Seek first the Kingdom of God and all these things shall be added to you."
—Matthew 6:33

MOST of us come to marriage and other relationships with a sense of need. We are empty and need someone in our lives to help us feel fulfilled or full. We are hoping that this person or relationship will give us a sense of fulfillment — that "feel good about me" feeling.

In this second "rule of the road," we will learn what I believe is the priority relationship of life. It works like this. Instead of coming to your marriage on empty with your battery drained, come in filled up with your battery charged and a life of fullness. This can only be done vertically with God. It's a skill or lifestyle that allows God to be your source of energy, letting Him fill your heart rather than sucking life from your partner.

We all enter life and relationships a lot like batteries — we're fully charged then we run down, lose energy and need to be charged back up. We get to the end and there's nothing left to give.

Each of us has a "life cord." We need to be filled with something that gives us new life. We need to have a full heart. This has to come from within, from God, the Creator, the Life Giver, and not from a created being … like one's spouse.

Instead of being needy and dependent on your spouse or even other externals like job and career, kids, parents, friends, possessions, you need to allow God to recharge your soul from the inside out. Instead of coming to relationships expecting to be filled up or fixed or to somehow find the source of satisfaction, you need to come to God and allow Him to "recharge" you. The source of your life comes from the inside out rather than outside in.

I was working with one man who had a lot of anger issues in his life and marriage. Because he had so many issues with his wife, I was meeting with him alone. I said to him, "You know, you'll never be happy looking to others, especially your wife. We need to plug you into what God has for you. Let Him renew you on the inside, so you become full instead of empty."

After talking a while, he said to me, "Let me get this straight — you're gonna fix my marriage by fixing me?"

And I said, "Yeah, pretty much."

His face twisted up in deep thought and after a long pause he said, "Well, OK, then we better get started."

Here's what I wanted him to know: In every marriage, there are three entities I call "you," "me" and "we." Couples come to counseling to get the "we" fixed. He thinks, "I just need to get her to do what I need her to do," while she thinks, "I just need to get him to do what I need him to do." Many marriage courses could be titled "How to Manipulate My Spouse to Do What I Want." Or even "Pray 'til You See It My Way." I don't think that's what God had in mind when He designed marriage.

> ## YOU CANNOT FIX THE "WE" UNTIL YOU FIX THE "ME."

Let's begin with an illustration. Close your eyes for a moment and picture a cross. If you were to build a cross, how many sticks would you need? The obvious, simple answer is two sticks. So now I ask you, which one is more important?

Again, the answer is obvious: the vertical, but why? Without the vertical stick, the horizontal or crossbar would fall to the ground. The horizontal has to have something to hang on to. The vertical is the base, the strength; it's what supports the crossbar.

So when I talk with couples about marriage, I say, "Before we talk about the 'we,' let's talk about where you are vertically with God. There's no sense in working to fix the 'we' until we fix the '"me."'"

I think of the vertical as one's relationship with God, one's walk with Him. The horizontals in life are made up of all one's personal "stuff": dogs, jobs, cars, houses, school, and career. My wife is happy with me, she's not happy with me — that's horizontal stuff. Every horizontal in one's life hangs on this vertical relationship with God. If you can learn to live out of your vertical, to come to your horizontals by walking with God first, then you won't turn marriage into something like "two ticks and no dog." Trying to suck life from each other just doesn't work. If she's upset then you're upset. If she's fine then you're fine. You need to change that. You need to bring to marriage a "live life vertically" perspective. That is your life cord to a successful marriage.

Life Cords

We all come to relationships with what I think of as "life cords." We tend to plug them into something that gives meaning or value to our life, like our job or our appearance or material possessions. We get what we think of as "life" from them — that "feel good" feeling about ourselves. I belong. I'm important. I have value. I'm appreciated, affirmed. I'm secure, protected.

There are eight basic things we plug our life cord into. I call these "I am who I am because ..." statements. These are the external things we tend to rely on to define ourselves.

1. **"I am who I am because of what I do."** The first thing we plug into is our performance. I am a performance-based person. Here's how performance works: I introduce myself to someone and say, "Hi, my name is Jim." He gives me his name.

What is the very next question a man will ask? "What do you do?" Women will ask "Do you have a family, are you married, how many children, who does your hair, where did you buy your outfit?" But not us guys. We're more into performance. And we rate ourselves.

That's the American performance-based mentality. What we do, how we perform, determines our self-worth. If we are afraid of losing our job or our finances tank, we struggle to find value in ourselves. But when we live vertically, our relationship with God, not our job, defines who we are. The fact is, vertically our God is all we need. What or how we do our job should not define who we are.

You may say, "I don't have this problem." Watch your heart (it's where life springs from). What happens to you when you don't succeed at some project at work? You didn't make the grades. You won't make the deadline. Your kids didn't put the puzzle together right. When someone lets you know by a look that you just don't measure up. That's the feeling performance-based value systems give you. You don't measure up.

2. **"I am who I am because of how I look."** Women deal a little bit more with this one than men, typically. When women dress, they have to look right. They have to put on clothes and makeup, and accessorize with their shoes, necklace, bracelet and purse. I can take seven minutes and I'm in and out; showered and dressed. I may not look very good when I get out, but I can actually make that happen. Meanwhile, she's taking 45 minutes to an hour to get RTG (Ready To Go). Presentation is important.

When two women introduce themselves, they look each other over. "Hi, my name is Cheryl," or "Hi, Nancy, how are you?"

"I'm fine ... so nice the way that you accessorized today ... love your earrings ... love your shoes ... who does your hair?"

With guys, it's a lot more subtle. The point is that what you do or how you look can define you. And you might plug your life cord into those definitions.

You may say, "I don't have this problem either." Look at your heart (it's where life springs from). What happens to you when your kids are acting up in a store or when you don't look as good as your co-worker? What happens when "church lady" comes up and gives you the "once over"? What happens when you and your spouse are having heated discussions? Do you get help? Ask your pastor? Why not? Because you fear you just don't measure up. That's the feeling presentation-based value systems give you. You don't measure up.

3. **"I am who I am because of what I own."** I love this one. I gravitate toward it so naturally.

I love stuff. I plug into what I have or what I own for value in life. Having my own stuff, new stuff, better stuff, more stuff is what makes me feel good. I stack stuff, store stuff, secure stuff, polish stuff, arrange stuff, move stuff, save stuff, trade stuff, argue about stuff, and pull stuff on trailers. I guard my stuff, put my stuff in a bank, build portfolios with my stuff, and get pretty irritated when people are "in my stuff." Then there's OPS (Other People's Stuff). Maybe theirs is bigger, better, faster, stronger, prettier, nicer, harder, softer, higher, or just plain "badder" stuff than my stuff. So now I'm just not as happy as I was. The feel-good feeling about me isn't right.

You may say, "I don't have this problem." Look at your heart (it's where life springs from). What happens to you when someone breaks your stuff, steals your stuff, keeps you from stuff, and takes your stuff? What happens when someone jerks your life cord?

4.   **"I am who I am because of the pleasures I enjoy."** This category includes your friends, your recreational times together, going to fun places, seeing new or familiar sights, and spending money, all for pleasure.

Sliding further, pleasure seekers turn to drugs of choice, caffeine, alcohol, antidepressants, or more — in other words, the things that bring you pleasure or feelings of euphoria. These are where you might get those "feel good about me" feelings, and they become what defines you.

You may say, "I certainly don't have this problem." Well how's the heart so far? (It's where life springs from.) What happens to you when you miss out on the latest event? When you weren't there to be part of the group? What happens when you have to double up work to meet a specific deadline and you can't take some time off? How do you feel when you can't relax or spend time just being by yourself or hanging out with all your friends? What happens when you can't say no to a glass of wine or alcohol?

5.   **"I am who I am because of what I can control."** Most of us desire or need to keep our lives under control, for obvious reasons.

But control of circumstances and people in our lives can become the life cord of feeling OK. We go from setting proper healthy boundaries to having to be in control of everything.

Some of us become perfectionists. We obsess over getting it right. Keeping people in line. Not being hurt again. Often that sense of control or security becomes our source of well-being. Our life cord is being charged by controlling our self or those around us. Usually this comes from a sense of fear — fear of being hurt ... again.

You may say, "Now I absolutely don't have this problem." Well let's do another heart check (it's where life springs from). What happens to you when someone backs into your car, or spills food on your lap, or your son wipes mashed potatoes on your new suit because he was trying to say "I love you"? What happens when the plans go bad and the vacation doesn't go exactly right? What happens when your family tries to help you accomplish a task at work so you can get caught up on something? Or what happens when you are building a deck and your family tries to help? What about when your health isn't right? You say, well I don't yell at people. But your family would say "No, he (or she) just pouts."

6. **"I am who I am because of what others say about me."** Simply put, these are the people pleasers. This is the need for acceptance and affirmation mentality. These folks find fulfillment when others are accepting of them. They feel good inside when others speak well of them or, at the very least, feel good when others are not upset with them.

7. **"I am who I am because of my life pursuits, my life agenda."** Here are those who cannot understand that life is not all about them. They play golf not to enjoy the friendships or the game but to be a killer on the green. They are the high-powered sales people who have to make all the quotas. These are the ones who drive to build out a legacy.

You may say, "Finally I can say on this one, I definitely don't have this problem." Well let's do another heart check (it's where life springs from). What about when your mother-in-law rejects you because you're not good enough? What about sisters and brothers? What about when you don't get that raise at work? What about when your savings or investment portfolio isn't as grand as it should be for retirement?

8. **"I am who I am because my wife or my husband defines me."** This world value system is driven by co-dependency. I honor prioritizing one's spouse, but you must not put him or her ahead of God. You can inadvertently make an idol out of your wife, or she can make an idol out of you. What is the result? Just like with every other idol, when you plug your life cord into another person, you become controlled by his or her mood swings, their wishes as priority over yours or their outright manipulative control. The questions you have to ask are, "Am I getting life from them or am I up when they're up and down when they're down? Is their rejection the end of the world for me? Am I sacrificing my vertical identity on the altar of their horizontal pride?"

(For a more extensive treatment of these eight external sources of value, see my book *Grace: Orphans No More*.)[8]

From the start of each of my counseling sessions, I want people to learn to build out their time with God in that vertical relationship first. Otherwise, if their definition of themselves is plugged into a lesser thing, they can be manipulated by someone coming along and "cutting their cord." If someone is plugged into his or her performance, possessions, what they can control, and so on, someone else can hack through that line with a look, a critical word, an obstinate response. Then what will happen is, they will react in one of three ways: *get big, get little, or get lost.*

Getting big means you become frustrated and angry because somebody threatens to cut or take away your life cord. Let's say you lose your job — you may get big, get little, or get lost.

---

[8] Dr. James G. Johnson, *Grace: Orphans No More: A Pastor's Journey into the Arms of the Father's Love*, (2015), http://www.amazon.com/gp/product/0985331704?keywords=grace%3A%20orphans%20no%20more&qid=1458519576&ref_=sr_1_2&sr=8-2.

Why is this important? Because what spills out of my "cup" of life reveals my true values and priorities. If I'm getting big about something, or I'm getting little about something, or I'm running away from something, it reveals who's in charge — who I'm allowing to fill my cup. So when I live vertically with God, I disconnect my plug from all those substitute "life" sources — they are all counterfeits — and I plug into Christ.

When I disconnect from the counterfeits and live vertically, my God is in charge of my life. My job no longer controls my thinking. I can tell my mind to stop thinking that stuff. ("I'm panicking, I'm sweating, I haven't had a job for three hours; what am I gonna do?") This is because you have your life cord plugged into your job instead of God.

How do you correct this? You need to learn the value of God's love in your life. Here's a key verse that literally changed my life: Psalms 73:25. Write it down on an index card and memorize it: "Whom have I in heaven but Thee, and besides Thee, I desire nothing on this earth." Living out that verse in my life is my goal, and I'm not there yet.

I also love the flavor of Psalms 87:7 — "All my springs of joy are found in you." When things get really bad in my life on the horizontal plane, I can live in a roller-coaster existence. When events go "my way," I'm up, then they turn around, and I'm down. I'm exhausted just thinking about it! I have a choice; I can get off that ride and live life vertically or stay stuck with the false horizontal cord.

My daughter Kristin taught me this lesson a long time ago. We had been waiting to buy her a new cell phone. Her old phone had horrible reception and dropped calls. Meanwhile, I was teaching this principle of "Whom have I in heaven but Thee?" I also define this principle with the question, "Is God's love enough or do you need more?"

Finally, we bought her a brand new cell phone — the best on the market. Less than a week after getting the new phone, Kristin gathered up an armload of groceries with the phone cradled in her arm. At the door she fumbled with the keys, and as she bent over, that cell phone slipped out and hit the concrete. She picked it up saying, "Oh, don't let it be shattered; don't let it be shattered." But the glass screen had exploded. Kristin says, "What went through my mind was, 'Is My love enough or do you need more?'"

That's powerful! Her cords were cut, but she was living vertically. How do you do that? Learn to daily abide in Father's love for you. Psalm 73:25, Jeremiah 31:3, Lamentations 3:22-23, John 15:9, and 1 John 4:16 all describe this love. Our identity as Father's child "in Christ" means each of us is loved perfectly.

Three times a week, I review these verses in my walk with Father God. This one is the core: knowing Father's love. If everything you do in your Christian walk with God does not flow from the starting point of God's love for you then you are a legalist trying to impress God with your good behavior.

Out of this core radiate four principles of godly living:

1. **Put God First.** Start your day with the prayer: "Lord, it's not about me."

You may say, "But I'm upset, I'm mad, I can't stand this, I'm really hurt by what she/he/they did to me, I'm going up and down." You know why that is? Because it's all about you! In your mind you are seeing your agenda, your concerns, and your personal interests. But by putting God first, you can break that pattern. God's promise to you in the Bible is pretty amazing: "Seek ye first the kingdom of God and His righteousness and all these things will be added to you."

The words of Jesus describe this principle even more pointedly:

> One of the scribes came and heard them arguing, and recognizing that He had answered them well, asked Him, "What commandment is the foremost of all?" Jesus answered, "The foremost is, 'HEAR, O ISRAEL! THE LORD OUR GOD IS ONE LORD; AND YOU SHALL LOVE THE LORD YOUR GOD WITH ALL YOUR HEART, AND WITH ALL YOUR SOUL, AND WITH ALL YOUR MIND, AND WITH ALL YOUR STRENGTH.' The second is this, 'YOU SHALL LOVE YOUR NEIGHBOR AS YOURSELF.' There is no other commandment greater than these."[9]

---

[9] Matthew 6:33.

Jesus is basically teaching that this is the highest priority in all we do. Love God first and love others second. Whew! That kind of reduces the list to just two. And that is just what Jesus means in another passage when He says, "On these two commandments depend the whole Law and the Prophets."[10]

Putting God first — it's what I call living vertically and it is the number one optimizing factor you can bring to your life and to your marriage as well. In fact, this principle works in all our relationships. You may ask, "How do you do that?" By walking with Him and putting Him first every day. Begin each day with some specific time to read in the Bible and then pray, dedicating yourself and your day to God as you close. I recommend the devotional *Our Daily Bread* as a starter. [11]

I have walked with the Lord for more than 40 years. Every day, I want to be centered in His presence. He is my primary relationship. I need to be vertical. I need Him first in my day, and get there by spending time with just Him alone.

Then I put Him first in my week. I dedicate time to have my family in church every single week; we rarely miss. God gave us six days to work and set apart the seventh day for us to focus on Him. He spent six days creating the universe. And on the seventh day, He rested. He's all powerful, He's omniscient, and He. He doesn't need to rest. And yet He did. Why? He was setting an example for us to live our lives in balance.

I also put Him first in my habits or actions. Before doing the things I tend to do without thinking, I start checking my habits. Is my family eating before giving thanks? Then change the habit. Am I neglecting to open doors for others? Then change habits. Turning on the television, I ask, "Is this a television show that will honor You, Lord?" Change habits.

---

[10] Matthew 22:40.

[11] You can find *Our Daily Bread* free online at www.ourdailybread.org. It takes just a few minutes each day and reaps huge benefits.

Typically we guys are notorious for putting ourselves first. But not overtly. We just think everyone else will be as excited as we are about what we are excited about. We want to get a new boat ... we get all the brochures and surf the Web, target the best price, and we bag it. We stalk it, hunt it, shoot it and bag it to carry it from the store. It's how we guys get into trouble so fast. It's like we have tunnel vision. Goal-oriented, we go for it. And somewhere in the process, we lose sight of the relationships. No matter what your agenda includes — golf, paintball, camping, building an addition, building your career — none of it will EVER be as important to God as your relationships, especially your marriage. Look it up: "Without love I am nothing."[12]

We can do the great stuff (God made us for joy) but never at the expense of others. Guys (and women too) if your dream doesn't include the words "to bless someone else" then it's not from God. We need to get into the habit of doing what we do to bless others.

I must put God first in my relationships with my family and friends. My relationship with God first in my life means I consult Him regarding my friendships. Nothing destroys a great walk with God like friends with compromised values. That's what the Bible means when it says, "Do not be deceived: Bad company corrupts good morals."[13] Even more pointedly, it warns us, "You adulterous people! Do you not know that friendship with the world is enmity with God? Therefore whoever wishes to be a friend of the world makes himself an enemy of God."[14] Pretty tough language.

God is first in my finances. Learning to put God first in my finances was tough for me. I had the attitude that God needs to keep His hands out of my pockets. I was born and raised on a Nebraska farm where we had to manage every penny. My whole life has been one of spinning on a dime and getting a quarter change.

The Christmas season was rough. Walking by the Salvation Army bell ringers, my wife would run over to drop money into their red

---

[12] 1 Corinthians 13:1-3.

[13] 1 Corinthians 15:33.

[14] James 4:4 ESV.

buckets. I'd think, *Are you kidding me? We can't afford that!* I'd even walk her in through a different door to avoid them.

But I began to learn that God will multiply the 90 percent if you give Him the 10 percent He asks for. He will make the total worth a hundred and fifty percent! Giving to God is not how He raises money. Giving is how God raises kids. Again Jesus said it this way, "Do not store up for yourselves treasures on earth, where moth and rust destroy, and where thieves break in and steal. But store up for yourselves treasures in heaven, where neither moth nor rust destroys, and where thieves do not break in or steal; for where your treasure is, there your heart will be also."[15]

Recently we needed some clothing for our toddler grandson. We couldn't afford department store prices, so we went to a garage sale next door. For sixteen dollars, we walked home that day with about two hundred dollars' worth of designer clothing. Does God take care of his kids? Absolutely! Learning to put God first in these five ways will change your life completely. You will start living for Him instead of for yourself.

2. **Brutal Honesty.** A second principle of the humble heart is learning to live your life in a way that allows other people (especially your wife) to speak into it. Does that mean you won't get frustrated? Of course you will, but God gave you your wife as a mirror to reflect what you need to see about yourself. She needs permission to speak into your life with brutal honesty. She will say things to you that you need to hear.

The key prayer with brutal honesty is, "Lord, change me." It's not about the other person. Jesus says:

> *Why do you look at the speck that is in your brother's eye, but you don't notice the log that is in your own? Or how can you say to your brother, let me take the speck out of your eye, and behold the log is in your own? You hypocrite, take first the log out of your own eye and then you are clear to take away the speck of others."[16]*

---

[15] Matthew 6:19-21.
[16] Matthew 7:3-5.

That principle applies to marriage. It also applies to other relationships. Marriage is the primary human relationship. Your marriage will show you every area you have not taken captive to the Lordship of Christ. Marriage is the first circle in the arena where God can work through you. His heart desires you to receive His love and give it away in random acts of humility. Marriage is the arena in which we practice our authenticity.

Brutal honesty is my attitude in all my relationships — with my wife and with my friends. If someone offers me a simple correction for, say, a spelling error, I can't let it be all about my self-image. *It's not about your self-image Jim, it's just about spelling the word correctly*, or whatever. You've got to be brutally honest to let people speak into your life. The Bible says in Proverbs 6:23, "For reproofs are the way of life." If I don't learn to let others speak into my life then I'll never see what they see, which probably are areas in which I need to grow or change. It's tough.

And yes, you have to let go of your pride. When you're brutally honest with yourself, the first thing you have to deal with is pride. We're all in that boat, but you will maximize your growth potential when you learn to accept other people's thoughts and comments. Does that mean you do what everybody wants you to do? No. But when somebody gives you a critique or comment, take it back to the Lord, and ask Him what He's trying to say to you.

You'd think since I'm a marriage counselor with all these degrees, I'd have my own marriage all figured out. But Cheryl and I miss the mark sometimes too. Then I find myself out in the garage thinking, *You know, that just wasn't flying at all*. And I begin to realize that God is showing me so much about things I need to change through this partner He's given me.

I'm very melancholy. I can go very deep and want to crawl off into a closet or something like that. Cheryl is the person who comes along and knocks a bit of sense into me when I need it. "Come on let's get in the game!" I really need that from her. Otherwise I'd be way too intellectual and too comfortable in my melancholy closet. When she speaks into my life, and approaches me with a sense of kindness and gentleness, she brings value to my life. And I can do the same for her. We can either defend ourselves and prepare our counterattacks like a couple of sword fighters, or listen to each other, give value to each other. It does work, guys!

3. **A Gratitude Attitude.** "Lord, I give You thanks." The Bible tells us, "In everything give thanks, for this is God's will concerning you."[17] Simply put, if you don't have the gratitude attitude, you cannot possibly be in God's will (no matter what other great things you are doing). People tell me all the time they just don't know what God wants them to do. Meanwhile, their lives are filled with griping and complaining and fussing and negative stuff. I learned a long time ago that complaining doesn't help, and frankly, nobody really cares. I can't say it in strong enough language: If you have a complaining, negative, griping spirit, you CANNOT be in God's will for your life. This is what the verse just said.

And it works this way. We are to give thanks IN everything. The verse doesn't say FOR everything. ("Oh, Lord, I just had a horrible accident. My family members are lying in the street bleeding. I just want to say thank You for my family bleeding all over the pavement.") No, that's not what we are asked to do. We are not expected to give thanks FOR what's happening in the middle of bad situations. But we do thankfully acknowledge that our God is in control of our destinies. Giving thanks IN our circumstances is the power of putting God in control because a thankful heart is a heart YIELDED to His Will.

4. **Unquenchable Faith.** According to God's plan for our lives, we are challenged to live with an unquenchable faith. We put God first, saying, "Lord, I put You first, it's not about me; it's all about You." Next we say, "Lord, it's not about them; rather change me." Then we choose to say, "Lord, in this I will give You thanks." And finally, "Lord, I believe." Several passages come to mind.

Jesus exhorted and implored us to great faith when He said, "Ask, and it will be given to you; seek, and you will find; knock, and it will be opened to you. For everyone who asks receives, and he who seeks

---

[17] 1 Thessalonians 5:18.

finds, and to him who knocks it will be opened."[18] There is a promise we should be claiming for our marriages every day. I challenge husbands frequently, "Do you know what the most powerful tool you have in your marriage is?" Most often the answer is a bewildered stare.

"I'll take that as a no."

The most powerful tool we husbands have is praying every day for our wife. As we walk in humility, as we get the agenda off our own interests, God promises that our "prayers will not be hindered."[19] It's an amazing promise, and as we walk with Him, He goes to work in our relationships.

Another passage that pointedly addresses unquenchable faith is the story of a blind man named Bartimaeus. He sat at the side of the road and begged people to give him money.

> *One day Jesus and his disciples were leaving Jericho when Bartimaeus heard the noise of the crowd. Learning that it was Jesus the Nazarene passing by, he began to cry out, "Jesus, Son of David, have mercy on me!"*
>
> *Many were sternly telling him to be quiet, but he kept crying out all the more, "Son of David, have mercy on me!"*
>
> *Jesus stopped and said, "Call him here."*
>
> *So they called the blind man, saying to him, "Take courage, and stand up! He is calling for you." Throwing aside his cloak, he jumped up and came to Jesus.*
>
> *And answering him, Jesus said, "What do you want Me to do for you?"*
>
> *And the blind man said to Him, "Rabbi, I want to regain my sight!"*
>
> *And Jesus said to him, "Go; your faith has made you well." Immediately he regained his sight and began following Him on the road.*[20]

I quoted that passage in its entirety because I want to demonstrate something. Here's a blind guy. He can't see. So in his despair he sits

---

[18] Matthew 7:7-8.

[19] 1 Peter 3:7.

[20] Mark 10:46-52.

on the side of the road hoping for some help. He hears about Jesus and yells for help. It's not a whisper; he is so intense the crowd is uncomfortable and shushing him. Jesus says, bring him here. So they bring him.

Now it's probably a good thing I wasn't living back then because I imagine Jesus saying, "What do you want?"

"Uh, duh, Jesus, the guy is blind, he's as blind as a doorpost, can't even walk without aid, what do you think he wants, a new car?"

I'm not trying to be disrespectful; I'm simply saying it's pretty obvious. So what is Jesus doing? Jesus is not surprised or caught off guard. He knows what the man needs, his hopes, his heart, his desire. What is Jesus doing? He is making blind Bart express EXACTLY what he is hoping for.

Jesus WANTS TO BE ASKED. He wants us to say specifically what we want.

Here is the point, if it's not obvious already: ASK. Ask Him. Seek Him. Knock at His door.

In prayer follow these four steps of ACTS:

- **Adore** Him by putting Him first
- **Confess** your needs in brutal honesty
- **Thank** Him in everything because it's a demonstration of your submission to His Heart, then ...
- **Specifically** ask Him

Ask Him for exactly what you want to change. Ask Him to work with your spouse, build into her or him, change her or him. Pray she or he will come to see His will in everything. Don't be shy and kick the dirt. Jesus wants to know "What do you want Me to do?" Engage.

I once read a saying printed on a coffee cup that quipped, "Life is short. Stay awake for it. Drink lots of coffee." I decided that Christians could edit that maxim to read, "Life is short. Stay awake. Live life vertically."

Here's a word picture for you: If both you and your wife put Christ first in all that you do, you form a triangle. As you and your spouse walk toward Christ, the natural and obvious result is you will move closer to each other. I can say with absolute certainty this works every single time.

Prayer:

Father God, thank You so much that we can learn to live our lives vertically. Thank You for teaching us to understand that You are our only source. That Your love, and not any created thing, powers our lives. So we live that out by putting You first, Lord. It's not about me. Help us to be brutally honest, Lord, and be willing to say, "Change me," then be ready to receive what comes. Lord, we give You thanks and believe You for great things. Father, help us to live our lives vertically. We ask in Jesus' precious name. Amen.

CHAPTER 3: GOOD, BAD, AND UGLY

"And God saw all that He had made, and behold, it was very good."
—Genesis 1:31

WHAT did God have in mind when He created man, (male and female) relationships, and especially marriage? In the pain and sheer frustration I often find when two imperfect people try to "make it work," I sometimes want to ask God, "Seriously? What kind of Mind would think of something like this? Did you have a reason for this, or was this a colossal cosmic wind-up toy that went amok?"

Was there a plan? What was our Creator thinking? Did He have an original design? I am passionate about this question because in my early years I neither saw nor understood God's plan for relational dynamics. But growing older I've realized that the intricacies of relationships done well, God's way, are a channel for incredible joy and blessing. Many counselors would agree with the observation that most people's hurts come through relationships. Likewise, most healing also comes through relationship.

This chapter could easily be called "The Smell of Marriage." Sometimes marriage stinks. I grew up on a farm. Cows and pigs were a mainstay for our financial wellbeing. Often my grandfather, driving us kids down a road, would take us past a huge feedlot. In the July summer heat, those places could be "ripe," I mean, REALLY ripe. Driving by, he would roll down all the windows with us gagging in the back and say loudly, "AHHHHH. Smells like money!"

As a 13-year-old kid, I didn't know what he meant. Why would somebody say that? Now, as an adult, I get it. In the Bible, Wisdom says, "Where there are no oxen, the manger is clean, but much revenue comes by the strength of the ox."[21] When you've been around a farm like I was, you know that the more oxen you have, the more "fertilizer" they produce. The larger the herd, the larger the pile. This verse acknowledges a

---

[21] Proverbs 14:4.

certain exchange. When you have no oxen, visitors say, "Wow, what a clean manger! You really keep your place clean — smells good!" But there's no profit without the oxen. Basically, there's a direct correlation: The greater the profit, the greater the poo.

How does this apply to marriage? God gives us a principle of marriage that is rarely quoted on a couple's wedding day, though it should be: "If you marry, you have not sinned; and if a virgin marries, she has not sinned. Yet such will have trouble in this life, and I am trying to spare you."[22] Entering marriage, from the very beginning, couples need to understand that it's not all a bed of roses. In fact, the way romance novels and "rom-com" movies portray marriage sets us up for disappointment.

People come to marriage with an overwhelming sense of love. Several neurotransmitters work within the brain in those months of dating and during the honeymoon period. One of them is phenyl amphetamine, which functions as a neuromodulator. It literally makes people delusional. The second one is serotonin, a neurotransmitter that acts as an antidepressant and a cognitive impairment.

So not only are you delusional when you're dating, you are also cognitively impaired, and you can't be depressed.

The third agent in people's systems when they're dating that wonderful person and thinking "Wow" is epinephrine, also known as adrenaline. It's another neurotransmitter that provides a burst of energy, which people may easily attribute to this new love interest. Whenever guys say, "I've never felt so alive," well, that's the reason.

Now you're delusional; you're cognitively impaired; you have energy bursting out of your system. But wait! There's a fourth one! Dopamine. It is a neurotransmitter that actually acts like an addictive drug in your system, like cocaine or heroin. It gives you feelings of ecstasy and excitement. So your body is pushing all this stuff into your system.

Here's another: oxytocin, which is called the "cuddle chemical." Your date thinks you're so cuddly because you're bonding and snuggling.

---

[22] 1 Corinthians 7:28.

And it builds that sense of trust and empathy. So in those dating and early marriage days, things seem to be all rosy.

But at the end of those days, things begin to change. Scientists — no kidding — actually have a name for this "honeymoon period." It's called "limerence" and is described as "an involuntary potentially inspiring state of adoration and attachment to a limerent object involving intrusive and obsessive thoughts, feelings and behaviors from euphoria to despair, contingent on perceived emotional reciprocation."[23]

So the first reason we have trouble is we come together in marriage all doped up. We're "under the influence," so to speak. A second reason is ... well, we marry sinners. That's the fact. My wife is a sinful person; she has sins in her life. The third problem — even bigger — is that SHE married a sinner.

I think of that guy who said, "Lord, why did you make her so pretty?"

"So that you'd be attracted to her."

"Why did you make her so soft?"

"So you would find comfort in her."

"Why did you make her so much fun?"

"So that you would want to be around her."

"But why did you make her so stupid?"

"So that she could love you."

Yes, you each married a sinner — an imperfect, prone-to-mistakes, blows-it, steps-over-the-line and-misses-the-mark sinner. So in this chapter, we'll see what God saw when He created marriage, how men fell, and then as a result of that fall, what happened to our hearts that affects the way we relate to one another. The good, the bad, and the ugly.

THE GOOD

The best place to begin something is in the beginning. Seems logical, right? Genesis, which literally means "The Beginning," is the owner's

---

[23] Lynn Millmott, *Love and Limerence: Harness the Limbicbrain*, (Lathbury House, 2012).

manual narrative describing how God created all that exists. There are five pictures I'd like you to see.

The First Picture: God Corrected a Problem

He made a woman. YOU'RE KIDDING! The picture comes to us in Genesis 1 and 2, where we see a summary of what God did. Day One, He creates heavens and earth and separates the light from the darkness. Day Two, He creates land and sky and separates land from ocean. Day Three, He makes bushes and plants, then Day Four, sun, moon and stars. Day Five, He creates animals, living creatures, fish and birds and whales and everything that moves. With each creative episode during the first five days, God gives something of greater glory and complexity.

Now note this: After each creative day — and this is really important — the Bible reiterates, "And God saw that it was good." Day One, "God spoke and … God saw that it was good." Day Two, "God spoke and … God saw that it was good." Days Three, Four, and Five, same thing: "God spoke and … God saw that it was good."

But the sixth day is completely different. God creates man. Now, instead of speaking, God forms something. God reaches down into the dirt and literally manufactures something called a man, His masterpiece. Man isn't something that God just speaks into being; He takes time and works His hands into the clay.

Imagine the detail God put into every sinew — muscles and tarsals and legs, eyes, ears, brain, jaw, hips and feet. This all shows the value God placed in His culmination of creation.

God forms man's every cell from the dirt then gives him the name Adam, meaning "the human." In the original Hebrew language, what God does next is most amazing — He bends over and kisses Adam, blowing breath into him. Man coughs, and the first face he sees is Father God. That is man's first breath.

Now imagine God looking at this first, perfect person. God steps back, He looks; the man blinks, and what does God say about man? Nothing. Genesis does not say, "And God saw that it was good." He doesn't say the finished product is good, as He did about everything else He made. He doesn't say anything.

Instead, God gives man the opportunity to start naming the animals. God gives man work, a job, a task, a mission. And as man watches the animals go by, he thinks, *Wow, male and female; I think I'll call that a giraffe. ... They're male and female; I think I'll call that a hippopotamus.* Eventually man begins to realize, *Hey, there's two of them and just one of me.* Then the Bible says, "Man gave names to all the cattle and to the birds of the sky and every beast of the field, but for Adam there was not found a helper suitable for him."[24] So God's solution to the problem was woman. (How's that ladies?)

The Second Picture: You Complete Me

The word "Adam" is from the Hebrew word ADAMA, which means "formed from dirt." ADAMA was the substance from which man was formed. So Adam, "the human," was made, "and there was not a helper suitable for him. Then the Lord God caused a deep sleep to fall upon the man and he slept. And God took one of Adam's ribs and closed up the flesh in that place. And He fashioned that rib into a woman. And God brought her to the man."

When I get to heaven, I want to see the DVD of this moment. Adam says, "Wow! This is now bone of my bones and flesh of my flesh!" He calls her woman, which is the Hebrew word ISHA, because she was taken out of "man," which is the Hebrew word ISH. From then on, God calls them "Ish" and "Isha." Now and only now, God finally says on this final day of creation that it is "very good."

You can see that the marriage relationship isn't just something that God coughed out one day because He didn't have anything to do. Or, like some of my counselees think when they first come in, "God made marriage because it's His way of getting back at us. HE WANTS ME MISERABLE."

Marriage is something God totally loves. God had a specific design in mind when He made marriage and joined husband and wife together. The description of Eve being pulled out of Adam makes a very clear statement of God's intention. Without woman, man is not complete. And without man, woman is not complete. In God's original design,

---

[24] Genesis 2:20-22.

human was complete with both halves together, but God reached down and literally pulled the fibers from the one to make two halves.

You must understand that man without woman is not complete and grasp the powerful realization that your spouse is the one who completes you. God intended for a one-flesh, one-spirit relationship to complete us. That's an amazing concept. Think about it. What was originally one person became two in a division whereby God created two halves from one. She got part of the original goo and he was left with the other part.

The Third Picture: To the Rescue

The language of this creation story is incredibly Technicolor. When God said, "I will make a helper suitable for you," He used the Hebrew word EZER for "helper." It means "rescuer." This word is used in scripture 21 times. It is used for woman as well as for God Himself. God intended that in all of the tasks a man faces, he would be assisted by an incredible gift — someone to help, someone to rescue. But modern Western society reduces life to "his tasks" and "her tasks." It wasn't supposed to be that way. Not in the original design.

> **MAN AND WOMAN WERE INTENDED TO BE COMPLEMENTARY, INCOMPLETE WITHOUT THE OTHER.**

The Fourth Picture: Matching Pieces

Man and woman were meant to match, his zigs and her zags, fitted together. The Hebrew NEGEV means a corresponding match. The word can also mean "suitable" or "to fit opposites together." Man and woman are opposite. They're opposite in their feelings, in their perspectives, in physical appearance. In nature, the males of most species look more colorful and flashy. Have you noticed that? Until you get to woman. Then she is the beautiful one. God made her in a special way. She's an opposite in personality, in the way she thinks, in the way she approaches situations. She's a helper, suitable for man, a matching rescuer.

In my experiences as a counselor and seminar leader in multiple formats with various audiences, I have concluded that God intended a beautiful complementary relationship for man and woman. I believe that in some way God pulled a part of woman from man so that neither could be complete without the other.

(My single readers might construe that I'm saying they can't be complete until they are married, and I don't intend that. Many single adults have multiple gender relationships that supply the differing balances between male perspectives and female perspectives. The intimacy of the marriage relationship makes the need for completion much more INTENSE).

Attract or Attack

Some fundamental reasons for the diametrical opposition of men and women stem from God's original design. We will cover these further in this book. Suffice it to say, we really need each other. We need to listen to each other's perspectives and hear each other's hearts rather than assume our spouse is the enemy. An explanation of these differences and so much more lie ahead. We will learn how to compliment each other rather than criticize. We will learn how to balance each other rather than push each other away.

I love walking on railroad tracks. The farm where I grew up was just beyond a set of tracks, and I would walk them almost daily. My goal was to walk as far as I could before falling off. One of the things I've learned is if you grab your wife's hand and each walk on a separate rail slightly leaning outward but balancing each other, you can keep going indefinitely. That's a picture of marriage presented in this book.

The Fifth Picture: A Gift of Great Price

God brought Eve to Adam as a gift. It wasn't as if Adam stumbled on Eve; she wasn't a discovery of someone who had been there all along. They weren't created in twos, male and female, like the other animals. God intended and accomplished in His plan something far different than what he meant for all of the other animal kingdom.

God prepared a gift for Adam. "So the Lord God caused a deep sleep to fall upon the man, and he slept; then He took one of his ribs and closed up the flesh at that place. The Lord God fashioned into a woman the rib which He had taken from the man, and brought her to the man."[25]

God BROUGHT her to Adam. He didn't say, "There you go, Eve, go find Adam." He didn't say, "Hey, Adam, there is something out there for you to go find." The Bible is VERY specific: "The Lord caused ... He took one of his ribs ... He fashioned into a woman ... AND BROUGHT HER TO THE MAN."

This was the first Father, walking the first daughter to the first husband. Now, guys, I'm not a touchy-feely person by nature, so I'm not saying grab the hankies, but seriously consider what was going on here. This is a phenomenal statement about God's intention. He planned it, He executed it, He fashioned her then He brought her to Adam as a gift.

Gentlemen, I will tell you this: We typically get everything messed up the moment we forget she is not a thing — "that woman" — but rather a very precious gift. Most marriages would start changing right at this point if we could see our wives as the gifts they were when we first started dating them.

And ladies, this scene has a message for you as well. Father fashioned you to assist and help and complete. Maybe you would do well to see your role as one who assists because that is what God intended.

And in this gift of marriage, this gift of a special relationship, there was the foreshadowing of the face of Christ. More on this idea later, but Paul said in Ephesians, "For this cause shall a man leave his mother and father, and will cleave as one. This is a great mystery, but I'm speaking about Christ and the church."[26]

Well, we guys say, "Something finally makes sense." If marriage is a complete mystery to Paul the apostle, I don't feel so bad, because it's a huge mystery to me. My wife confuses me so fast I can't believe it. And then I'm angry, frustrated, irritated, mad, quiet, and out in the garage hammering things.

---

[25] Genesis 2:21-22, *New American Standard Bible: 1995 Update*, (The Lockman Foundation, LaHabra, CA).
[26] Ephesians 5:31-32.

Marriage is a complete mystery. Paul says it. The picture is Christ and His Church. God intended marriage to ultimately be a complete picture of how Christ treats His church. "I'm speaking of Christ and the Church," Paul says. In marriage relationships, God built the potential reflection of the love of Christ for the church.

The Sixth Picture: Passion

The original Hebrew language was very picturesque, literally. The shapes of the ancient letters themselves displayed underlying meanings within the words they formed. The word pictures for Ish and Ishah reflect their root word meaning, "fire." Marriage is a place of fire, a place of passion. We were intended to be passionate people.

THE BAD

God created man and woman, Ish and Isha, and He gave them some requirements, lots of do's and only one don't — not to eat from the tree of the knowledge of good and evil. Then Satan arrived and offered them an opportunity to change the field. In Genesis 3:5, Satan proposed that they eat from the forbidden tree, "For God knows in the day that you eat from it, your eyes will be opened and you will be like God, knowing good and evil." Man and woman made their declaration of independence from God. *We can do it ourselves*, their actions declared.

Focus on this point of Satan's. What was he really offering? When God created man and woman, He made them in His image and likeness — they were already like God. What was Satan really offering man? He was offering man the opportunity to become like God through his own self-effort.

I've read lots of articles, spent years studying theology about what sin is and is not. You can look at all sorts of behaviors and make judgments, *this is sin, and that is sin.* I've studied 1 John 2:14, which demonstrates that sin will manifest one of three ways: lust of the flesh, lust of the eyes, and the pride of life. But those outward shows are not the core. The core of sin is *self-dependence* rather than *God-dependence*. Every other sinful behavior springs from that core of self-dependence. All our self-centered, self-justifying, self-vindicating, self-promoting, self-righteous, self-exalting, self-defending attitudes and behaviors spring from this core that beats away inside of us. And every one of us has it — that desire to be like God through our own effort. Let's follow this idea to its conclusion.

The "bad" is that Adam and Eve were already like God. Satan's offer was for them to have God-likeness on their own terms. The core of sin is not pride, lust or desire — those are manifestations. The core is self-dependence to the exclusion of God. We must realize that this drive toward self-dependence affects all of us in our marriages.

THE UGLY

Now the consequences start getting "ugly." Remember what Adam and Eve did once their eyes were opened by sin? There were five consequences. First, they covered themselves up. Hiding, cover-up and defending now became the relational stronghold. Can you imagine their thinking, "Oh, I wonder if God can see me behind this bush?" They hid from Almighty God!

Second came fear. For the very first time in their lives they felt fear. Until that point they had never been afraid of anything. Now they had FEAR. Before the fall, when Adam and Eve went to bed at night, Adam never turned to Eve and said, "You got anything in the refrigerator for tomorrow?" He never had to say, "The cupboards are empty."

Eve never said, "You'd better get out and get a job buddy, 'cause we don't have anything to eat." She never said anything like that. She didn't have to. When Adam and Eve went to bed at night, they had no idea what they would eat the next day. They just knew that God was taking care of them. Not anymore. Now fear entered the scene. They would become afraid of everything. Not just what was outside the home, but now also on the inside.

Third came judging. They ate from a really, really bad tree — the tree of the knowledge of good and evil. Before then nothing in creation had experienced evil. Nor was there an experience of good in comparison. All creation was dependent on the goodness of God. Now Adam and Eve would have open eyes not just to see it but, even worse, they would become judges of it. They would judge each other, and they would judge themselves.

They would develop "I" problems. *I want this, I want that, I need, I desire, I can't stand, I don't like, I won't take this from you.* Gone was a self-less heart. Gone was humility. Now came judging the other. *You're not good enough, you don't meet my needs, you don't provide, you don't measure up, you don't perform, you don't look right* and so on. One became a controller and the other became a survivor. Each now had a sense of right versus wrong that didn't exist before. Now they were not just judging, they had become judges.

Fourth came blaming. God confronted Adam saying, "What have you done?" Like all good males, Adam responded with two-directional blame, "It wasn't me (deflection), it was the woman (blaming) You gave me (justifying)." So it was not just *her* fault; it was actually God's fault for giving the woman to him.

Fifth, betrayal. So the woman is standing there with her fig leaves on, when she hears this guy, who was her trusted best friend, say, "God, it's the woman You gave me …." Imagine her shock! "You mean … what?" Now another horror enters the picture. Woman is betrayed by her husband, her head, and she will not trust him again. Leadership betrayal. His leadership will no longer be about her, but all about him.

And when God turns to her with His question, the woman says, "It was the serpent you sent. That serpent caused me to sin." Sin has taken its toll; for the woman, too, rationalizes and defends. What might have happened if they had just said, "We have sinned; help us, we are broken"?

But self-dependence was what Satan offered, and they took the bait. Instead of dependence on the Lord, they declared Independence Day at that sad moment. Part of what has to happen in marriage rebuilding is the realization of how selfish we are. How self-dependent. How protective.

What a beginning we make when we come to the foot of the cross and confess that Independence Day is over! We so need to admit that we are all selfish people. There is a selfish person inside every single one of us, even as we're learning to be more Christlike. Marriage will expose every area that you have not made subject to the Lordship of Christ.

Now, what each of us does with what we know is problematic, because we will take God's principles and start to turn them around. Instead of being courageous, we will be fearful. Instead of telling the truth, we will hide. Instead of bringing our faults and sins to the surface, we will cover things up. And we will blame others.

I've determined in my marriage that I need to see myself as someone who needs to change, that the core issue in my marriage is my own selfishness, and that I need to see that I don't need to hide the truth anymore. I need to be open and willing to be examined — no blaming and pushing off responsibility on my wife or family members. I love that in my family we can joke about each other and laugh a lot. But there's also this piece: Nobody seems very cautious about telling me when I do something wrong. No hold is barred, no pain is spared. I love it. I have nothing to prove.

I believe you can change your marriage when you start to see that your helper is suitable for you as your Isha. You are Ish. You need to backtrack through the original Ish and Isha's process of *living in fear, hiding the truth, covering up, and blaming*. Those four ugly responses were never intended for marriage at all. Yet now they exist worldwide.

We need to be willing to be open, willing to let people speak into our lives, to share their hearts with us. We need, by God's grace displayed at the cross, to be the person to come with bended knee and a humble heart, saying, "Lord, change me." *Marriage Made Simple* is all about "Lord, change me."

When couples head into divorce, they think nothing can change the outcome. But I know a couple on the East coast who played out this concept of "Lord, change me." They went through the legalities; the divorce papers were signed. They had become bitter and angry. Then one day, he said to her, "When I look at the children's feet, I see yours." That statement melted her heart, and she said, "What are we doing?" They got help and now they teach marriage seminars.

Can we begin to see the essence of sin in our lives — that self-protectiveness and self-centeredness hold the idea that "it's all about me and I'm not willing to have anyone speak into my life"? Instead, let's begin letting God build us out and make us the husbands, fathers, and sons He created us to be.

That's the challenge. Remember, God uses your marriage to show you every area you have not subjected to Christ's Lordship. Learn to live unselfishly.

Some people are givers, and some people are takers. Some will give and give and give, and the others just take and take and take. I knew someone who wanted so badly to get reconciled with her husband that she would jump in after a conflict and say, "I'm sorry, I'm sorry it's all my fault." And her husband would say, "I forgive you." And that was it.

Then she'd think to herself, "Wait a minute, what about you? Don't you have to apologize to me?" And her husband was thinking, "You just said it was all your fault."

She thought she was doing the right thing, but felt whipped and defeated. Finally a counselor told her, "It's not 'all' your fault; you need to take responsibility only for your part of the conflict. That frees him up and releases you, so that he can take responsibility for his part."

In one marriage I counseled, the husband was apologizing for this and apologizing for that, and I realized he was sacrificing his self-image on the altar of his wife's ego. She'd say, "You're right — you were wrong." But there was no mutuality. He had become quite co-dependent (or a better term, "henpecked"). So we started addressing this issue in a specific scenario.

I asked her, "In all of this, do you see yourself wrong?"

She thought and said, "No, quite frankly I don't."

I said, "Well, in the whole vast scheme of things, was there a way that you could've been wrong in some way?"

"No," she replied, "I don't think I was."

"In the terms of eternity," I said, "when you see how all things can play out, is there one possible way that you could have been at fault here in some way?"

After careful consideration came the reply, "Nope, I don't think so." She was totally sincere.

I wondered where I could go with that. The Holy Spirit gave me wisdom to say, "So, what you're telling me is that you're perfect?"

Since she knew she was a sinner, this question broke open her whole understanding of her self-centeredness. She started learning to take ownership of her own "stuff." She started admitting her faults and confessing her own apology. Some people will give and give; some take and take. Later, we will see the balance in giving and taking. In our hearts, we need to be right with God, to walk in humility.

The Shepherd's heart is to learn to be unselfish, to be brutally honest with ourselves in marriage. It's coming to give rather than coming to get. We need to stop using relationships for what we can get and start looking for what we can give. I once heard a pastor say to the bride and groom in a wedding ceremony, "I challenge you to out-serve one another."

Prayer:

Father God, thank You for Your Word and for your Spirit at work within us. Thank You for Your blessings. Thank you, Jesus, for the Hebrew language and for Genesis and for the beauty of marriage and for the changes that we need to bring to the table. Thank you, Lord, that we also need to be cautious, to not just sacrifice ourselves on our spouse's ego, but to let You have Your place in our life. Amen.

CHAPTER 4: ALIENS AND STRANGERS

"Therefore, confess your sins to one another, and pray for one another so that you may be healed. The effective prayer of a righteous man can accomplish much."

—James 5:16

WHEN I start marriage work with a couple, as mentioned earlier, I usually tell them I am dealing with three personalities or entities: "you" plus "me" plus "we." The preceding three chapters have focused on the "me" in the triangle these entities form. We've established that the priority relationship is vertical. And each of us needs to fix the "Me" before fixing "You" or "We."

The first problem we each face in marriage is our own wholeness or fullness. When the vertical walk is in place, we can start to manage horizontal relationships. This is true in all of life. Rather than manipulating our spouse to do what "I" want her or him to do, our foundation must become what God wants to show each of us and how "I" need to change. It's called ending the blame game: *It's all her (or his) fault. If she (or he) would just change, …. If it weren't for her (or him), I'd be happy.*

Think of flying on an airplane. As soon as you board, the flight attendant warns you that in the event of "the unlikely evacuation over water" — which always gives you that really great feeling, anyway — "your seat cushion turns into a flotation device."

Seriously? Have you ever checked to see if it turns into a flotation device? The flight attendant also reminds passengers in that pre-flight instruction, should there be a loss of cabin pressure, there is something you have to do first. The instructions are very clear: Do not put the mask on someone else. You are not to assist your children, your baby or someone else until you have taken care of yourself. In marriage, I need to have the mask on me first, so that I'm taking in oxygen before I begin to assist others in applying their masks.

Moving forward, we'll shift gears to the "We." But as we examine men and women in all their differences and determine how the complex pieces of our relationships fit together, you must highlight, bold, and underline the importance of your vertical relationship with God. You need to remind yourself repeatedly, "When I get healthier, we get healthier." *Work on you first.*

OK, let's start by looking at the male/female differences. They are mind blowing. I've counted more than 30 major categorical differences between men and women. We live out *Alien Nation* (and sometimes *Zombie Apocalypse*). I know; I'm married, too.

Remember how men want to slay dragons and rescue princesses? And women want a knight in shining armor and to live happily ever after? And that men think linearly, like a strand of Christmas lights in series? And that when one light burns out, the whole string burns out?

That's how guys tend to be. They usually can't multitask. I am that way. My wife will say to me, "Let's do such-and-such," and as I'm trying to make a phone call, she'll start giving me a list and, all of a sudden, I'm all frustrated and she's saying, "Why would you be frustrated? I'm just trying to tell you everything that needs to be done."

I love the story of the couple who have been dating for six months. She is thinking they need to DTR (you know, the words that drain the blood from a man's face: "Discuss the Relationship"). It goes a bit like this:

She says, "You know, we've been dating for six months."

He thinks, *Six months. Has it been that long?*

She: "Well, I was just wondering where we are going."

He: *Six months, I just can't believe that.*

She: "I mean, if we are to go on further we should think about where we're headed."

He: *Wow, six months. I don't think I changed the oil in the engine.*

She: "Maybe you don't want to talk about it."

He: *Hope that guy at the auto shop put in the right oil; he's not that sharp sometimes.*

She: "Maybe you just don't want to go further with me at all."

He: *I have got to make an appointment and get that taken care of next week.*

She: "You probably have no intentions of going on; maybe you don't like me that much anyway."

He: *I think I can do that next week on Wednesday.*

She: "PULL OVER THIS CAR RIGHT NOW! I WANT TO GET OUT."

He: "What?" *Now where did that come from?*

And so it starts.

Men just aren't wired like women are. We burn out one light over here, and our whole string is burnt out. Women, on the other hand, are wired more parallel. They can take out bulbs, put them in, take them out, and put them in. We guys absolutely cannot do that!

Remember what James Dobson writes in his book *Bringing Up Boys* about that chemical wash that occurs in boy babies as they develop in utero, and separates the hemispheres of the brain? So guys really can't think from both sides of our brain at the same time. It's what makes guys very goal- and target-oriented, and very command-oriented.

It also makes guys on the wild side. When my wife and I go shopping, I'll say, "Let me have the cart."

And she'll say, "I'm not giving you the cart!"

And I'll say, "Why, Honey?"

Then she'll say, "Because I know what you'll do with it."

Pretty soon I'm scootering along going up and down the aisles riding on the back of that cart. You'd think at my age I'd probably have that under control, but I'm always going to be kind of on the wild side. Guys, we're meant to be that way.

John Eldredge's book *Wild at Heart*[27] declares that guys were intended to be wild. When we shop, we hunt it, we bag it, and we drag it to the car and stash it in our cave. That's just the way we do things.

In further contrast to men, women think in a kind of tangled-spaghetti sort of way, and can multitask and do things several different

---

[27] John Eldredge, *Wild at Heart: Discovering the Passionate Soul of a Man*, Thomas Nelson, (Nashville, TN: 2001).

ways. Guys, on the other hand, tend to think in boxes. We have mental boxes for everything. For example, I have my work box. I have my church box. I have a hobby box, a friend box, a television box, a sports box, a leisure box and a sex box. And according to pastor and speaker Mark Gungor, we never allow those boxes to touch each other.[28]

When I was in the army, everybody was upset about the food they served, but I thought it was great. They had these trays that separated things. So my peas never touched the potatoes, and the potatoes never touched the roast beef (or whatever the meat was that we were getting). I loved that! Now I had a box for everything, even the way I ate.

Guys have all sorts of boxes: their electronics box, their sports box, their television box. Then there's the "nothing box." That's where most of us guys like to go a lot. We'd like to live in that box. My wife will say to me, "What are you doing?"

"Nothing." I'm really not doing anything. I'm not lying.

"What are you thinking?"

"Nothing."

"How do you feel about that?"

"Don't really feel anything at all."

"What did you do today?"

"Not much."

"Who did you talk to?"

"No one particularly."

Yeah, nothing. And my wife thinks I'm LYING. I'm not. She thinks I'm avoiding her, but I'm not really. I'm just ... in the zone.

Women love to connect; we guys just love peace. Literally, not thinking anything. And we will sit in front of the TV and live in that beautiful nothing box until somebody rudely interrupts us from our nothingness to ask us what we think of this outfit, or what did we think of someone's

---

[28] http://markgungor.com/products/laugh-your-way-to-a-better-marriage-hardcover.

shoes, or to say we can go to the store and buy another this or that. And we are, like, there in our nothing box! And we want to stay there!

Here's another one. Men come to relationships with a *command-to-control* mentality. It's our default. We learn early on to control our environment by being in command. That's inherent in guys. We control or watch over or manage our environments by making command-level decisions. Women, on the other hand, come to relationships with a (now watch this) *connect-to-control* default. That is how they control their environment — by connecting.

So a man wants to command to control and a woman wants to connect to control. The originator of this interesting concept is Dr. David Clarke, in his excellent book *Men Are Clams, Women Are Crowbars*.[29] He writes that he discovered this "command control" and "connect control" behavior by playing Barbie dolls with his three little daughters. They sat down and he thought, *Grab some clothes, slap them on the doll, let's go. This won't take very long at all.*

The girls spent a significant amount of time dressing and accessorizing and making sure that everything was right. And as he was doing this with his daughters, he began to realize they were synergizing to make decisions, rather than the way we guys do it. They would put on one thing and all of them would comment about how that doll looked. Now, if you put a 4-, 5-, 6-year-old little boy in there, he'll be sliding those Barbie dolls across the floor like a boat, flying them through the air or making siren sounds, like a fire truck — command to control.

Those little girls were all about connecting with each other. They would comment on how they were accessorizing and they would comment on this one, that one, oh, and then they would change. David Clarke watched one of them say, "Let's go to the beach. Let's take our Barbies to the beach." The other little girls didn't want to do that. This began a huge discussion on where they were going to go, and it ended up that they were going to the marketplace.

Guys, this drives me nuts! We just aren't wired this way.

---

[29] David Clarke, *Men are Clams, Women Are Crowbars: Understand Your Differences and Make Them Work*, Promise (Uhrichsville, OH, 1998).

Let's say my friend Jimmy and I are out on the baseball field, and I hit the ball, and I hit it pretty well. I'm pretty proud; I take off toward first base running hard and slide in. Jimmy jumps up, grabs the ball in the air, pulls the ball into his hands; it's an amazing catch. I might have complimented him, but he's caught my double-base-hit ball. It falls out; I'm in luck. He scoops it up and runs over to the base. We both arrive there together.

I yell, "I'm safe! Yes!"

He says, "No, you're out!"

I say, "No way, ya clown, I'm safe!"

He says, "You're nuts; you were out!"

I yell, "You want to settle this outside?"

Jimmy yells back, "We ARE outside." Obviously, not a successfully negotiated agreement.

Now, in the midst of this, across the field comes a guy dressed in a zebra outfit, who says when he arrives there, "What seems to be the problem?"

I say, "I'm safe and he says I'm out."

The umpire replies, "Well, you were out."

I look at Jimmy and Jimmy looks at me and I shrug. "Guess I was out." Problem solved. He's in command; we're under his control. Rules! Code!

We were about to fight each other because we were so mad. And some well-accessorized guy in a zebra suit was able to come over and solve it, because there is a system and he has the rules.

Men are all about a "code of honor." We're all about a man code that exists among us. And we don't relate in a synergistic way. When women are playing whatever they're playing — softball or whatever — unless they're competing at a very high level, they're going to be more concerned about the relationships they have on the field than about winning the game. I'm competitive; I could care less about relationships. I'm so competitive, I had to quit playing softball. I was so frustrated with our players because they weren't working together and we weren't winning the game when somebody yelled across the field, "They're only 8 years old!" At that point I had to learn some things about not being too competitive.

Let's not miss the point here. Guys, our wives have the ability to keep us from being shallow people. They help us do what we need to do to learn a little more about relationships and relational values. It's hard for us guys; we don't naturally relate. We naturally kill things. We naturally bag them. We naturally drag them to the car. Our wives can help us to be more relational. Remember, relationships are what God is all about. It's called loving others more than ourselves.

Let's start with first learning that there are *Five Levels of Relationships.* And believe it or not, they can be measured.

Level One is Acquaintance. The bottom level of relationship is an acquaintance level or a cliché level. Small talk. It's where people use words like, "Hey, how are you doing?" "I'm doing well." "What do you think of the weather?" "Did ya see that Cornhusker game?" (Yeah, I'm from Nebraska.) "What do you think of this, what do you think of that?" That's the acquaintance level. It's shallow communication. It doesn't take much time or commitment. You can know approximately 75 to 150 people on a first-name basis as acquaintances.

Level Two is Informational. Shop talk. "What do you think of the Bears?" "What do you think of the Cardinals?" "What did you think of this?" "Did you see how so-and-so made that play, caught that ball, and so on?" People can generally handle 35 to 75 relationships at this level. (These are general, not specific, figures.) I call these first two levels "news, sports, weather."

With my own dad, until he had a stroke, it was always news, sports, weather. We could never get any further beyond these levels because that's just where he liked to talk. "What do you think of the news? What do you think of politics? How is the weather?"

"Oh, it's been really cold, it's snowing." I kept thinking life's got to be more than this. Then my dad went through a stroke, and as he came out on the other side of it, he realized that relationships are more important.

Both of these levels are important in a marriage. It's necessary for couples to have fun, to share events and schedules. To laugh with chitter chatter. But marriage is deeper.

Level Three is Teamwork. It's about working together toward a common goal, a common understanding. In this relational level, there is a joining together with another person or group of people because you share a common goal. The teamwork level of relationship is designed to accomplish a specific task. And it is based on or empowered by unity. Commonality. It is a performance-based relationship. And it's crucial in order to accomplish the team's task.

But I would venture to say most marriages never go beyond Level Three. It's because most of us guys don't know how to get there. And the longer we're married, the more we stop trying. And I think that's the tragedy. The challenge is to keep trying, keep figuring out how this works, and keep trying to move beyond performance-based Level Three. And, guys, we do this level really well. We can work with each other based on common goals all the time. So far, nothing has been all that threatening. We'd be so satisfied to just stay at Level Three. Right up until we arrive at some point in our marriage and realize we missed it.

I kept getting wake-up calls in life — buddies who died or were injured, families deeply wounded. One day I read about some best friends from Minnesota who went fishing every single weekend, had been doing it for 20 years. Minnesotans love to fish. During the winter, they are so passionate that when the lakes ice over, people take their fish houses and tow them out in the middle of the lake and park them there. Seeing them, I thought they were outhouses. (I'm from Nebraska, remember.) And I thought, that's the most disgusting thing I've ever seen. Imagine my relief to find out they were fish houses (no pun intended).

One day I read in the paper how four of these guys who fished almost every weekend for 20 years drove up in front of the fifth guy's house and honked the horn like they always did. They knocked on the door, and, it seemed really strange, their buddy wasn't there. His wife and kids were gone for the weekend. He'd always been there for 20 years; they were friends since before high school. They walked to the back, opened the garage door, and there he hung. From the rafter. He had killed himself the night before. What a horrible loss!

But you know what the greater tragedy was? Not one, NOT ONE of those other four guys knew why he had killed himself. They were buddies for 20 years and not one of them had gotten out of that teamwork, let's-go-fishing stage. And they were friends! They drank beer together. Bought bait. Talked about spinners and sweethearts and kids and stuff they were into. Fishing partners. But not one of them knew what was going on personally with the others. So let's call it ... shallow. Empty. Alone in a crowd.

I want to challenge you, as we explore this idea of relationships, to understand how we go from Level Three to Level Four and Level Five. And, guys, you're not going to be very comfortable with this, but it actually involves learning to get in touch with your emotions.

The Apostle Paul wrote, "If I speak with the tongues of men and angels ... if I give my body to be burned, ... if I preach with great words, ... and I have faith to move mountains, ... but I do not have love, I am nothing."[30] I don't like that. I want him to say I am something. But those words hit me. "I am nothing." Everything we do and build and grow and strengthen, all our goals outside those two circles will ultimately burn away. Tough to hear. We can learn these relational levels and we can practice them, but they take some work.

The benefits are amazing. Where do you think God wants to go in His relationship with you? In your prayer time, do you think God wants you to come to Him as you go about your day, and you're praying and talking to God and giving him news, sports, and weather? Do you think God's really excited about that? Like, "You can't believe the weather down here, God, we really need better weather over the weekend ...." I'm not trying to knock your prayer life. But I'm saying that many guys could go a little bit deeper instead of coming to our Father God in the teamwork mode.

I'm a seminary-trained pastor, a "godly man." I'm in love with God because of what He's done for me, but you wouldn't know that by what I give to Him. That's what hit me in 1996. I couldn't get any further than that third level, that teamwork, church-building relationship. *God, we're*

---

[30] 1 Corinthians 13:1-3 (my paraphrase).

in ministry, we're saving the world, we're discipling, we're doing this, and we're doing that.

I want to tell you that emotions are the vocabulary of the spirit. Let's say I take a guy to the Cardinals game, and we're jumping in the air, popcorn flying all around! We're beating each other on the arm, "Did you see that? Did you see that play?" Of course, I saw it. I was sitting right here next to you. All the emotion in the world is right there. Now you take that same guy, that 250-pound guy jumping up and down at the game, and he goes home and cringes in front of his wife because he has never been taught to go beyond Level Two or Three with her.

But you will have to learn to use what I have learned to call my rational mind and my emotional mind. Want to hear a secret? Your wife is hugely wired in both sides of her brain. She has an internal radar that knows where you are at One, Two or Three; it is acidic to her heart.

Level Four is Sharing. It's where we share our feelings and opinions and judgments. In this fourth level of relationship, people are exposing their inner heart, understanding each other's opinions. We have a mutual sense of knowing each other, specifically, in terms of what we feel about things.

I never want to drive 100 miles in the car sitting next to my wife and not saying anything. I'm thankful that Cheryl will see a cactus and say, "Look at that cactus!" I'm thinking, *You've seen a cactus before. It's a cactus. We've lived in the desert.*

But Cheryl will get excited about little things and in that way, she has pulled me out of this person who is all about goals and performing and helps me understand that I need to be much more about connecting relationally, because relationships are the only thing that will survive in God's eternity.

In fact, there are only two things besides God that will last forever. One — God's Word. Two — other people. Here's a hard-hitting statement: If your mission statement in life does not include the phrase "so that I may benefit others," you are self-consumed. Marriage will teach you that if you let it.

This sharing works with your kids, too. So often we guys would like to have our kids on remote: "Be Quiet!" (Click) and they "Mute."

I could do that with my son, Jeremiah, from across the room. I'd give him "the look," and he'd be like, "Oh, boy, I'm in trouble." He would shape up. Remote-control kid, right? Yeah, right up until they hit the teen years and then leave for college. Why? Because you've been parenting at levels one through three and never getting inside your child's heart.

You're not connecting with them. You may be controlling their behavior, but you're not connecting. It's not until you get into sharing your heart and hearing theirs that you connect with your kids. Some parents let their kids share their hearts for about two seconds. Then they're busy telling them all the things that they should be feeling. Kids can say some really stupid things, that's true, but you've just got to hang in there. And you may just step over that line of teamwork as a parent into sharing and being real.

One of the things I did with Jeremiah when he was about three years old — I was learning a lot of these things — and I realized that I was 5 foot 11, and he stood at about 36 inches. I would pick him up and set him on a kitchen counter to have a talk. Now, 3-year-old boys will not stand on counters very long, I get that. But he and I used to look each other eye-to-eye. Jeremiah and I would talk together eye-to-eye, and I would listen and he would teach me, his dad, a lot.

From brain studies by research specialists Dr. Jim Wilder and Dr. Marcus Warner, we know that we can do four things to change established relational circuits with another person and build a deep feeling of awareness and understanding.[31] These four change agents are (1) Become curious instead of criticizing, (2) Be appreciative instead of dismissive, (3) Be kind instead of harsh, and (4) Speak in an "ice-cream sandwich" style of communication, which I'll explain in chapter 12.

We thereby move from Teamwork talk that is critical and controlling into mutuality and awareness and discovery.

---

[31] Marcus Warner and E. James Wilder, *Rare Leadership: 4 Uncommon Habits for Increasing Trust, Joy, and Engagement in the People You Lead,* Moody Publishers (2016).

> ## IT'S NOT ABOUT FINDING THE RIGHT ONE.
>
> ## IT IS ABOUT BEING THE RIGHT ONE.

Learn in marriage to hear your spouse's heart. Give her the value of wanting to know her emotional heart. Why does she feel the way she does? What is really going on in her?

Level Five is Connectedness. I use this word because the word I really want to use would have every guy going weak at the knees and shutting down. What I actually mean is "intimacy." So I don't use the "I" word; I say instead, "connected," because it's also a very powerful descriptor. It doesn't mean that you are this touchy, feeling-all-over-each-other, google-eyed, pedicure provider. But you learn to be personal and open and safe and genuine and honest and transparent. Soul-to-soul, so to speak. It takes some work and effort but then, good things always do.

The key to this level lies in something Jesus reiterated frequently. This is the level of humility. It is seeking another person's interest over one's own. It is not coming to be served but to serve, especially one's spouse and their heart needs. This is where a marriage goes beyond expectation. Two people not blaming, not judging but out-serving each other. Level Five is so hard to do, but it is powerful when it happens. And its biggest deterrent is spelled ... S-E-L-F-I-S-H-N-E-S-S.

I've heard people say they're marrying their soulmate, and then a year and a half later, they're divorced. I don't believe in soulmates. I never have. After my years of experience as a counselor and mentor, I believe a successful marriage is not about finding the right one; it is about BEING the right one. The one God gave you is the one God gave you, and you need to work and learn how you can make that person your mate. Here is my mate. Let's make that relationship honest and transparent; soul-to-soul. How do you get that?

Let's see if I can help you understand how to get that. Most guys know how to "level up" in a video game. So how do you level up relationally? You need to go through life experiences. Going from Level One to Level Two to Level Three and into Levels Four and Five involves four things.

Prioritize

First, you must prioritize your mate, your spouse. Make her your priority. Go places together. If she is gracious enough to not ask you to go shopping for women's clothing, you can still accompany her to the supermarket. Why? Because she can't handle grocery shopping on her own? No, because shopping with your spouse is priority bonding time. Who assigned her that job? You and she both have busy lives, but try to prioritize going shopping with her.

What are some other ways to prioritize your wife and family? How about taking a family outing instead of watching a football game on television? Here's an amazing truth: *The score will be the same whether you watch it or not.* Listen, guys, television is leisure; it is not a lifestyle. So shut it off or watch a family-friendly show with your wife and family. Prioritize your family. That's my challenge to you guys.

You need to cultivate a sense of wife and family first, so you don't grow apart. If you work backwards through those levels, starting at four then three then two, then pretty soon your marriage relationship is all about clichés and connecting as acquaintances because that's all you know how to do. Become friends. Never stop dating. After God, she becomes your first priority. For life.

And that means invest your time. Every one of us has the same amount of hours in a week given us by God. Time is not elastic. Sometimes we think we can give away time to others when we really don't have it. So we need to use our time purposefully. Your schedule demonstrates your priorities. It shows you where your true priorities are.

Picture your life in terms of a circle cut into different pie shapes. The pieces of the pie represent all your activities: work, fun, leisure, church, family, spouse, God, and so on. When everything is in balance, that circle is a true circle. But what happens if your boss at work asks you to work nine hours instead of eight hours? Well, you have to, or you will lose your job. *Uh oh, you're defined by your job!*

So you start working nine hours, but soon that's not enough. Then you're working 10. Then, "Oh, we need you on the weekends. Without you we can't succeed." Now, because you're working 10-hour days and on the weekends, the other guy in the office who was going to take a stand for his family is also forced to work those insane hours. Because of your compromise! You need to stay balanced. You can say, "I'll give you a certain amount of time and that's what I'll give you."

Since time is not elastic, what happens if you dedicate more of it to work? Somewhere, something has to pay the price. Time is not elastic. So what are you losing? Time for God, time for spouse, time for family, time for church. And in this day and age, we need to be people of commitment for God. So when you start to see that pie bumping out of shape, you need to pull aside in your life and re-assess. You need to understand that you can't just respond to everything or everyone that comes down the road. Your priorities determine what you can and cannot do.

Have you ever heard of "The Tyranny of the Urgent"? Good becomes the enemy of better; better becomes the enemy of best; because somebody runs into the room and says, "You have to do this right now!" God has taught me two wonderful words that both start with N. These are the most magical words in the English language. If you can master them, God will bless you richly. N-word number one: NO. When people respond, "But you have to," I can say, "What part did you not understand — the N or the O?" When life is screaming to grab my time, I can stop it with one word. NO!

The second N-word is Next. I have learned the hard way to not waste my time with people who waste my time. Sometimes I just need to move on to the next one. Sometimes people pull my time away from the important things. Friends, family, work, others ... all have voices we hear, and they are demanding our time. "Sorry, I just can't do it. My wife (or my family) is first in my time circle."

Demanding people and circumstances always have the potential to emotionally hook us, to draw us into their vortex because of urgency. Yet our priority system tells us what we can and cannot do.

The best way to manage your time is to put God first. When God is at the center of your life, when you put Him first, then your priorities have a foundational place and God is in the midst of it all. He can tell you when and where to back off and make you aware of the levels of your relationships. Learn how to prioritize your time with God.

Commitment

You need to do more than put in your time with your spouse; you need to engage with her (or him). It's not just going down the road from point A to B. It's not just spending time together in the same car; it's the commitment to learn about each other, to actually talk. To relate. To connect. It's letting her in to engage with you. It's accepting your wife or your husband into your thinking. It's listening and talking. It's about hearing their heart. It's about the commitment to engage.

Sometimes your wife is at a Level 2 relationally when you're at a Level 4 or 5. You know what? You can't force people from one level to another. You invite them to go from one level to another. A wife might say, "I can't get my husband out of Level 2. He never wants to talk about anything but news, sports, weather and sex. I can't get him to step outside his box." You need to accept your spouse where he or she is. Let him or her come alongside in their time.

Commitment means standing in tough times rather than getting freaked out. Commitment is unwavering when conversations are tough, hanging in there and saying, "I need to learn from this." Commitment in relationships is about setting someone ahead of ourselves. Yes, this can get out of balance, but partners in real marriages have learned to invest in each other. Marriage isn't about two perfect partners, it's about two imperfect people who are committed to partner together.

Safety

The third way we "level up" into more connected relationships is by being safe with each other. Often, couples end up in emotional swordplay. She's trying to get in and connect while he's trying to keep her out. Parry and thrust. In and out. What you need to do is open up and get into the relationship together. There is a wonderful peace that comes with safety. Keep each other safe. Allow your spouse to speak his or her heart and hurts and be there to listen and help clean up the mess. Safety means we leave a lot of the judging behind.

Most guys will shut down immediately and never talk again if they feel judged. Yes, we do stupid things. Yes, we need help at times. But people — and guys especially — if they feel like they are coming home to a critic or a judge, move out. They move to the safety of Level 1 or Level 2. That is why guys verbally abuse each other. I know, ladies, it sounds crazy but when I verbally abuse my friend, I communicate the opposite ... you're safe with me. I'm not judging you. Not finding fault. Not going to say "told you so." Most guys learn — now get this — BY FAILURE. It is how we are wired. (More on this later.) Help each other feel safe and supported and encouraged as much as you can.

There are times in all relationships when we truly believe we have married an alien. "What the fat are you talking about" ... "Where did that come from" ... "Seriously, who are you" ... "Get a life" ... "Grow up" ... "I hate you ...." All words of alienation. That's why I call this chapter "Aliens and Strangers." We start polarizing right here. Instead of building out our relationship, we grow further apart. Safety means you protect, you care for, you encourage, you listen, you find the good in the bad.

Safety also means you allow yourself to be vulnerable. You ask for help. You listen to what your spouse is saying even when she is speaking harsh words about you. You listen. You hear the reproof and admit your own failures. It's ownership. You become a safe place where she or he can speak the truth in love regarding what you may have done differently. You're the first to say, "You're right, I blew it, I'm sorry." Safety means you're vulnerable to being told what to do once in a while. Vulnerable to allow conflict to occur without being defensive.

And safety is about trust. Extending your trust in the other person's intentions. People get married and then, in about two years, get injured by each other and start closing gates and doors and windows. Sometimes people have to do that in abusive relationships, but generally we need to open up, not just to be vulnerable but also to rely on and trust our partner again.

Some people are taught, "If it's not nice, don't say it." That's not biblical. The Bible teaches *if it's not truthful and can't be spoken in love, don't say it.*

Paul addresses that concept when he writes, "Speaking the truth in love we are to grow up in all aspects into Him who is the Head."[32] Your partner may not be the kindest person at times, but listen for the truth. Trust your spouse with your heart and entrust him or her with your confidence. Some may say, "Wow, I will just get killed." Then bring in added safety. Get a marriage coach. Talk openly and vulnerably. Find places of safety for each other.

If you share with your wife that you're about to make a discovery and say something, she will track with you. If she's running circles around you at 22,000 words with gusts up to 25,000, you have to ask her to slow down. You can say, "Honey, slow down, I'm about to give birth to an emotion. I'm about to give birth to a new thought. So be gentle with me, I can only translate one emotion at a time."

Cheryl and I use humor a lot. We tease each other and laugh at each other. Our friend John Riva was driving us to the airport, and Cheryl and I were involved in a conflict of wills. We worked our way through it and ended up teasing and laughing with each other. John said, "I would love to see you guys have an argument." And immediately Cheryl and I both responded with, "You just did."

Cheryl is safe for me. I know her. I trust her. Sometimes when she moves in to tell me I've blown something, I don't want to but I become vulnerable. I listen and hear and change. That's the core of levels in relationships.

As you do this, you will find each other as best friends. You will be able to share your hearts and connect in incredible ways. You'll do things together more as a team (Level Three). You'll share your thoughts and dreams more (Level Four), and you will find each other in connec-

---

[32] Ephesians 4:15.

tion (Level Five). You will start having more times of saying in wonderment and appreciation, "I can't believe we have each other."

Don't tell me it can't be done. We did it.

Breathe

One last thing — as you learn the relational levels in your marriage, *you must be careful not to force it beyond news, sports, weather when your relationship needs to breathe.* Relationships breathe back and forth. Sometimes we push our relationships to make them do something or other, but in reality, they need to breathe.

Learn to let your relationship breathe. One day you may both feel very close together, and the next, one of you may want to be closer while the other one is moving away. Then positions may reverse. Relationships do this. It doesn't mean you're not at the same level with each other. It's just that everyone needs to breathe, and conversations need to breathe, too. Relationships need time to mature and grow. It's in this normal relational cycle that you stay the course. You are committed. When one or the other feels distant, it's OK. You are committed to each other for life.

Prayer:

Father God, thank You for Your blessings. I pray, Father, that these principles would be an encouragement to others. Thank You, Jesus, for Your presence. Thank You for Your Spirit. Thank You for Your leadership. Thank you for giving me my spouse, who is different, so I can mature and grow to be more Christlike. Help me move deeper in relational levels. Help me learn to share without being defensive. Help me trust my spouse, who seems like an alien sometimes. Show me, Lord, how I can grow. Amen.

CHAPTER 5: BENT BEARINGS

"Bearing with one another, and forgiving each other, whoever has a complaint against anyone; just as the Lord forgave you, so also should you."
—Colossians 3:13

WE all know there is really nothing simple about marriage. But I want us to recognize the most basic, foundational principles. It's like driving cross-country. No matter where you drive your car in the United States, everyone must obey the same set of rules. We may see different sights out the window and stop at different scenic overlooks, eat different foods, engage in different conversations. But we utilize the same traffic laws: Don't run red lights, stop at stop signs, go on green, watch out for road hazards, obey speed limits, and drive on the right side. *Marriage Made Simple* is all about understanding the basic "traffic laws" that make marriages work.

One of the simple basic rules of the road in relationships is learning that we are all different in some pretty cool and some very frustrating ways. I've learned through my own marriage and in counseling many others that we all arrive in marriage bent.

Growing up, I played pool and often saw players take a cue and roll it across the pool table. I wondered why they did that. I learned that a good player knows the different points to hit on the face of the cue ball; they all give the ball different tendencies when the cue hits the other ball. This is called using "English." If the stick is bent, the point that you're aiming at on the cue ball will not be the point you hit, and your ball won't do what you want it to do. You can't shoot pool with a bent cue. You may know where the shot is supposed to go, but with a bent cue stick, it's not going to get there. Like certain pool cues, we are all "bent" certain ways. So we will look at our various temperaments and how they affect us.

The way I am "bent" has much to do with the temperament that God gave me. Typically my "bent" determines where I get my energy from, how I take in information, how I process information and how I live it all out. Historically, temperaments are not a new revelation. Hippocrates, a physician in 390 B.C., observed there were different characteristics in people's behaviors. Dylan, a philosopher in 190 A.D. differentiated four general categories that people appeared to be shaped in. He actually, gross as it seems, applied them to body fluids. People were classified as choleric, sanguine, phlegmatic or melancholic.

Much more recently, Myers and Briggs, actually a mother-daughter team, studied people in the workforce during World War II. Industry leaders wanted to analyze how people thought and felt. So Katharine Myers and her daughter, Isabel Briggs, tested people to figure out how they perceived the world and made decisions. They published their findings from 1958 to 1962 as the Myers and Briggs Temperament Analysis. Myers and Briggs observed 16 different types. They defined the differences as the extrovert and the introvert, the intuitive and the sensory, the thinker and the feeler, the judger and the perceiver.

Furthermore, industrial psychologist Walter Vernon Clarke developed the behavioral assessment tool called the DiSC® system.[33] And Christian counselor Gary Smalley more humorously called all the different personality types interacting together "The Family Zoo."[34]

The point is we come into relationships built differently from birth. It's not about environmental shaping, it is all about the way God designed us. Mothers know this all too well. Kids come in different flavors. The Bible even alludes to this early developmental personality when it says, "Train up a child in the way he should go; even when he is old, he will not depart from it."[35] As Chuck Swindoll points out, the words "in the way he should go" reference the way the child is made. He restates the verse more accurately, "We are to train a child according to his or her characteristic manner."[36]

---

[33] https://www.discprofile.com/what-is-disc/overview/.

[34] Gary Smalley, *Making Love Last Forever*, Word Publishing Company, (Dallas, 1996).

[35] Proverbs 22:6.

[36] https://www.insight.org/resources/article-library/individual/a-better-way-to-train-up-a-child.

Think of temperaments as the way each of us is bent from the time we are born. Each of us comes with a natural shaping or style. Our brains are already built with hardwire. Temperaments affect how we relate to one another, how we absorb information, how we make decisions and how we orient to our world. Those things are all going on in our brains as we perceive our world and gather information for making decisions.

Temperaments can also be shaped by negative or abusive-childhood and early-adult experiences. Temperaments can have multiple expressions; some can be dominant, some regressive, some are social and some can only be seen under stress. A complete listing goes far beyond the comprehensiveness of this chapter.

Precision is necessary in relationships. To illustrate, I formerly worked as an insurance claims adjuster. My very first fire-loss allowed me to see the bearings and equipment that go inside a very high-speed jet engine compressor. Those bearings vibrate less than one-seventh of the diameter of a human hair. They have to be unbelievably precise because they rotate at 50,000 rpm or more. (Your car runs at about 1,500 to 2,700 rpm). Just the smallest variance at that speed would vibrate the engine into pieces. Having "an engine vibrate to pieces" while flying makes the rest of the trip rather nasty. Precision and balance are extremely important in pool cues, in jet engines and in relationships.

Now let's apply this principle to marriage. As soon as I said, "I do," I began to realize that my bride is slightly bent. She's strange; she's different; she moves in different directions from the way I move.

Obviously in marriage this bent will cause partners to be out of balance with each other. If both spouses operate in that bent condition, the vibration in their relationship can be self-destructive. The extrovert (sail) will drive the introvert (anchor) crazy. The suggestion "Let's go out and do something tonight" can be very challenging when the other partner wants to sit with a book and read. Let's see how you can understand and use this knowledge to bring balance to your relational engine.

Temperaments: What They Look Like

Imagine a huge room full of people, with two perpendicular lines dividing the room into four rectangles. These four quadrants will represent four basic personality types. The first two types of personalities are Extroverts and Introverts. An extrovert gets recharged by being around other people. Some people become energized when they're in highly social situations for a while. Others don't mind being around people for a while, but sooner or later, they will want to retreat to quiet solitude, because that recharges them. These people are more introverted.

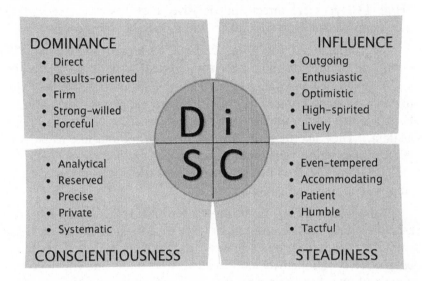

DOMINANCE
- Direct
- Results–oriented
- Firm
- Strong–willed
- Forceful

INFLUENCE
- Outgoing
- Enthusiastic
- Optimistic
- High–spirited
- Lively

D i
S C

- Analytical
- Reserved
- Precise
- Private
- Systematic

- Even–tempered
- Accommodating
- Patient
- Humble
- Tactful

CONSCIENTIOUSNESS

STEADINESS

So we will put all of our extroverts on the far side of the room and all of the introverts on the near side. Next we will divide the two groups again. On the left side of the room we will put the highly goal-oriented people. These folks like to have a plan, get things done, be on time, and take no prisoners. On the right side of the room are relationally oriented people. They are more concerned with how people feel than whether or not the mission is accomplished. They are more interested in helping others than in achieving an objective.

As different personalities have been observed over many years, researchers have typically defined them in four categories: The DiSC system identifies them as: (top left) "Dominance" or "Driver" or "D," (top right) "Influence" or "I," (bottom right) "Steadiness" or "S," and (bottom left) "Conscientiousness" or "Creative" or "C." Other systems identify them as the "Choleric" or "Lion," the "Sanguine" or "Otter," the "Phlegmatic" or "Golden Retriever," and the "Melancholic" or "Beaver."

So a "high D" refers to an extrovert (far side of the room) and goal-oriented (left side of room). This is this person's "bent." He or she is very energized by people and loves getting things done NOW. This person is direct, results-oriented, firm, strong-willed and forceful by nature. "High D" types are direct and decisive; they have high ego strength; they're problem solvers, risk takers and tend to be sole starters.

The "Influencers" (or "I" in the DiSC system), also known as "Sanguine" or "Otters" in the family zoo, are extroverts (back of the room) and people-oriented (right side). I love this group because they simply like to have a good time. They like being around people. They don't have huge agendas and want to have fun. No worries, be happy, "Hakuna Matata." They like to smile, like to be positive, and like to be part of what is happening. They want everyone to be happy, and I like that. "High I" types tend to be enthusiastic and trusting, optimistic and persuasive, communicating and impulsive.

In the front half of the room are the introverts. To the left are the goal-oriented, creative, compliant people, also known as the "Melancholic" or the industrious "Beavers" in The Family Zoo. The "high C" people are contemplative, tend to be very accurate, analytical, conscientious, cautious, fact finders, precise, and systematic with high standards.

Finally, to the right below the midline are the steady stabilizers, the people-oriented "Phlegmatic" or "Golden Retrievers." These are the "high S" types, and they tend to be good listeners, team players, a little bit on the possessive side but that's because they are loyal; they tend to be steady, predictable, understanding and friendly.

Step One: Know Thyself

To understand how these "bents" affect your relationships, you must first know your own. Obviously, this presentation is just an overview. I encourage you to call a counselor or coach and have yourself tested in this area. Some simple, but very insightful tools are available to help give you a greater understanding of who you are. My favorite is the MBTI (Myers Briggs Temperament Inventory).

The MBTI reveals how your personality type becomes the base for four different things you do:

- How you get energy
- How you process information
- How you make decisions
- How you choose your lifestyle

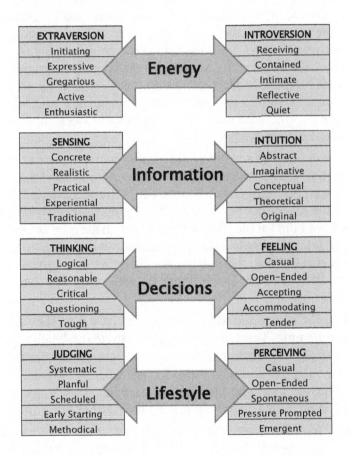

But first, learn to observe yourself. Do you see yourself as more people-oriented or more introspective? Do you like to be with others or like to be alone? Are you more goal-oriented or more relationship-oriented? Those questions will give you a basic idea of who you are.

Next observe how you deal with others. Whom do you like to be around and who frustrates you? Typically you will understand those of like temperament and be more frustrated with those who are different.

Step Two: Opposites Attract and Opposites Attack

As a pilot I learned of a dynamic that occurs in a twin-engine aircraft. If both engines are not working at the same speed and in the same direction at the same time, you can hear a terrible vibration and a pulsating noise between the two. This dissonance can be nauseating. A good pilot learns to "synchronize" by listening to the sounds the engines make as they work together. Modern planes do this electronically with a "sync" mechanism. A similar principle works for marriage and relationships. Being out of sync with each other causes bad "vibes" and a feeling of nausea in those involved.

Let's say you put a "high D" in a room with a couple of "high C's" or a "high I," like maybe taking the family zoo to Disneyland. The "high D" will start off and say, "Get in the car — we've got to go! We have to stick to the schedule." So quite frankly, he makes everybody miserable. That's what I did for the longest time … just made a lot of people miserable. But I did get people to Disneyland and we did get there on the right day and checked into the hotel at the right time and arrived at the ride on time. *OK! Time's up! Lunch!* That's the idea of being strong-willed; we take leadership.

"High I's" want to go to Disneyland and have fun. They simply want to enjoy the time. These people totally frustrate the "high D's." ("High D's," actually, are frustrated by just about everybody but themselves.) Picture a "high-D" dad who wants to "get 'er done," and he's got a couple of "high-I" kids who just want to have fun. They're loose and running off in their own directions, driving their dad nuts.

As a "high D," I get frustrated with "I's" and "C's," but the "high S's" are my biggest challenge. When I managed a church staff, God gave me mostly "S's." as co-workers. Staff meetings were hard — while I appreciated the S's loyalty, they didn't get a lot of stuff done. "I want you to do this and that," I'd say. And they'd answer, "We'll get to it, we'll get to it."

"When? Next year?"

So "high S's" and "high D's" can be in conflict. "High C's" and "high I's" will often butt heads too.

Before we dog the "D's" and "C's" too much, think about who you'd rather have performing open-heart surgery on you. Imagine a roomful of "high I's" kind of high-fiving one another and clapping and yapping about last night's work and everything's fun for them while you're squirting a bleeder. Or maybe someone says, "Why don't we get some anesthesia over here for this guy?" And you're lying there hearing all this chatter going on. Wouldn't you be thinking, "I want 'high D's' and 'high C's', and the rest of you people are out of here"?

Let's transfer this picture to a family. Everyone's sitting around the table talking and sharing, and the "high C" is busy about where the silverware is placed, or how the food should be served. We "D's" may criticize those people for being so systematic, but we certainly need them. The "high S" wants the family to stay together — *let's do Christmas, let's call each other more, let's go to a movie.* The "high I" says, "If it's a party, I'm there!" We can drive each other nuts if we're not careful to accept one another for who God created us to be. We need to reflect on who we are and to whom we're married.

As a marriage counselor, I see couples with these different personalities. Let's say she's a "high C" and she knows everything needs to be in order. She's a believer and they need to be in the Bible and hold to the Word. They have to watch exactly what they do and how they do it because that's just the way she's "bent." He, on the other hand, is a "high I" and just came to Christ for the joy of coming to the Lord. They provoke each other immensely until I can help them see "This is who you are and this is who he is." Then they begin to realize, "That's why we are the way we are!"

Step Three: Not Necessarily Wrong, Just Different

God wants us to realize how to work together. He wants us out of our "selfish," depend-on-me attitudes. In His Family, everyone has a place.

Each brings a BALANCE to the engine if they work together. Back to the illustration of the twin engines: Often the propellers rotate in opposite directions. There is a reason behind this: If they both operate in the same direction, they tend to twist the aircraft. By rotating in opposition, they balance each other.

You must learn your spouse is not your enemy. Some people get so angry that they start viewing the other person as nothing more than a problem. You must see and understand that God made everybody different. He knew what He was doing. So you have to say to each other, "I am willing to bet you are a good person; I trust you; you're not wrong, you're just different and I need to see our situation through your eyes."

This viewpoint has helped in my own marriage and in those I serve. At times I ASSUME I know what Cheryl is thinking. One time I could tell she was irritated and frustrated with me. Instead of ASSUMING I was right, I started listening and hearing her point of view. Then I said, "Honey I get it now, I really see it, I see what you are saying." (I really could see it.) But I had to start with *she's not wrong, just different from me.*

Step Four: Synchronize, Work Together

As couples, learn to examine all the pieces of your personalities and spend time talking about how you relate and how you do things together. Become students of each other; it is actually kind of fun and provides opportunity for some playful teasing. I love taking couples through personality inventories and watching their eyes open — the huge sails realizing they are married to very big anchors. *Not wrong just different.*

Opposites attract and opposites attack. What's up with that? The strengths that you loved in the person you married often become the weaknesses that frustrate you the most. You end up criticizing the very characteristics that initially attracted you to your spouse. Learn that God uses others in your life, especially your spouse, to teach you the intricacies of grace and how it works. God uses the one who's the opposite of your personality so He can straighten your bent perception.

Here's an illustration: Hold up your left hand —four fingers and one thumb. If you traced your hand (as I do with my 3-year-old grandson) the tips of your fingers are your strengths and the valleys between your fingers are your weaknesses. Put your right hand together with your left, fingertip to fingertip. This is what happens when you are in attack mode. Tip to tip. All of the things you liked become the things that irritate you. Your spouse is so carefree, and on the opposite side can pick up laundry, put stuff away or manage money well. You like to be quiet and enjoy restful periods, and your spouse wants to go do something. You are sitting in your chair and she/he is ready to go already.

I've learned that I need Cheryl's counterbalancing tendencies. I depend on her, and as we've worked together, she has come to trust me and depend on me as well.

When you and your spouse allow each other to build into each other's life, you will find that your strengths will match your partner's weaknesses, and your partner's strengths will match your weaknesses. So instead of hands pressed together fingertip-to-fingertip, the picture becomes clasped hands, strong fingers gripping the other's weak areas. WOW!

When you learn to respect each other and allow for each other's bent, to use your mutual strengths and cover your mutual weaknesses, you become strong like clasped hands. When you are tip-to-tip, you are easily divided. When you are clasped, you are nearly impossible to pull apart.

Learn to respect each other's perspective.

Step Five: Get the BIGGER Picture

I challenge you with this idea: Jesus was all things to all men. When He needed to be Dominant or a Lion or "get it done," He would be that person. I wouldn't classify throwing the moneychangers out of the temple as the actions of a "high I." There was a lot of "C" and a lot of "D" going on there. He did not just tip over a few tables. He threw them — money and all — out of the temple. "High D," "high C."

But at times, Jesus also rejoiced greatly in spirit. He saw Satan fall from the heavens because the disciples were out there sharing His salvation with a broken world. At other times, He was a "high S," very loyal, very steady.

So here's my challenge: Learn to respect each other's perspective so that you become all things to all men. Deeply respect others, see how they react, and understand their perspective. Allow others to pull you toward them rather than polarize you.

Listen to them, see their point, and understand their perspective. Start saying in your marriage, "She's not wrong, she's just different." Allow the Lord to use that person in your life so He can straighten out your bent. Here's the secret: This is how God straightens relationally bent bearings and cue sticks. He puts you with your opposite to pull you toward the center.

Let God use others to do a work in you. Don't let your pride keep you from listening. In other words, allow your spouse to pull you toward the center, and get over your pride. And remember these words from Proverbs 12:1 — "Whoever loves discipline loves knowledge, But he who hates reproof is stupid." And these from Proverbs 14:21 — "There is a way *which seems* right to a man, but its end is the way of death."[37]

God uses others — especially your spouse — in your life to balance you out. If I let Him, God can use someone's "high S" on my "high D" to pull me toward the center. And He can use someone's "high I" to make me more people-oriented, maybe less frustrated, and less irritable.

That center is where you will find Jesus. In that center, as you allow God to straighten your bent, you'll see God in the process of making you more like Him.

Living Life Vertically means putting God first in your life, becoming brutally honest with yourself, developing a gratitude attitude and believing God for great things. As I allowed others to speak into my life, I began to see my "orphan spirit" at work in me. He used my marriage to show me how selfish I was. God will use your marriage to show you

---

[37] AUTHOR'S NOTE: These wise sayings put a sword in our heart of pride. If we love knowledge, we'll love discipline and reproof. We often get all puffy ... *"Imagine them saying that to me!"* Reproofs are "the way of life." The older I get, the more I regret not listening a hundred times more to what people were saying to me. And the way of death? Want to see it? Look behind you and count the bodies of broken relationships. If there are a lot of bodies, that is the way of death.

how self-centered you are — self-defending, self-vindicating, self-promoting, self-justifying, self-rationalizing.

I learned to live my life vertically, letting God speak through others into my life, and as a result I started coming to my marriage and relationships FULL instead of empty — giving instead of needy. Then God taught me how to love His way. It's called "loving by faith" and it looks like this:

> *Seeking the best interest of another not based on the behavior of the object loved but based on the character of the one doing the loving.*

Jesus teaches that your love for your spouse is not based on your spouse's characteristics and behavior but on your character as his/her lover. That sets you apart from the world. It sets your marriage apart from the world's standard of marriage. Ninety-five percent of all the marriages that I work with can be improved by this one principle: "Not wrong, just different."

You need to choose to love your wife or husband and seek his/her best interest, not based on their characteristics but based on your character. You say, "I choose to love you not because of how you look, but because of who I am in Christ." This is life changing, especially in marriage.

God loves us because of who He is, not because of what we do. We don't earn His love. He loves us because of His character. As His children, we need to apply that same type of love to our marriage.

People say to me, "Where did you learn this?" I learned this by watching Christ work through other personality types in the break room, in the bathroom or out in the garage. "God, why in the world did you put me next to that person? Of all the people out there, why couldn't I have been with a group of people just like me, bent the same way?"

Because Cheryl and I are similar, bent the same way, we often agree. But when we don't see eye to eye, our relationship can be tough. Then I'm out in the garage saying, "Lord God, why can't you help her see it my way?"

In those times alone with God, standing in the garage, allowing Him to work in my heart through others, I learned to seek the best interest of the other person, because of my character. As I stared at the face of

Christ, I heard, "It's not about you, Jim; it's about her. And you need to seek her best interest, not your own." We need to be able to say to our spouse, "Your way is not my way and my way is not yours, but that's OK, I can learn from you."

So no matter what personality type you are — a "D," an "I," an "S," or a "C" — if you are in love with Christ, you will move closer to the center in a heartbeat. There's no movement of the Spirit in a person who doesn't love Christ.

Prayer:

Father God, thank You so much for this specific subject of personalities and temperaments and showing us how we're bent and shaped. God, please allow us to stop seeing each other as wrong but, rather, to see each other as different and to let it be OK. "Your way is not my way, my way is not your way, and it's OK." Those are good words. Help us live vertically. Help us live our lives dedicated to and passionately in love with You. Press what we're learning into our hearts and allow us to walk in the power of your Son, Jesus. Amen.

CHAPTER 6: BARRICADES AND BARRIERS

"Regardless of which season your marriage is now in, learning to speak your partner's love language will enhance your communication, fill your spouse's love tank and strengthen your relationship. If your marriage is in fall or winter, learning to speak your spouse's love language may be the key to turning your marriage around and heading forward into spring and summer."

—Gary Chapman

WHEN I was in the military, I spent some time overseas in Turkey. I quickly noticed there were lots of dynamics that occur when you don't know the language.

One thing I noticed was certain foreigners who didn't understand Turkish would say, "Me no speak your language," or, "Me no speak Turkish." Hilariously, the non-Turkish speaker would start talking louder and faster. Helping someone understand a foreign language doesn't work that way. It just hurts their ears and frustrates them.

Flat out, I didn't speak Turkish, and when I was trying to buy or negotiate or order food or even find a bathroom, the locals could gang up on me as an American and increase the price. They would talk behind my back right in front of me because I didn't speak their lingo. So, with no greater motive than self-defense, I learned to speak Turkish.

Not speaking the lingo occurs in marriage too. Spouses actually speak two different languages. This chapter will talk about the languages we speak to each other and why we're so hard to understand because, "Me no speak the language."

Sometimes there are times when I just want to say to Cheryl, "Me no speak your language." Trying to verbally convey one's meaning to someone can be hard; trying to figure out what they're saying can be harder.

This is so true in marriage. I know I'm married to a good-willed person; I know she loves me; but we have those moments during discussions when I will begin to doubt her motive, and question if I should or should not have my guard up.

Often when my wife is speaking to me in a language I don't understand, that's what I will do: question her motive or assume she is saying something with an underlying negative connotation. Then we start doing the dance; she's trying to get in and I'm trying to keep her out.

So let's see if you can learn the language of that other person in your marriage. It takes time. You have to understand your own language first before you can speak somebody else's language.

> ## CONFLICT IS GOING TO HAPPEN. THERE WILL BE COMMUNICATION DIFFICULTIES IN ALL RELATIONSHIPS.

Dr. H. Norman Wright said the following: "Well, this comes as a shock to most couples, and I do share this with almost everyone I work with now. You and Sue are similar. But you were raised in different homes with different parents, siblings and experiences and, in effect, different cultures. You may eat the same types of foods, but they were prepared differently. You have different customs, different rituals in your families, different beliefs and values, and you each learned a different language. You even have a different dictionary. If you want to have the kind of marriage you described to me, your biggest task is going to be to learn about the other person's culture, to develop the flexibility to be comfortable with either set of customs, and above all, to learn your partner's language so that you can speak it!"[38]

Some of the first "languages" we learn to "speak" are "love languages." Gary Chapman set the pace more than 20 years ago when he

---

[38] Wright, H. Norman, *Communication: Key to Your Marriage: The Secret to True Happiness* (Kindle Locations 1132-1137). (Gospel Light. Kindle Edition, 2000).

wrote a book that catalogued five different "love languages" couples speak.[39] Millions of copies later, it's fair to say there has been widespread acceptance of the principles.

These are five ways we say or show another "I love you":

- Words of affirmation
- Quality time spent together
- Gifts, cards, flowers
- Acts of service
- Physical touch

Imagine that my love language is words of affirmation, and my spouse's is acts of service. She's speaking English; I'm speaking Turkish. She's trying to show me she cares for me by doing things for me, but she never says anything affirming, like "Thank you for taking out the garbage; I love it when you help me." Then, speaking Turkish, I'm trying to tell her "I love you," but I never do anything to physically shoulder some of her work load, like helping her wash the dishes after she's fixed a nice meal. I just talk a lot. Eventually there will be conflict because we are not talking each other's love language.

I've been there. Conflict is going to happen, there will be communication difficulties in all relationships. One person raises his or her voice to be heard and understood. The other partner raises his/her voice in return. Conflict is the result. Let's see if we can flesh out these languages and understand exactly how they work.

Words of Affirmation

Words of affirmation typically are unsolicited and speak encouragement to affirm another's efforts, build them up, and make them feel good about themselves. The word "encourage" means to give courage to someone.

I saw a couple demonstrate this beautifully. I could tell she was trying hard to make the marriage work and she was pretty angry. She was

---

[39] Gary D. Chapman, *The Five Love Languages: How to Express Heartfelt Commitment to Your Mate*, (Chicago: Northfield Pub., 1995).

speaking words at 75 with gusts to 120. He sat non-expressively, saying almost nothing. I finally said, "Could I see you individually? I would like to meet with each of you separately." (Sometimes if I can get together with a guy one-on-one, a lot more will surface.)

We made an appointment, and when he came, I basically said a few words, probably a couple of sentences and then asked him, "Where are you at?" He talked for 45 minutes, he had that much to say.

What happened in that conversation was amazing! He said, "Do you know Magic Johnson?"

I replied, "I know the name. I'm not a basketball player, but I do know the name."

He continued, "Magic Johnson is the greatest player on the team, and he doesn't need anybody else to play with him. He can win the game all by himself."

I'm thinking, *That's how you see yourself? The Magic Johnson of communication?*

He went on to describe Magic Johnson and obviously had an admiration for this player. I was thinking, *He sees himself as Magic Johnson. The team comes out on the court and he sees his wife as one of the team players. But she's not being submissive to Magic Johnson's leadership.*

He said, "The other guys know they're around the greatest player ever in basketball. They all know to look at him to give them direction, where they should go in, how they move, and what does he want them to do."

Finally I said to him, "Can I ask you a question?"

He said, "Yeah."

"Who are you in this illustration?"

"I'm just one of the team. My wife is Magic Johnson." (My mouth literally fell open.) "She doesn't need me; she can do everything so well. I would just like to have her tell me where she wants me to be and when she wants me to receive the ball so that I can be a part of the team."

I was speechless for a minute. This man was so resistant and strong and cold. He wouldn't communicate, yet here he created an illustration he could relate to.

So I said, "I want you to take what you just told me and share that with your wife, because I think she needs to hear how you really feel." He did that the next time we got together. She said almost nothing; she just rolled up into his arms, and leaned back on his chest and they both smiled.

Words of affirmation — they are so powerful and so strong in communication. In fact, Proverbs 12:18, says, "There is one who speaks rashly like the thrust of the sword, but the tongue of the wise brings healing." Words of affirmation have the power to communicate that you think your partner is worth something.

Words can create or destroy. When God created, He did what? He spoke. He didn't have to. He could have snapped divine fingers, but He spoke. Why? Because words demonstrate creative (or destructive) intent. Learn the skill of creating joy in your spouse's heart.

Here's a little insight. If you want to affirm your spouse, make sure to speak to what she or he said or did. Like, "I love you when you take the garbage out for me." Don't just flip off some "I love you," but actually define the why. The comment will show that you really understand her or him.

Another way to affirm your spouse is when you arrive home from your workday, let him or her know that you appreciate them for all they have done in your absence.

I have the opportunity to interview and work with many couples, so I get to witness the effects of this affirmation. After one couple I counseled tried it for a week, he shared with me, "These words of affirmation tricks were a really big encouragement." His eyes welled up with tears, because she used the principle to verbally affirm her husband about some handyman things he did. She recognized that it made him feel loved. She had never entrusted him with doing stuff around the house, and she'd make fun of his non-mechanical nature. He stated, "I waited to hear those words for twenty years."

Typically, husbands need a lot more encouragement than they get from their wife. In this case, she explained, "I'm very detail-oriented and he's not. It's not my norm to take time to affirm. It's really hard for me to say, 'You did a great job.' But I see how he really needs it and it does make such a difference when he hears the words." The tongue of the wife brings tremendous healing.

Quality Time

The second love language spoken in relationships is quality time together. This refers to time spent together WITH someone else. It is not quality time together when you say, "Come sit beside me and let's watch the sports channel together," if your partner hates sports. Or if your wife despises guns, you don't take her out to shoot a few rounds with you and then call that quality time.

The key to this quality time is the word TOGETHER. Spending time together. Time that the TWO of you get a recharge. That is the basis of this love language.

As a counselor/coach, I like to have couples incorporate the quality time of the first ten minutes after a day of work. Making it a priority to take those first minutes back home again to affirm each other is a very powerful statement of your love for each other.

Another method of sharing quality time is to hug each other. I often ask couples, "How much time do you spend hugging each other?" One will reply, "I'll get a peck on the cheek and a little bump on the way out."

Oh no, no, no, no, no! I actually set a timer. "I want you to hug her and time it," I'll instruct them.

One wife told me, "He was counting while he was hugging me." That is not how we should do it. Usually if you give each other a meaningful hug (5 ... 10 ... 15 seconds) you will find your bodies relax in an amazing way. Try it.

Another method of spending quality time together is learning how to listen. It's easy to think you already know what the other one is thinking or going to say because you have been living together for so many years. Frankly, you don't.

Most of us think we're listening simply because we are waiting for our turn to talk. Instead of listening, we are thinking of what we are going to say in response. Look at your spouse. Focus on what he or she is talking about. Time spent together means you are focused on the other person. Not on the TV, not on the car, not on your own thoughts, but really focused on your partner.

Give eye contact; don't over-talk, and don't interrupt. Grant you, some people take 15 minutes to describe a two-second event. But because you're not focused on your agenda or getting back to your program but on spending time together, you can listen and let your spouse enjoy you hearing their story.

Eye contact — huge. You are listening with intent. When most of us see a couple sitting next to each other talking, sharing and laughing, we think, "Oh, cool, they're dating." But we see another couple across the way, sitting face-to-face, staring at cups or magazines or phones not saying a word, and we think, "They must be married."

The Bible states, "Better is open rebuke than love that is concealed."[40] Basically, you cause less damage or hurt to someone by being angry with him or her than by giving them the silent treatment. Just because you told your spouse, "I love you" on your wedding night doesn't mean it's good for the rest of your life together. Don't be like the guy who said, "I told her I loved her 30 years ago; if that changes I will let her know."

We need to say "I love you" every day while looking straight into our spouse's eyes. Take the quality time to sit next to each other or work on a project together. Make sure to spend regular date nights together. The key is spending time together. You can go to a zoo or have a picnic or go on a field trip or to a gun show or auto show together (if she'll do it). Then take some time and go antique shopping or visit a consignment outlet or a novelty shop. Spend time together.

Gifts, Cards, Flowers and Post-it-Notes

Cards, small presents, flowers, Post-it Notes, text messages, a quick phone call, a cold sack lunch with a hot note — these are all simple

---

[40] Proverbs 27:5.

things that we can do for each other that say "I love you," especially if these tangible gifts are our love language.

I know an explanation seems unnecessary to those folks who don't need this type of material demonstration of love. But to those who do, it says you took the time to think of them in some special way. Sometimes, putting sticky notes in different places, like on the car's radio dial or on the steering wheel or rearview mirror, speaks volumes to those who relish such gifts.

Cheryl once bought a card and sent it to me. I don't speak that language, probably because I'm tight and maybe a bit lazy on gift things. I took the card out of the envelope, read it, wrote another note under hers then put it back in the inter-office memo bin (we worked in the same company) and sent it back. She loved it. She kept it at her desk a while and then sent it back to me. I loved it because I thought, *What a way to get the most bang for your buck.*

Isn't it amazing? I know people who have kept their 300 cards and notes for 30 years. That's how you know someone's love language is gifts. Small gifts say a lot to them.

I was always at a loss as we approached special occasions regarding what to get for my wife. Our anniversary would be coming up and I'd be thinking, *What should I do?* One day I was driving by a little theater, so I bought two tickets. Man, did I hit the jackpot! It was a dinner theater. We dressed up and watched a show called *Pump Boys and Dinettes*. It was FUN! She loved it! The theater shows we watched for years after were entertaining and some of my best gift giving. I even developed some "culture." And guess what? I didn't have to think of something to do.

So brainstorm about a gift your spouse would love to receive. What things touch his or her heart? The gift doesn't have to be super fancy — just think of something fun or special. One wife told me that on her husband's day off, he comes by the school where she works to drop off a vanilla latte for her. This speaks love to her.

Acts of Service

Acts of service (or helping out with things that need to be done) occur when your spouse is trying to accomplish something and you jump in to help. This type of service especially communicates love when you see your partner is stressed or overwhelmed. You jump in alongside, automatically assisting and helping as needed. That is called an act of service and it says, "I love you."

You can serve your wife and show her that you love her by putting gas in her car or washing it when it's dirty. You may stop to pick up some groceries on your way home from work, or take the kids to their afterschool program.

One wife said her biggest love gift is when her husband takes the kids out once a month on a Saturday morning so she can have a day to sleep in or take time for herself.

Jesus committed His whole life to serve. Listen to His words: "Just as the son of man did not come to be served but to serve and to give his life as a ransom for many."[41]

Acts of service reflect the life and the character of our Lord because that's who He was on earth — He served. Here He is, the Creator of the universe, bowing in front of his disciples to wash their feet.

Physical Touch

Physical touch probably doesn't need a whole lot of explanation, except to say that it is not necessarily sex. It can lead to sex, which is really great, but not always necessary. We guys need to be especially cognizant of that. Physical touch communicates, "I'm connected to you."

Physical touch is more about holding hands, walking arm-in-arm, scooting close together, touching each other in the car, taking her hand, putting your hand on her leg, or touching her side as you walk to a table.

Guys, listen, it's just being next to your wife, touching, taking her by the hand, putting your arm around her, giving her a small kiss in public. Touch can speak volumes of words in her love language.

And here's a secret: Ask her.

And ladies, you too. Ask him what he likes, what he needs. Figure him out.

---

[41] Matthew 10:28.

Apology

You will probably find this eye opening, but there are actually several languages of apology. Some of us say very quickly, "Oh I'm sorry." For Cheryl and me, our home and our lives are filled with apologies. We bump each other, cut in front of each other, talk over each other, forget an appointment, don't communicate clearly, and we are extremely quick to say, "I'm sorry."

But there is more. There are actually five methods of apology. For some the simple words, "I'm sorry" are good enough. But for others those words lack a sense of sincerity. We don't realize the other person doesn't understand because we aren't speaking his or her language.

Your spouse may be looking for the language that speaks about how you can fix it. It gives her a sense of security. Another person needs to hear the question, "What can I do to make it right?" For another, a sense of sincerity is communicated with an expressed commitment: "I will try to not do that again." Another person may need you to be specific about what you did or didn't do. Yet another may hope to hear, "Will you forgive me?" Sometimes deeper injuries from past trust broken will be at the core of the most effective apology language.

The one offended needs to hear why you're sorry or think you blew it. Once after I'd spoken at a conference, a woman caught up to me in a hallway and said, "I have lived with my husband for 35 years and he has not one time, ever said the words, "I'm sorry."

Guys, let's start here, leading by example. If we want to see the heart of the lady we're leading, then we'd better be there first. We need to be the ones who are there to apologize and say "I'm sorry" and to mean it sincerely.

So where do we go with all this?

First, Make an Effort

Learn your spouse's language. When you speak in your spouse's love language, it's timeless for them. They remember it because you are talking in a way they understand. But you have to make an effort to see their need and respond. It's what love does. Love sees another as more important than one's own selfishness. Not that you are a doormat, but you care enough to learn, to listen, to watch and act.

I watch the occasional chick flick — the World War II GI falls in love with a French girl. (Yeah, I know, corny.) But he works so hard to understand her and what she is saying. Marriage is about really trying to figure out what makes him or her tick. It's being a student of your spouse, watching and learning.

Know Your Own Language

Secondly, know your own language and let your spouse know what it is. Again, I think of the non-French-speaking GI and the mademoiselle who goes to great lengths to teach him her language. You and your spouse need to teach each other. Figure out your language.

You may ask, "How do I do that?" It is pretty simple. What do you like? Words of affirmation, time spent together, physical touch, cards and gifts, or acts of service?

What speaks to your heart? What do you long for? How do you express yourself? What do you complain about the most? What do you most frequently request? What makes you feel most loved? What makes your spouse feel most loved? What do you desire above all else? What things seem to meet your deepest needs?

Get in touch with your answers to these questions and share them with your spouse. Then he or she can know what your love language is. In return, ask your spouse, "What do you desire above all else?" Notice what makes his or her face brighter. What makes them smile? Help each other understand.

Caution: Your Love Language May Not Be Theirs

Remember how the foreigners in our earlier illustration would raise their voices when the Turkish person didn't understand? We do the same thing. We get more intense; we may get angry or upset or yell at our spouse.

Sometimes we express love in the language we want to receive. We're talking German; they're hearing French. Even though you think you are talking in a way they understand, take it from me — they don't. A wife will tell me, "He doesn't talk to me; we don't spend time together." Then he will say, "I come home, I cook dinner, I help with laundry and she doesn't even care." Two people, lots of language, no communication.

> ## SERVE ONE ANOTHER BY CONNECTING WITH EACH OTHER'S LOVE LANGUAGE.

We May Have More than One Love Language

Is it possible to have more than one love language? Yes, absolutely you do. There's a dominant one and there are recessive ones. Some of us have three, some of us may have four, and some of us may have all five. However, we are talking about the one that really hits you the strongest, and then the second one, and so on, so that your partner knows how to speak your language.

The Acid of Rejection

Relationships can get more intense because one spouse becomes critical and assumes the other doesn't care. One's expression of love doesn't measure up to the other's standard of perfection. This can verge on manipulation, and you have to be careful of that.

We'll discuss expectations in a later chapter. But rejection can be a powerful tool of injury; and when you don't take the time to help your spouse but instead assume he or she doesn't care, you can set up a cycle of cascading hurts.

It's Never Easy

Gary Chapman summed it up when he wrote, "Speaking in your spouse's love language probably won't be natural for you. We're not talking comfort, we're talking love. Love is something that we do for someone else, so often couples love one another but they aren't connecting."[42]

---

[42] Gary D. Chapman, *The Five Love Languages: How to Express Heartfelt Commitment to Your Mate*, Northfield Publishing, (Chicago, 1995).

A couple may love each other, yet lack connection. They may be sincere, but sincerity is not enough.

You can tell you're speaking each other's love languages when you start connecting and committing to each other. That's what God's love does in our hearts. It's not about "me" anymore. Marriage is not about "me," it's about a commitment, a covenant, and a desire to put someone else ahead of one's self. We'll discuss this in the next chapter.

Let the grace of Almighty God impact your life. Let that sense of "I am coming to this relationship because I'm here to give my heart" rule within you. That's the change that grace does. It's "living life vertically, going back to the cross" again and again. Learning how your spouse responds and reacts makes it a lot easier for you when you're trying to communicate with him or her.

Serve one another by connecting through each other's love language. Don't be suspicious of your spouse's motives if you don't understand what's going on inside him or her. You may not realize that your spouse may be acting out of hurt when it comes to displaying anger. Anger does neither of you any good.

It benefits both of you when you let go of some of your perfectionism and give much-needed words of affirmation and encouragement. This is what it means to be a student of your spouse.

In what areas of your marriage can you speak to your spouse that will bridge your languages?

So you're not connecting with your husband. Is he an evil person? No. An ill-willed person? A malicious person? No, of course not. Do you trust him with the children? Yes. Then maybe his language is different from yours. Maybe if you become students of each other, you can learn how to talk to each other.

Prayer: Father God, thank You for these principles about understanding languages that we use with each other in the areas of love, how we relate to each other, how we apologize and how we talk to each other. Help us to affirm and to spend quality time with one another, and to give those gifts that express our love. Help us to serve unselfishly and to touch each other with hints of affection. And most importantly, Father, give us courage to apologize with sincerity when we blow it. Father, we pray that You would press these things into our hearts so we can see them as real in our marriages. I pray that you would cause our hearts to be quick to run into the joy of grace, the joy of Your love, the joy that comes from having a relationship with You. Give us a sense of rest and peace, and fill our hearts with Your love for each other. Help us each to love the other not based on what we see in them, but on the character that we see in ourselves, so that we can be like children who are following You. We commit this to You, in Your name, Jesus. Amen.

CHAPTER 7: SUPER GLUE

"Busyness rapes relationships. It substitutes shallow frenzy for deep friendship. It promises satisfying dreams but delivers hollow nightmares. It feeds the ego but starves the inner man. It fills a calendar but fractures a family."
—Chuck Swindoll[43]

"What does a man get for all the toil and anxious striving with which he labors under the sun?"
—Ecclesiastes 2:22 (NIV)

WE'VE been considering the relational rules of the road. In the preceding chapters we've discussed some of the different languages we speak. With your differences, you and your spouse may sometimes seem nearly alien to each other.

This chapter will provide even more insight as you learn the different gender languages men and women speak. Women speak the language of love while men speak the language of respect.

Though men and women share a mutual need for respect and love, it has been shown that guys tend to be much more sensitive to the issues of respect. Women tend to be much more sensitive to the language of love. Bluntly, gentlemen (and ladies), she speaks the more romantic language of French — sweet, kind, flowing. We guys, on the other hand, speak something more like German. We speak in nods, looks of the eyes, and gestures and grunts and innuendos and moans. You know — Klingon.

Let me illustrate. After a particular response to my wife, she said to me, "What does that mean?"

I said, "What?"

"What does that mean?"

---

[43] Charles R. Swindoll, *Growing Strong in the Seasons of Life*, Multnomah, (Portland, OR, 1983).

"What does what mean?"

"When you go *uuuhhh,* or *hmmm,* or *uh huh….?*"

"I don't know … really. I guess I had no idea I was doing that."

"Well you do AND your son does it too."

"What?"

"He grunts the same way."

My next response might have been "Well, I guess I'm in good company." But that would not have been the thing to say. As we talked about it, I began to realize she was right. I don't talk when I don't agree or I don't want to speak harshly or, like most guys, I'm processing how to get out of this situation and save my life.

Characteristically, men speak the language of respect, and women speak the language of love.

Background

Four decades ago, Dr. John Gottman surveyed 2,000+ couples (in a small city) over a 30-year span. In his book *Why Marriages Succeed or Fail,* he discusses rebuilding friendship, intimacy and partnership in marriage.[44]As he observed couples under a variety of testing methods, he saw that they struggled, negotiated and fought in their attempts to resolve inevitable problems.

Gottman documented a communication ratio of five to one. Couples who had five validating, appreciating or approving actions countered by one demeaning or discounting action, grew increasingly distant, and, more often than not, their marriages ended in divorce. In fact, based on this research, Gottman said he could predict divorce in couples with 94 percent accuracy.

He observed four kinds of demeaning or discounting word phrases. Comparing them to the four horsemen of the apocalypse, Gottman called these phrases *criticism, contempt, stonewalling and defensiveness.*

---

[44] Drs. John and Julie Gottman, *"The Art and Science of Love,"* https://www.-gottman.com/couples/workshops/art-science-of-love/.

Conversely, very successful marriages commonly contained two powerful undercurrents in their actions — love and respect.

Love and respect. Gottman identified these as antidotes to the horsemen of contempt, criticism, stonewalling and defensiveness. Gottman wrote, "But the ways partners show each other love and respect ensure that there's this positive to negative ratio in their marriage that's always tilted towards the positive side."[45]

In my own study of couples, I find the four horsemen are used as guards or protectors against being hurt (real or imagined). We want to be quick to see and quick to get rid of them.

Gottman continued, "The bottom-line difference that is causing the conflict between you and your spouse is you need to understand and learn how to live by honoring, loving and respecting each other."[46]

Dr. Emerson Eggerichs began to see a parallel in the Bible while working through the Gottman material. He contended that according to the Bible, love and respect are the specific needs of women and men in marriage.[47] Specifically, women need to know they are loved and men long to feel respected.

This research was further complemented by the work of Jeff and Shaunti Feldhahn.[48] Their well-documented research with 15,000 couples reached the same conclusion. The Feldhahns discovered two shocking facts: 1) Men, by a great majority percentage, choose being respected over being loved, and 2) women, by a great majority percentage, have no clue what their men mean by "respect."

But beyond these experts, the Bible is our true final authority. Four primary biblical passages specifically speak to the love and respect lan-

---

[45] John Gottman with Nan Silver, *Why Marriages Succeed or Fail And How You Can Make Yours Last*, Bloomsbury (London, New York, Berlin, Sydney, 1994).

[46] John Gottman, *The Seven Principles for Making Marriage Work*.

[47] Emmerson Eggerichs, *Love and Respect*, Thomas Nelson, (Nashville, TN, 2004).

[48] Shaunti and Jeff Feldhahn, *For Men Only: A Straightforward Guide to the Inner Lives of Women* and Shaunti Feldhahn, *For Women Only: What You Need to Know About the Inner Lives of Men*, http://www.shaunti.com.

guages of marriage in the Bible.[49] It behooves us as spouses to figure out that language and understand their application.

Let's Go To Work

I want to help you understand some of the specifics of these two languages, love and respect. The most pregnant passage in the Bible starts off the discussion like this:

> *And do not get drunk with wine, for that is dissipation, but be continuously filled with the Spirit, speaking to one another in psalms and hymns and spiritual songs, singing and making melody with your heart to the Lord, always giving thanks for all things in the name of our Lord Jesus Christ to God even the Father and be subject to one another.*[50]

That passage solves most of the misunderstanding about Paul's next statements. Many times wives feel a bit beat up and husbands will argue, "Well she's supposed to follow my lead, submit to me." She will counter with "He's supposed to be loving to me." Both are Bible-based concepts, but they're frequently misused. So it's imperative that this passage be properly understood.

Paul begins his argument in verse 18 by saying, "And do not get drunk with wine, for that is dissipation, but be continuously filled with the Spirit."

Remember our concept of living life with God vertically first? That's what this Spirit-filled concept is all about; it's a relationship with Him. That's God's idea.

The health of your marriage is completely dependent on the health of your walk with God. God intended neither spouse to be looking to the other to meet all their needs, but for both parties to be looking to God, walking under the control of God's heart.

Then the succeeding verses teach that each of you is to speak to the other in encouraging, uplifting ways. Furthermore, the flavor of your lives should be thankfulness. (If this sounds familiar, remember John Gottman's research.)

---

[49] Ephesians 5:18-33; 1 Peter 3:1-7; Colossians 3:18-19; 1 Corinthians 7:1-40.
[50] Ephesians 5:18-21.

> ## MARRIAGE IS SERVING EACH OTHER; LEARN TO SERVE EACH OTHER IN LIFE.
>
> ## MAKE IT YOUR GOAL TO OUT-SERVE EACH OTHER.

Really? I'm to Be Submissive to Her?

Here comes a shock-and-awe phrase in verse 21: "Submitting to each other in the fear of Christ." It is my firm conviction that submission in marriage starts with each other. The Greek word is HUPOTASSO. It means to get underneath and lift someone up, just as if you have both fallen into a hole.

The black hole is dark, cold, damp. You try jumping to the top; it doesn't work, and it's too high. You try climbing up the wall, but it's too soft and caves in. Then you come up with a plan — One of you stoops to let the other one stand on his shoulders. BOOM! You're out! That's HUPOTASSO, getting underneath and lifting someone up.

In marriage, God intends for us to start right here. I'm subject to Cheryl and she is subject to me. We serve each other. In the Godhead, the Trinity of Father, Son, and Holy Spirit have role identification. The Father leads, the Son responds, the Spirit serves. All are equal in nature, yet different in role. In spouses serving each other as God intended, marriage was to literally demonstrate this amazing synchronistic relationship of Father and Son and Spirit.

I love to tell a couple, "It's not about you." Selfishness is your greatest enemy. It's like two people both injured, both in wheelchairs, both with their own pain and agendas, taking care of each other. For life. It's not about 50:50 — THAT'S THE SPIRIT OF DIVORCE. Marriage is all in — 100:100 — 100 percent of the time. Always learning and growing. Always setting your task to take care of the other.

At a marriage ceremony I heard the officiating pastor say, "Marriage is serving each other. Learn to serve each other in life. Make it your goal to out-serve each other."

It's not about "Well, you're not doing this right," and "You're not doing that right." It's about you guys being subject to your wives, and you wives being subject to your guys. I have a sense of passion about this because we so often play Holy Spirit in the life of our spouse. Why do we need to do that?

I learned that the power of a praying husband is far greater than the mouth of a selfish one. Too often we're playing Holy Spirit; too often we're not fleeing back to being filled in the Spirit.

Submission: Wives

So from the very beginning of this passage, we see that spouses are to be submissive to each other.

Paul continues in Ephesians 5:21-22, "Wives, be subject to your own husbands, as to the Lord. For the husband is the head of the wife, as Christ also is the head of the church, He Himself being the Savior of the body. But as the church is subject to Christ, so also the wives ought to be to their husbands in everything."

In marriage-counseling situations, as we start dealing with this issue of submission, some guys question me, "Isn't my wife supposed to follow my lead? Isn't she supposed to be subject to my leadership?" Or worse yet, "Pastor you need to tell my wife to submit to my leadership and then everything will be fine in our house." They usually point to the Ephesians verses quoted above.

So I will respond with "Do you know what the penalty is for reading someone else's mail?"

"What?"

"Do you know reading someone else's mail is a federal offense, and the penalty is $10,000 or 10 years in prison, or both?"

I'll ask, "Could we read that passage together?"

"Sure, right there, it's right there, 'Wives, be sub...'"

I interrupt him, "Wait, hold on, who's that written to?"

"Oh, wives."

"If that verse is addressed to you," I'll say, "read it; if it's not addressed to you, you better put it back in the mailbox, because this is a felony. You need to read YOUR verses and when you have accomplished those then you can start pointing fingers." They get the point.

I have learned that a wife's resistance to following her husband extends back to the garden when the first husband threw the first wife under the first proverbial bus.[51] Naturally, women don't trust. Further, part of the curse placed upon a woman is the desire for her relationships to all work well, and when they don't, she seeks to master them, husbands included. "To the woman He said, 'I will greatly multiply your pain in childbirth. In pain you will bring forth children; yet your desire will be for your husband, and he will rule over you.'"

H. Norman Wright notes that in all of the passages on husband and wife, the word HUPOTASSO is not in an active voice but in a middle voice, which indicates that this is not a military directive BUT A PERSONAL APPLICATION FROM THE INNER HEART OUT. Wright says, "The submission we are called to in marriage is never anything that is externally imposed; it is a definite act on your part that comes from inside you. And it is a mutual submission that involves both of you."[52]

Submission: Husbands

So this HUPOTASSO submission is God's idea. You guys need to stop playing Holy Spirit and realize you're reading somebody else's mail. You need to let God speak to each of you individually, rather than reminding your wife and playing Holy Spirit in her life.

Let's look at the passage in depth.

The word for "subject to" is not a quantitative or qualitative statement; it is an organizational or a role statement. It's learning to respect; it is not a woman's natural language, and we'll address that specifically in later chapters.

---

[51] Genesis 3:12-16. Adam blames Eve and then transfers to God, "You gave her to me."

[52] H. Norman Wright, *Communication: Key to Your Marriage: The Secret to True Happiness,* (Gospel Light, Kindle Edition).

Husbands, love your wives, just as Christ also loved the church and gave Himself up for her. ... So husbands ought also to love their own wives as their own bodies. He who loves his own wife loves himself for no one ever hated his own flesh but nourishes and cherishes it, just as Christ also does the church because we are members of His body.[53]

The same question now goes to the ladies. Whose mail is this? Husbands. So ladies, you also need to not read someone else's mail, right?

YOUR MARRIAGE HAS PRIORITY OVER EVERY OTHER RELATIONSHIP.

Guys, love is not our natural language. Most of the marriage books out there are written to women. They talk about love. Hallmark cards are written for women. Statistically 85 to 90 percent of them appeal to women. Why? Because that's who buys them. Those greeting card companies don't write cards about respect language.

For us guys, love is not our natural language, so we have to learn from this Ephesians passage how to do that, and the standard is clear. Love like Christ. Because of this I realized God had called me to love my wife irrespective of what she does. Christ loved and gave Himself up for us. That is His love. Guys, honestly? I would rather have the wives' job. This one is a nightmare. Look at Paul's words: "Set her apart," "cleanse her," "present her," "having no spot or wrinkle or any such thing," "holy and blameless." Add to that Peter's directive, "live with her in an understanding way,"[54] and the task becomes daunting.

And your personal relationship with God rides in the balance. Isn't that amazing? Your ability to converse with God is directly connected to how you treat your wife.

---

[53] Ephesians 5:25, 28-30.
[54] 1 Peter 3:7.

How Do We Do This?

OK, so how do we put love and respect together? The cool thing is God gives us the keys at the end of Ephesians 5:

> For this reason a man shall leave his father and mother and shall be joined to his wife, and the two shall become one flesh. This mystery is great; but I am speaking with reference to Christ and the church. Nevertheless, each individual among you also is to love his own wife even as himself, and the wife must see to it that she respects her husband.[55]

Leave

Step by step let's walk it through. The first action word is to LEAVE. Paul says, "For this cause shall a man leave ...." Leaving carries a picture of departing from, leaving behind, getting away from, choosing to reject. In biblical culture, a man's family was his job, career, stability and inheritance. God simply says, "Gentlemen, there is one relationship that is priority over all others. Ladies, you are not off the hook either. Your marriage has priority over every other relationship."

This is the second most common problem in troubled marriages. First, spouses don't walk with the Creator of marriage and second, they forget the meaning of prioritizing one another. What happens is sinister. It's much easier to migrate over to a career or friends or family or hobbies or even somebody of the opposite gender. To leave in this sense means to prioritize. There are innumerable forces in our world today that tear us away from that perspective.

Your home should be your priority. To prioritize, you have to push into second place all the things that cry out for your attention, your thoughts. *First is first.* After the Lord, your wife is your first priority. Your husband is your first responsibility after the Lord.

Far too often in the counseling room, I hear a wife or husband say, "I just don't matter to him/her." Or "I am at the bottom of the totem pole." In other words, everyone and everything is more important than I am to my spouse.

---

[55] Ephesians 5:31-33.

One wife said, "I am so many after golf." I thought, *What in the world?*

She said, "Look at the way he holds that club; he treasures it. He polishes it; he puts it away carefully. He shows them all off to his friends, spends hours reading about how to use them effectively. HE HAS EVEN GONE TO CLASSES TO USE THEM BETTER. If he held me just half as gingerly, if he spent just one hour of time with me, I would literally melt and follow him anywhere."

I coach and counsel with people daily and frequently hear, "My spouse is my first priority."

I say, "Really? Let's test that. Where do you spend most of your time? And where do you spend most of your money?" Now the push back begins.

"What? What? You want to see my check book?"

"Yeah, I want to see how you spend your time and I want to see how you spend your checkbook because that's going to tell me what your priorities are."

Guys, I fall down on this all the time. I'm not perfect, far from it. But we must each set our spouse as our Number One human relationship.

I learned this the hard way. Early in my life and ministry I put the Great Commission before the Great Commandment. I placed my work before my wife. That's backwards.

Priority. Who do you think about? Who do you plan for? Who do you train with? Priority.

Leaving is a statement of priority. "I will choose my spouse over everything else — pressures from parents, pressures from children, pressures from my job." All of these are priority issues. You must choose her (or him) before them.

Cleave

"The two shall be joined together." The New and the Old Testament words for "joined" are very similar in meaning. The Hebrew word for "joined" refers to a powerful glue, like a bond that can't be broken. Super glue. Cyanoacrylate. $C_5H_5NO_2$. (Just in case you want a conversation starter.) God says, here's My plan. Leave others and GLUE yourself to your spouse. Two imperfect people bonded for life, overcoming self-ishness and seeking the other person's best interest.

You leave others and cleave to her or him. As "leave" is a statement of priority, so "cleave" is a statement of commitment. It's like traveling on a train. You leave FROM the Omaha station so you can travel TO the Lincoln station. You relegate other relationships to a lesser priority because you are cleaving to or committed to something different.

Cleaving is the glue. Cleaving says, "I'm committed to this for life, and it doesn't matter if I get my way in everything, because I'm sticking to this."

Cleaving demonstrates gluing oneself to that relationship, not letting other things divide or separate it. I've learned that this takes a conscious decision on my part. When I cleave to something, I grip it tightly.

One way you demonstrate cleaving is by fighting for your relationship. Marriage is going to be trouble — the Bible says it. But when you want something badly enough, you will stick with it. That is cleaving.

A dear friend told me after a particularly rough episode of "cleaving" to his spouse, "I don't care. I'm in this for the long haul, and I may be bruised and battered but I will promise you this: I will not be beaten, I will, no WE WILL cross the finish line together even if I have to drag us."

Making your spouse number one in your time and prioritizing others second is one part of it. But the other part is committing to her or him. It's placing your spouse first before your job choices, before your career advancements, before your friends or hobbies. Cleaving is a commitment that places your marriage before your dreams, desires and goals.

My successful marriage is my dream, my desire and my goal. If my other commitments tear this commitment down, then they aren't worth it.

Cleaving says "no" when someone of the opposite sex says "yes." Cleaving says "no" when hobbies demand more time than they should. Cleaving says "no" when the strains and pressures between you are forcing you apart. Cleaving says, "I'll fight for my marriage." Cleaving says to a spouse who asks to get counseling, "Sure, you bet; I'd love to go, because this is too important to me to lose."

Cleaving is the glue. It says, "I'm committed to this for life, and it doesn't matter if I get my way in everything, I'm sticking to this." It's the "for better or worse" clause. It means honest-to-goodness, down-and-dirty, I'm-committed-to-doing-whatever-it-takes-to-make-this-relationship-work commitment. If so, then shouldn't a couple who take commitment seriously be able to work through infidelity — in whatever incarnation it comes to them — and keep their marriage intact? Wouldn't that be the "better or worse" part of their marriage vow? Or does commitment include an asterisk for infidelity?

Before we go on, infidelity is any crossing of a line that breaks the glue. While a sexual affair is a definite leaving-the-rails situation, an emotional affair from which you derive your emotional needs of belonging, importance, value, appreciation, and provision/protection can be just as devastating. The rudder of commitment is what steers us through the waters of emotional storms.

In my counseling and coaching, I have had the great privilege of witnessing the power of commitment when a spouse confesses an infidelity. It isn't easy. It isn't simple. It isn't painless. It requires a "won't give up" attitude. This is why Jesus gave very little option for divorce. The Bible basically gives us two: infidelity and abandonment. But neither is mandated. God looks at marriage as a "covenant" relationship. That means both partners stick it out.

In a UCLA research study, the authors, Thomas Bradbury and Benjamin Karney, wrote, "It's not just that I like the relationship, which is true, but that I'm going to step up and take active steps to maintain this relationship, even if it means I'm not going to get my way in certain areas." This, Bradbury said, "is the other kind of commitment: the difference between 'I like this relationship and I'm committed to it' and 'I'm committed to doing what it takes to make this relationship work.' When you and your partner are struggling a bit, are you going to do what's difficult when you don't want to? At 2 a.m., are you going to feed the baby?"[56]

---

[56] Thomas Bradbury and Benjamin Karney, http://newsroom.ucla.edu/releases/here-is-what-real-commitment-to-228064.

The couples that were willing to make sacrifices within their relationships were more effective in solving their problems, the psychologists found. "It's a robust finding," Bradbury said. "The second kind of commitment predicted lower divorce rates and slower rates of deterioration in the relationship." Of the 172 married couples in the study, 78.5 percent were still married after 11 years, and 21.5 percent were divorced. The couples in which both people were willing to make sacrifices for the sake of the marriage were significantly more likely to have lasting and happy marriages."

Cleaving avoids a "bank account" relationship. In relationships we make deposits and withdrawals, but this doesn't mean we have the right to keep tabs on what we're getting so we can make a break for it when we're at our limit. According to one definition, cleaving is the act of "binding yourself to a course or action." It's a commitment to accepting someone else's baggage; to being willing to compromise; to hold to integrity and open honesty; to guard the dignity of the other person.

I hear people say this all the time: "Well, I love her but I'm just not IN love with her."

To cleave or live out a commitment is the highest expression of God's love. God's love or grace can best be defined as "the commitment to seek the very best interest of another not based in the behavior of the object but in the character of the lover." True love is all about the lover's character and not about another's behavior.

I experienced the joy of this cleaving type of commitment while hiking with my wife. Cheryl and I were out climbing rocks in Arizona. There is a principle about rock climbing that says, "What goes up must come down." Well not always; what goes up may stay up there and yell back, "I can't get down; you better get a helicopter."

We were out climbing, and I tend to run up rocks because I'm part mountain goat. Arriving at the top I yelled, "You gotta come up here! You gotta see! This is amazing! The sunset is so beautiful! Come on! Hurry up, hurry up!" Doing the typical "D" thing.

After much exertion on her part, Cheryl joined me. It was awesome. Right up to the point where she said, "I don't know if I can get down."

I said, "You'll get down; we'll be fine." Cheryl took a look at the distance, which now had grown because going up is much shorter than going down — another principle of rock climbing in Arizona. I realized we were in a bit of trouble. I could hear panic in her voice. Women have a special way of constricting their vocal chords that really touches the heart of a man.

So I skipped down the rocks, turned around and thought, *I'll get her down by words of affirmation.* "Come on, come on. You can do it, you can do it, come on." And I'm kind of starting to panic because the sun is now down; it's getting cold and I can't get this woman off this rock. As she is coming a few feet forward she stops. She's done. Frozen in time. I could have yelled, "Get over yourself! You got up there; get down...." My options were many ... but none of them would have worked.

I went back up on that rock and said, "Sweetheart, we can do this." I put my hand over her shoe and literally became her stairs coming down.

She said, "I am never doing this again. I am never doing it, I promise. I will never. Why would I do it?"

But what was happening in my heart was amazing. With every step my heart was changing in love with the Lord and in love with this very special lady whom He and I were getting down off that rock.

We walked away from the rock, and she turned around and she said, "You know, that's pretty cool. I bet we can do that again. We should try it again."

"Absolutely! Let's do it," I heard myself say.

Leaving my selfishness, and cleaving to my commitment to care for her resulted in amazing joy in both our hearts. Guys, that is the win.

> **WE WEAVE OUR LIVES TOGETHER, AND WE LEARN TO ENJOY THE MOMENTS, BUT IT DOESN'T HAPPEN OVERNIGHT.**

WEAVE

"And the two shall become one flesh." I like to call this "the weave of marriage." Two points stand out here. First is the obvious "one flesh" statement.

The word "weave" means to put threads together so they become entwined with each other in such a way as to make the resulting material stronger than the parts alone. Marriage was designed with the goal of oneness. Unity. A team. The sexual relationship, which is the picture of "one flesh," was intended to be a reflection of this God-given unity.

Most of us guys possess an intense desire to be part of a team. A certain peace and excitement and exhilaration accompany that kind of participation. Marriage was meant to be one of those life teams. Unfortunately it's fragile, it's pretty easy to mess up, and it takes some practice to make it work. But then, what sports team doesn't have those same characteristics?

Frequently, divorced people I've counseled will come back to me and say, "I feel like the fabric was torn, and part of me is still in that other person, and part of them is still in me." The reason for that is because that's the way God created us — to weave our lives together. And if we could see what He's actually accomplishing, I think we would fall more in love with being the kind of people that God wants us to be. Instead we worry about the things we don't have or we mope over the things we wanted to get but didn't.

But God designed us to feel an immense sense of accomplishment, being part of a team that scored the goals, won the game, because as a partnership, we built a great home.

One of the participants in our Marriage Made Simple conference stated, "We recently have started working out in the morning or going for walks, things like that, together. It's made a big difference, the time spent together, that sense of weaving our lives with each other. And the times we can't get up and go for walks in the morning, we really miss that. It's not the walk but it's the time together."

Cheryl and I have lived our lives to the max many times. From hiking way back into the mountains and bringing home huge rocks, attending and celebrating family and social functions, long road trips (we love to drive together), rearing a grandson from infancy forward, buying and selling a couple of houses, building …. We have lived and woven together so much of our lives.

Another piece of "two becoming one" is often overlooked. Weaving your lives together and learning to enjoy the moments doesn't happen overnight. "And the two SHALL BECOME one flesh."

It doesn't say we ARE one flesh, immediately. It is a becoming process; in it for the long haul; it is growing together and learning together. Frequently Cheryl and I will say, "Well, we've just learned a new way to do that."

Never get stuck in the perfectionist addiction — you can't make it perfect. But you also can't stop trying. Relationships are fluid. Stop seeing some end point and just enjoy the trip. You are human beings, not human "doings." Be together and learn to cherish moments. Make your home a place you enjoy coming to. Let there be mistakes, failures, shortcomings and blunders and just stuff. Roll with it and love it. Become a team. Become one flesh.

Prayer:

Father, thank You for these principles of leaving, cleaving and weaving. Press this stuff into our hearts so we can live vertically with You, and walk with You in such a way that we build into and encourage our spouse. Thank You for the time that we are able to share that love and respect, those commands that we accept from You, things that we can do for each other. Give us the passion to do that. Jesus, thank You for Your presence. Help us see it and do it: leave, cleave, weave. Please bless us as we do those things in humility and see that flow of Your love through us. It's in Your name we pray. Amen.

CHAPTER 8: AUTO SHOP

"So husbands ought also to love their own wives as their own bodies. He who loves his own wife loves himself; for no one ever hated his own flesh, but nourishes and cherishes it."

—Ephesians 5:28-29

THE next several chapters deal with ways men and women can connect with each other. Since we'll focus first on the husband then the wife, I'm calling this section "Auto Shop." It's a simple word picture that should save guys countless hours of frustration.

Just as your car needs maintenance, so does your marriage require regular tune-ups. Take small daily steps to protect your marriage before it demands a major blown-engine overhaul.

Guys, I know you know what I'm talking about. You're coming through the door some evening, exhausted, dreading conversation, avoiding eye contact, waiting for the "DTR" (Discuss The Relationship) hammer to fall.

Think of your car — you fill it with gas, check the oil every 3,000 miles, replace the tires when they start slipping in the rain, hang an air freshener, change wiper blades, clean and polish the exterior regularly to preserve the paint from fading. Well, in the same way, you need to take care of your wife. You need to REGULARLY check the noises she's making, establish a pattern of checking what's going on under the hood — basically DTR-ing the DTR-er before she DTR's you. Try it sometime; you'll blow her mind: "Honey I think we need to talk about our relationship." It might backfire, but it's worth it for the shock value.

A husband is driving down the road and he turns to his wife. "Did you hear that?" He's far more tuned to the car than he is to the relationships in the car.

So I challenged myself to maintain my marriage by maintaining my wife with love and attention. I learned to focus, listen, and become proactive rather than reactive. Instead of waiting for something to blow up, blow off or blow out, I started trying to hear the noises, check the oil, mend repairs and work with my family.

Remember Ephesians 5? God states in verses 18 to 21 that we are to "continuously be filled with the Spirit and be subject to one another." Why? Because of reverence to Christ. Because Christ has worked in us through grace and we live in that relationship of being subject to one another.

Wives, there is also clear instruction for you: Be subject to your husband. In the next chapter we'll take on the specifics of the word "respect."

Husbands, here's your passage, Ephesians 5:24-33:

Husbands, love your wives as Christ loved the church and gave himself up for her so that he might sanctify her having cleansed her by the washing of water with the word that He might present to Himself the church in all her glory, having no spot or wrinkle or any such thing, but that she would be holy and blameless. So husbands ought also to love their own wives as their own bodies. He who loves his own wife loves himself, for no one ever hated his own flesh, but, nourishes and cherishes it, just as Christ does the church because we are members of his body. For this reason a man shall leave his father and mother and shall be joined to his wife, and the two shall become one flesh. This mystery is great; but I am speaking with reference to Christ and the church. Nevertheless, each individual among you is to love his own wife even as himself, and the wife must see to it that she respects her husband."

Here's an acrostic for you using the word "cleave," six letters and six tasks:

C Connect and Engage with Her

L Lead by Example

E Encourage and Affirm Her

A Appreciate with Affection

V Vows, Virtue, Live with Integrity

E Excitement and Mystery

These six cardinal maintenance items are things we guys can work on daily.

C Connect and Engage with Her

The secret to a great marriage is not commitment or communication or conflict resolution; those are skills. The key to a great marriage is connecting with your spouse. No one says learning to connect is easy.

Let's say my friend Jimmy and I are having a conversation. I say, "Jimmy, how was your week?"

Jimmy replies, "It was a good week," and I say to him, "My week was terrible; I just had a hard week. You know, I was struggling with this and struggling with that. How's your work?"

Jimmy says, "Work was good."

I respond, "My work was bad. I had all these sale obstacles and deadlines to overcome."

Jimmy goes on, "Well, my car was really bad, I had this problem and I had to buy that."

So I say "Well, I got a brand new car and it's great…" On it goes.

So what's the connection? Precisely, there is none.

We're not having a connecting conversation at all. I'm not seriously listening to Jimmy; I'm all about me, thinking about how I can tell Jimmy what I want to tell him. I'm just being polite to let him finish his sentence before I get my turn to talk. That's not connecting. And in essence, what am I saying? "I really don't care about your story."

> **NOURISHING SOMEONE'S SPIRIT AND MIND MEANS I DO THOSE THINGS THAT PROVIDE A GROWTH ENVIRONMENT.**

When you don't really listen, when you don't connect, when you don't give someone your attention, you are handing him or her a value statement.

Connecting says, "I seriously want to hear how you are; I'm interested in you and I want to share my life with you, too." It's what Paul means in Ephesians by "nourishing and cherishing." Nourishing someone's spirit and mind means you do those things that provide a growth environment. You listen and pay attention, encourage, find ways to learn together, figure out problems mutually. Nourishing means you find ways to cause growth between you.

You connect by listening reflectively. You learn to be focused and interested in what the other person is saying by not polarizing. What do I mean by "polarizing"? I mean provoking each other on opposite sides of an issue or circumstance. When she brings up something that you don't like to hear, you can choose not to step back and roll your eyes with a sense of opposition. When you are engaging with her, you make an effort to keep from becoming polarized.

You also connect through cherishing her. Cherishing has different perspectives. Instead of "same old, same old," you regard your wife as a valuable gift entrusted to you. You cherish and treasure that gift. It means you think about her during your day; you are concerned for her safety. You spend time with her and engage with her.

Try giving her the first ten minutes of your time when you get home and listening to what she has to say. Desire to hear from her — there's no better way to show her value and to nurture your relationship with her than spending quality time with your wife.

Go with her on activities that she enjoys. One of the things I do to connect with my wife is to go shopping with her. It's easy for us guys to say, "Shopping is her job," but that's not what God says. "Shopping is OUR job." So I go shopping with her. Maybe your wife likes to camp or fish, so do those things with her. My wife, Cheryl, loves road trips and hiking. We do a lot of that together.

Connecting means doing some of the things she likes to do. I once asked a wife during counseling, "What do you do to connect with one another?" She responded, "It's a small thing, but when I get into the car to go to work in the morning, I have to carry a lot of stuff with me. And every single morning, regardless of how much or how little I have, my husband grabs my stuff and he walks me out to the garage. He puts the stuff in my car, waits till I get seated and then he kisses me and tells me to have a good day and he loves me."

Other quality ways you can connect with your spouse are filling up her gas tank, sitting down and having a meal together, listening reflectively. Let her vent after having a frustrating day and help her adjust to the evening. Don't just "hear" the words coming out of her mouth, but listen to what she's saying, and in your own words (without adding commentary) say it back to her. This is called reflective listening. A great way to connect and keep your mind from wandering is to ask questions. For example, I might say, "When I heard you say you 'had a good week,' what did you mean? What was it that you did? What happened this week?" Or "What about your work, what was good about it?"

Along those lines, guys, you need to be willing to share with your wife *your* challenges and *your* deliberations. You need to seek your wife's input and opinions, rather than just telling her what you think. Give her the right to share her thoughts and opinions regarding your days and circumstances. This shows her respect. Slow down when she asks a question about your day. Rehashing what you might want to forget allows her to connect with you over the challenges you face.

Maybe she spent her day with a one year old or had no adult conversation. So when you get home, she wants to connect while you want to remote. Men shield, women probe. That's their natural bent. Women become investigators —"How was your day?"

"Good."

"What did you do?"

"Nothing."

"Who did you talk to?"

"Nobody."

"Well, how did everything go?"

"Fine."

What begins to happen? The guy starts to get frustrated. Is that what she is trying to do? Irritate him? What's with the 20 questions?

She's trying to get him to connect, because that gives her a sense of value, of being treasured.

I learned to designate spots along the drive home — a bridge or a traffic signal. When I pass that point, I start thinking, *OK, what can I say, what can I do, how can I engage with my sweetheart when I get home?*

This connecting idea is found in the example of Christ. He sacrificed Himself for His Bride. He gave Himself up for her. That is a value statement. Bottom line: Her life is more valuable than mine.

Wow! Think about that for a moment. Your wife's life is greater than yours, guys. You're called to give your life in exchange for hers. Does that mean you just do everything she says? No, you're not meant to sacrifice your self-image on the altar of another's ego. That's foolish. Do you accede to being henpecked or emotionally whipped? No ... read on.

L LEAD by Example

In Ephesians 5:28-30, Paul speaks of Christ's love: "... sanctify her ... to present her ... cleansing her so she has no spot or wrinkle or any such thing that she should be holy and blameless." This breathtaking portrait of Christ and His Bride becomes the model that a husband follows. This section identifies Christ as the head, but now we get to see the amazing expression of His leadership with His Bride. He became a servant leader. He didn't lead by position — "I'm the boss; do what I say." He led by example; he showed Himself unselfishly. There's our model.

> **GENTLEMEN, YOU WILL ONE DAY PRESENT YOUR WIFE BACK TO THE ONE WHO GAVE HER TO YOU.**

Yes, we guys will be held accountable to report to Christ on the how's and why's of the way we treated our wives. Wives also will give an account to Christ for their treatment of their husbands, but *we* have the greater responsibility.

Notice the commands above in Ephesians 5:25-30:

- Love her
- Give your life for her
- Sanctify her (set her apart as valuable)
- Wash her, holy, blameless, even as you take care of yourself
- Get her ready to be presented.

Wait, what? What? Yes, so that He might present her. Gentlemen, you will one day present your wife back to the One Who gave her to you. This is sobering!

In his personal testimony, *The Family Quarterback*, former University of Nebraska quarterback Travis Turner describes a vision he had one night. His life has come to an end and now he is standing before Jesus Who says, "Give me a report of your life, and show Me what you've done."

Travis starts going through all of the people he has mentored and touched. He can tell the Lord is not pleased, but, in fact, bothered. Furthermore, he sees something rustling to his left that looks black and dark like a garbage bag. It annoys him. Becoming increasingly anxious, he begins recounting this service and that organization and this program and that group he had developed during his years of ministry. More rustling from the left, a movement, a sigh. All the while, he can see that Jesus is not impressed. He actually looks rather bored.

Desperately, he digs deeper. "I've been a Christian for 30 years, I've given this much money to the church, I've sacrificed this, I've sacrificed that."

"Are you finished, is that all you've got?"

Standing alone and empty with nothing left Travis says, "Yes, Lord."

The Lord says, "What did you do with the gift I gave you?"

Gift? He looks to the Lord. "I'm not sure what you're talking about, Lord."

Jesus says, "My gift, standing right beside you." Travis turns to look at the black, rustling garbage bag next to him. It is his wife, and she is empty. Nothing left. Used up. Uncared for. Very sad. Finally he realizes that he had failed to prioritize his wife. She had gotten the leftovers of his life and time.[57]

As you lead, you are to give of yourself with intentionality, knowing you will present your wife to Christ one day as someone for whom you have cared for very well. This concept scared me when I started looking at what husbands are supposed to do and wives get to do. I thought, *I really need to get another job*, because I have the responsibility of leading my family. I need to see leading my family as something the Lord has entrusted to me.

When I see our family start dropping emotionally or I observe them making demands of one another or they're losing their sense of humor and I realize my family is not going the way we should be going, then it's my responsibility as the leader to build their family spirit back up.

Our responsibility as husbands is to lead our families, and I challenge us guys to achieve this by example. Do it by illustrating rather than controlling. In chapter 6, I pointed out that men interact with their environment by controlling, while women try to find common ground and synergize to connect with their environment. Men tend to control. But we need to lower the controlling part and learn to lead by example. We guys need to learn to offer compassion rather than try to fix our wives and children, learn to listen with compassion rather than always try to step in and make things right.

Leading by example is, quite frankly, getting rid of pride. Pride says, "I'm better than she is." Pride says, "I don't have to apologize." Pride says, "My life goals and dreams are more important than hers."

> **IF I WANT TO CHANGE WHAT'S GOING ON IN MY MARRIAGE, I NEED TO BE THE INITIATOR.**

---

[57] Travis Turner, *The Family Quarterback*, Divine Romance Ministries (Scottsdale, AZ, 2014).

E Encourage and Affirm Her

First connect, then lead and third, encourage. Encourage her with words of affirmation. Refer to the love languages you learned in chapter 6. Encourage by sending a text or writing a message or leaving a voice mail, by refusing to do things apart from each other.

In coaching and counseling people, I observe that couples will get to the point where they don't do things together at all. I start asking questions: "Why aren't you taking your husband with you? Why aren't you taking your wife with you?" They reply, "Well, it's just because that's how we do things; we just get together with all the girls, and he wouldn't want to be part of it anyway." Or he says, "She doesn't like to do the things I do, and she doesn't like my friends."

I understand "girl time" and I understand "guy time," but I want to challenge couples to always remember that this is an engagement process. Guys, you need to engage with your wife.

I heard a story of a missionary to Hawaii. He met a very rich man who had chosen as his bride a young woman who was average in beauty. He was expected to go to her father and present him with a cow, which, according to their custom, showed the value of his wife-to-be.

But this rich man said to the girl's father, "I want to pay you much more than one cow for my wife."

Surprised, the father said, "Two cows?"

"She's not a two-cow wife."

"Three cows?"

"No, I want to give you eight cows for my wife."

The missionary asked him, "Why did you do that?"

To which the rich man replied, "Not because the father needed the cows, but because I wanted the look that you will see on my wife's face when she comes into the room."

Sure enough, when this man's wife entered the room, the missionary saw her face glowing; she was radiant. All because her husband had given so much to ensure that she knew she was appreciated in his sight. That's an eight-cow wife.

So, husbands, you can each tell your wife, "I want you to be an eight-cow wife; I want you to know that I appreciate you."

If I want to change what's going on in my marriage, I need to be the initiator. People ask me, "Which one of us is supposed to start this process?" My response is, the more mature one.

So we step up. Wives are designed by nature to respond; they want to respond. Men by nature are designed to initiate. So we have to focus our minds on moving in a way that prompts our wives to respond. These principles, by the way, prove true with women universally, not just those in Christian circles.

One lady said to me, "So you think you understand women?"

I said, "No, I absolutely don't."

"Yeah, but you think you understand some things about them?"

I said, "Well, I think I do."

"OK, if you understand so much about women, what do women really need?"

I said to her, "They want to connect with their guys, they want us to lead by example, they want us to engage in conversation, and they want us to appreciate them with compassion. Women want their men to be men of our vows, in integrity, and they would like to see us be men of excitement and mystery."

The point is, if I live out these principles to the best of my ability, I may still fall down, but when she sees I'm trying, she knows I'm trying to connect, take the lead, and set an example.

A Appreciate with Affection

Appreciation means telling someone thank you. I have a system I teach to those I mentor: Place yourself in the love God has for you and then live it out in humility. Part of humility is the core value of a gratitude attitude. Every Thursday I make "Gratitude Attitude" my reminder for the day. I want to be ever thankful. It spreads to other days of the week, but Thursday is my day to emphasize gratitude.

Tell Father God thank you, and spread your thankfulness to others in your world. Saying thank you and appreciating others is part of His humble heart, and for us guys, it starts at home. "Thank you for supper." "Thank you for all the work you do with the kids." "Thank you for letting me watch the game (or play paint ball, etc.)" "Thank you for changing the diaper." "Thank you for making my breakfast (or my coffee, etc.)" "Thank you for telling me what clothes match and for showing me when I'm messing up a relationship." "Thank you for finding my cell phone." "Thank you for being my wife!"

Think about sending a thank-you text or leaving a thank-you note in her lunch or her day planner. You'll be shocked at the change in your home because now you are emphasizing all the good gifts instead of the few things that are wrong.

We'll finish this topic of Cleaving as it pertains to men in chapter 10 when we discuss more about being a man of your vows and being a man of excitement and mystery.

The Benefits

As God has continued to work on me and my family, He's given me the ability to listen with ears that hear the hurting side and to develop compassion.

A friend has worked very diligently on many of these principles. At his very technical job, he sensed that a fellow employee was frustrated by another employee's habits. Because of his heightened sensitivity, he approached this person to express appreciation and to encourage him, at the same time connecting with him at a greater level than clichés or information. The other employee revealed that because he hadn't been heard or appreciated at work, he was turning in his notice that day. The loss of this individual would have been very costly to the company. My friend averted a disaster, saving the company thousands of dollars, because he allowed the Holy Spirit to train him in this type of sensitivity to others.

My point is don't merely read about these principles. Pray about them and apply them in your life and marriage. Manage your household well, and your business will profit. As you work through the information in this study, you will find God expanding your understanding in many other areas. Let the Holy Spirit have His way with you.

Prayer:

Father, thank You for the opportunity to live out the role You have given us and to be the kind of men who truly honor Your Son. It's a high calling, Father, and it is really beyond some of the things that we can do. Father, please don't let these words go out as just more information in an information-saturated culture, a culture that has lost the high calling of leading by example, where we rate ourselves based on selfish desires and the opinions of friends. Help us live like we will give an account to You. Help us to be the kind of men who reflect You, Jesus. Amen.

CHAPTER 9: LUXURY RIDE

"The man with basic goodwill wants to serve his wife, and he would even die for her. When his wife shows him unconditional respect, in most cases he will feel like a prince and be motivated to show her the kind of unconditional love she desires.

"She is a princess who is loved."

— Emerson and Sarah Eggerichs and Susan Mathis
"The Language of Love and Respect"[58]

THE preceding chapters discussed the rules of the road for marriage and relationships in general. Regarding marriage, we've highlighted several differences in how God created men and women. The preceding chapter focused on what God called husbands to be. Now we turn our attention to specific principles God gave to wives. We could say this chapter is FWO (for women only).

In Ephesians 5:31, Paul explains God's guiding principles for husband and wives. "For this reason shall man leave father and mother and shall be joined to his wife and the two shall become one flesh." We've identified this process as *leave, cleave and weave.* Man leaves his father and his mother (priority), he shall be joined to his wife (cleave or super glue welding), and the two shall become one flesh (weave together, become, grow).

Paul continues, "The mystery is great, but I'm speaking with reference to Christ and the church." I'm fully convinced that God created marriage to teach us the intimacy that He desires to have with His children as depicted in the intimacy of a marriage. The relationship of husband and wife was designed to demonstrate the intimacy that God wants with us — to know and be fully known.

Beyond intimacy, the Genesis blueprint includes an incredibly synchronized dance that occurs between Ish and Ishah. Woman is man's

---

[58] www.focusonthefamily.com/marriage/communication-and-conflict/the-love-and-respect-principle/love-and-respect-a-royal-marriage.

completer, his ally, his deliverer and rescuer. Proverbs 31 shows her as having what Dr. Frank Seekins describes as a warrior heart, as she protects her family and competes in the market place.[59]

That original divine blueprint planned for a complementary oneness, a unity in which the couple was synchronized as they worked together on everything. This is how God intended it to be. Ish led by serving, Ishah followed by desire. Their conversations would have demonstrated this unity, unlike couples since the Fall. Imagine with me a modern-day Adam and Eve:

"Hey Adam get up! You've got animals to name and a garden to weed."

"Back off! Leave me alone! I know what to do. I'll get it done."

"Yeah, well, the kids are going to starve."

"Listen, I'm working on some new names right now. Why can't you just support me?"

"I'd support you if you supported me once in a while."

"What?!"

No, that scenario didn't happen. It didn't have to. They were one. Adam and Eve functioned as a team, probably anticipating each other's movements and desires before they happened. But today we rarely see couples in sync this way.

Cheryl and I love doing projects together. But often she moves one way and I move another. We were loading wood on our car one day and as I went to the left, she went right. I had my reasons, logical and well thought out — BUT uncommunicated. Cheryl is strong-willed, too, so her passion shot to the surface. Passions can be awesome, but they have their place. Fire in the fireplace: AWESOME! Fire in the curtains: not so great.

So God had a solution expressed in Ephesians 5:33. "Nevertheless, each individual among you also is to love his own wife even as himself and the wife must see to it that she respects her husband."

---

[59] Frank T. Seekins, *Hebrew Word Pictures: How Does the Hebrew Alphabet Reveal Prophetic Truths?*, Hebrew Heart Media (1999).

The past couple of chapters used the word "cleave" to help give clarity to the meaning of loving your wife. It's her mother tongue, her default language. When I use the term "cleave," guys, I visualize you connecting with your wife, leading by example, instilling value by encouraging and appreciating.

I've learned this: If I want to see humility, I model humility; if I want encouragement, I demonstrate encouragement; if I want to see an attitude of apology, I speak apology; if I want respect, I show respect; if I want affection, I give affection.

So ladies, how do women do this leave, cleave and weave stuff for their guys? Ephesians 5:22 says clearly that a wife is to respect her husband. Now, the word "submit" does not occur in the original language. It is an implied word carried over from verse 21. The point taken from that verse is that spouses are subject to each other, submissive to each other. And notice the words, "to your own husbands."

Paul's instruction to wives includes a strong sense of respectfulness. This idea occurs in the Scriptures with great consistency, time and again. Husbands, love your wives; wives, respect your husbands. It's never the other way around. There's a very specific pattern here. I'll use the acrostic RESPECT as a guide to help shed light on what the word means in the context of husband-wife relationships.

Men Speak a Different Language

Ladies, understand that guys speak a very specific language, and it is the opposite of yours. This is important to understand because it is the key that opens the relational door. Men have a "bro-code," a "man code;" it is the language of respect. "Klingon," right, Trekkies? From IT specialists to *America's Deadliest Catch* fans, guys — every single one of them — speak the language of respect and have little clue what the language of love is. Remember the research by Shaunti and Jeff Feldhahn from chapter 7? The Feldhahn's discovered two shocking facts:

1. Men by a great majority choose being respected over being loved and

2. Women, by a great majority have no clue what their men mean by "respect."

Ladies, please let that sink in. I would recommend you re-read the preceding paragraph five times, out loud. Write it down on a card; repeat it as you drive your car. Yes, it's just that important. Say these words: "I have no clue how my guy is wired." You may think you know your man, and most women will agree with you. But pink doesn't "get" blue!

One of the things that women can do well is multitask. They see things with an investigative mind that connects ideas like a spider web. Men, on the other hand, process in a linear sequence.

Imagine two guys talking about repairing a car. They process their thoughts and resolve the problem to "tie a knot" before they move on to a new problem. They don't multitask like women do. Men's linear, goal-driven, fix-it thinking, starts with one point, which they have to see through BEFORE beginning the next agenda item.

Guys' minds work like a string of Christmas lights. One light goes out; the whole string shuts down. All the lights are off and they have to stop and fix that broken one before moving to the next item. That's just the way their minds work. Meanwhile, women, who are multitaskers, live in the moment. One light goes out, and they say, "Oh well." All the rest of the lights have stayed on, so they move to the next task.

Remember, ladies, guys are "brain damaged." So respect means you understand that your man speaks a different language than you and that's OK. You want to learn to pause when communicating with him because you respect him and don't want all the nonlinear ideas and emotions you express to be overwhelming for him.

Additionally, guys are just as sensitive as or more sensitive than women. It's true; studies have demonstrated men's emotional sensitivity. In these studies that measure galvanic skin responses, and observe tear ducts, and heart and breathing rate while both sexes watch the same scenes, men are as sensitive as or more sensitive than women. Women will cry and reach for the Kleenex; guys will tear up and hide the tears. ("Uh, I've got something in my eye.")

In counseling, I consistently witness this with men. I'll approach a guy heart-to-heart and all of a sudden he just starts pouring out stuff. I asked one guy, "Do you have anything to share with us?"

"Nope."

"Do you want to add anything to the way you understood the situation?"

"No."

Finally I got him off alone. We sat on a picnic table and I said, "What's going on?" The guy talked for 45 minutes without stopping. I began to realize guys are just as sensitive as or more sensitive than women.

> ## GUYS CAN BE JUST AS SENSITIVE AS OR MORE SENSITIVE THAN WOMEN.

Another study that grouped boys and girls based on age discovered that the group that communicates the most is not girls. It's 13- to 18-year-old boys. They communicate at the deepest level and they communicate the most. Other studies indicate that when a male college student breaks up with a girl, it typically takes her about 9 to 18 months to get over that guy. But when a guy gets dumped, it takes him about 36 months to recover emotionally, and some guys never get over being dumped.

This is the sensitivity that guys bring to the table. Guys can be just as sensitive as or more sensitive than girls. Don't believe me? Conduct your own survey. Ask your mom friends raising little boys; they'll tell you that by far, little boys are more sensitive than little girls.

But boys are taught to hide their emotions. For instance, if a guy breaks his arm, he says, "Oh, oh, I broke my arm," while holding back the tears from the pain. He has to be that way. But you let that same guy get a little sliver in his finger, and he acts like he's going to die.

Shaunti Feldhahn, Emerson Eggerichs, and the Gottmans have studied thousands of people. They put men and women in a room and asked the men, "Which would you rather be — loved or respected, and which would you rather be — nurtured or seen as incompetent?" Ninety percent of men will say, "I would rather be on a desert island alone and unloved than to be disrespected or seen as incompetent."

When researchers questioned the group of women, they came up with an exact opposite answer: "I would rather be loved than respected." The implications of this difference are huge for guys, especially because most parents and classroom teachers and Sunday school lessons and marriage courses and TV shows do not teach this concept of respect. Rather, they focus on the concept of how we love each other. The women in these studies were shocked to learn that men desire respect more than love.

When I mention the word "respect," people I counsel often bring up the word "submissive," "submission" or some derivative. The common application of Ephesians 5:21 has been that wives must be "submissive." As I mentioned in chapter 7, the word translated "subject to one another in the fear of Christ" is the Greek word HUPOTASSO, which means "to get underneath and lift someone up." I refer again to Dr. Norm Wright, who points out that the Greek middle voice infers "I order myself from inside." It's not about the husband's authority over his wife but is instead an honor she bestows upon him as she is led by God.[60]

This usage implies: *This is the ideal of what God would have us as wives to be, coming from the inside out, respecting our husbands. It's what we look like in Christ.*

These words were written FOR WOMEN, and this is something that they are to be working on. This is NOT something that their husbands need to be reminding them to do.

So don't read her mail, guys; don't be her Holy Spirit. God may be working on her heart as she responds to your godly CLEAVE leadership. Let's re-examine Ephesians 5:22-24:

Wives be subject to your own husbands as to the Lord for the husband is the head of the wife as Christ also is the head of the church, he himself being the

---

[60] H. Norman Wright, *Communication: Key to Your Marriage: The Secret to True Happiness*, Gospel Light (Kindle Edition).

savior of the body. But as the church is subject to Christ so also wives are to be subject to their husbands in everything.

It's an issue of learning to walk in the Spirit so that both husband and wife portray that sense of honor and respect just like they do to the Lord. This is not an issue of better versus best; it's not a position of value. It is a position of roles.

In our world, everything about being underneath — looking and helping and lifting someone else — is about value, the servant being of lesser value than the one being served. *In God's intent, these positions are not about value.* One person in a family acts as the "vice president" and another acts as the "president." This doesn't mean that the "president" is more valuable or important. According to the world's interpretation of submission, the man and the woman are not equals, but the man is superior and the woman is subservient. That is simply not true.

It reminds me of the lady whose husband went on and on, "You're the wife; I'm the husband. You're the wife; I'm the boss. You're nothing; I'm the boss and you're nothing." Finally he stopped.

She waited for a minute and said, "Oh, big deal — boss of nothing."

Guys, we're nothing without our wives; likewise, they without us. So let's see what the Word is trying to teach us: The complementarian view. Equal in value, but distinct in roles. A reflection of God. Father, Son, Spirit —equal, but distinct. Each in a distinct role or function but both equal in value. Women who long for loving care and men who are desperate for respect.

Now for the Ladies

We've addressed husbands, ladies. Now let's work with you.

RESPECT

R Rules Have Changed

E Eyes of Honor

S Shoulder-to-Shoulder

P Paint Word Pictures; Pose Questions.

E Expectations and Assumptions

C Competitive Nature of Men

T Touching the Sexual Side

R Rules Have Changed

Ladies, when it comes to marriage, you need to understand that the relationship rules with your husband are different than they are with any other relationship.

John Gray's popular book, *Men Are from Mars, Women Are from Venus* alludes to this different playing field. Our two genders are planets apart. All women will sympathize with one another a hundred percent when they hear all the bad stuff that their husbands are doing. "Why, you poor dear. You're just so sweet! How could he treat you that way?"

"I can't even believe it; what's wrong with him?"

"It's men; it's always men. Men are always the problem in everything. MENtal anguish, MENstrual cycles, MENopause, MENingitis … men, men, men! It's always men!"

Women can get together, dogging their husbands because "he's the problem." But truthfully, the problem is that often wives don't understand that the rules guys operate from are planets away from where women come from.

Guys don't talk and think the way women do. So when I say that the rules are different, I mean you need to learn to respect his language because it's his code that he's sensitive and you need to understand that he is a sensitive human being. Respect begins when wives see that guys' rules are different.

This issue of respect was made obvious in a discussion I had with two very dear friends, Frank and Judy Gerald. I call it the "Chips Ahoy" moment. Frank had bought a package of Chips Ahoy cookies, but, using it as comfort food, he managed to eat the entire package. When Judy got home, she exclaimed, "You didn't even leave me one cookie?"

Frank realized what he had done and said, "I'm going to go to the store right now and get some …"

"Oh, just don't bother …"

"Nope, I'm going."

"Don't bother. It's OK. Don't worry about it ... just forget it."

Back and forth it went. Finally, Frank went out the door saying, "This wasn't right; I was selfish." (Guys don't often say this.) "I'm going to the store."

And Judy is thinking what? *What a hard-headed, stubborn man!* But, ladies, here's what you don't get: You don't get his language, his mother tongue.

So what was he truly thinking? To him it was an issue of honor. Of respect. His man code kicked in. The "Code" says, "You do not eat the last cookie, you do not take the last piece of cake, don't smoke a guy's last cigarette," so to speak. *I blew it, I gotta fix it. I made a mistake. I'm to take care of my wife. I selfishly ate all the cookies. I was wrong. I have to fix this.*

According to his code, this was a major violation. And he had to go to the store to make it right.

"Well," you may say, "it's just a Chips Ahoy cookie." Not to a man. It's a statement of respect. Ladies, your difficulty understanding this is a meter of how unnatural this language of respect is to you with your language of love.

See? The rules have changed.

E Eyes of Honor

One of the most powerful ways you show respect, ladies, is with your eyes. He can see in your eyes when you respect him and when you don't. You may think he's a block of concrete; he's an emotional zombie. But that's not true. He may not talk but he watches. He also listens. And it's not just eyes; it's all of your body language.

Ladies, you have a very powerful voice. It's not very loud, but when you start to get stressed, your vocal chords tighten and all of a sudden there are tones that come from you that wring your husband's heart and make him absolutely nuts because he doesn't know what's wrong and he's trying to fix you. You're his best friend; he needs to make sure that you're OK. You think he's hard and nothing affects him. Not true. Inside, his whole day is ruined and finished, but he is trained not to show it.

He can see in your eyes and he can hear in your voice and he can read your body language. Folded arms, crossed legs, no more hand holding, turning away — all of this and more he knows. You don't have honor for him. He somehow dropped the ball. He failed you. Doesn't mean much to you, just a conversation. But to him it's ACID in the face. Literally.

Honor his way of thinking and he will think differently. Remember, when one light goes out for him, the whole Christmas tree is out — that's just it. He loves peace, longs for it, and goes crazy inside when he can't produce it. Guys love peace; wives love connection. Guys don't think like their wives do; the whole structure is different to them. You wives know the names of all your kids' friends, know all your kids' birthdays, know where their hair is done, know how many shoes they have, etc. … and that is extremely important to you; you're wired that way.

He's vaguely aware there are little people running loose in the house. He compartmentalizes his life into different boxes. He has a "work box," which is a fairly good size because he works in his work box and he really doesn't like to be interrupted. He also has a "sports box," and that's how he can sit there and watch television with a remote in his hand, and the world can come crashing down beside him, and he will never hear it because he's in his sports box. He has a "car box." A guy's whole house can burn to the ground and the question will be, "What happened to my car?" He has a "sex box," he has a "friends box," he has an "enemies box" and there is another one, a big one.

A "nothing box." As noted in chapter 4, in our nothing box we guys are all by ourselves and we're alone and we're very happy. Our nothing box is huge and it's where we go to repair the day. When you wives come and you're trying to connect to your guy, trying to get into his life, hoping to get him to talk and he's like "nothing there," that's because … he's not home. Lights are on, no one's home.

You might have one of those "nothing" conversations where you ask, "How did your day go, honey?" And no matter how you word your follow-up questions, you basically get, "Nothing."

You need to know he's come out of his work box and gone into his nothing box, and that's where he rests. And this becomes insanity when you and your husband are out with friends and someone asks him what happened today ... and he starts chattering like a teenage girl. Come to find out the wall blew off the building. So you wives are just fit to be tied.

Somehow you have to help him change boxes. Honor his efforts to communicate. Guys don't know what they feel, or how to communicate. So honor the few sentences you get at times; it may be the best that he can do at the moment. Let him cool down and give him this space, and he'll start to open up and share with you a lot of the things that are going on in his life.

Honor him publicly. Ladies, you can joke with him privately, but joking about him in public can ram him in his fragile spots. You are out with friends and you joke about the fact that he can't fix a garden hose, let alone a kitchen sink. As I've said, some guys are very sensitive, and what you think is just fun kidding, to him is an exposure of his incompetence. The "I can't do that" thoughts are hard for a guy to swallow.

Over-talking is a huge problem in communication. Watch what you do when he talks. Are you respecting him as he talks? Can he complete a sentence or two before you start talking? Your mind is thinking five times faster. Furthermore, he is on trial and he can't think of every conversation you've had like you do, and can't come up with the examples you can. But listen to his heart. Hear the guy behind the face you are irritated with.

The way guys listen is one of the greatest methods of respect they give to each other. In serious conversations, we get very slow and precise and we do not interrupt. When we are lighthearted, we joke, make fun of others, use sarcasm, and are free-hearted. You wives need to be aware of these different modes.

S Shoulder to Shoulder.

Men love to have their wives shoulder-to-shoulder with them. That means not telling us what to do. Cheryl and I have been married for many years, and we share a rich trust. But even now, when she tells me to do something that I am "about" to do ... welling up inside me comes this sense of anger at being told.

We guys want to do things with our wives without talking sometimes. We like being together. When you look at how parents relate to their infants and toddlers, women are nurturers and guys want playmates. We love it when our wives do things with us. So honor your guy by teaming up with him, by being side-by-side with him.

Awhile back, a lady came to me and said, "I tried to get in, side-by-side with my husband, but he said, 'Please, I can't have you here.'"

Ladies, often when a guy says such things, it is because historically you have been more trouble than it's worth. (Sorry, I don't mean to hurt your feelings.) He doesn't need directions on how to paint the wall; he just wants you there. You may good-heartedly volunteer your advice: "Well, you could push your toolbox over here or there."

After a few moments he starts to clam up. Then he says, "Why don't you go inside?" Think before you say something, because it may be simple to you but huge to him. You may have great intentions and simply want to help, but your suggestion in "French" may be heard by your "Klingon" man as a statement of his stupidity, i.e., *Why didn't he think of that?* So, ladies, remember this as you offer him an idea. (A word to us guys: Drop the pride and learn to listen to your wife more.)

Honor his opinions, ladies. Let him win once in a while; it's really important, and this is one of the ways you can honor your husband.

One day in a session, I said to a guy, "What's your dream?"

There was this long pause — and I knew he was afraid to say because his wife was sitting there — and he said, "I really want to go to Thailand and be a missionary. I'd give anything if I could do that." Pounding in the heart of that man was a passion to go to Thailand and be a missionary. I looked at him thinking, *Wow!*

I glanced over at his wife and said to her, "How do you feel about that?"

She said, "I'd give anything to go because it's my dream, too."

P Paint Word Pictures; Pose Questions

Ladies, did you know that guys view criticism as contempt? Criticism in the heart of a man is like acid on his soul. Often ladies ask me, "What are other ways I can honor him in our relationship?" I tell them they can paint word pictures and pose questions.

Start by figuring out what you are thinking then put your brain around what you feel emotionally. Then paint him a word picture that helps him see and understand that feeling.

When my son Jeremiah was nine years old, he and I were talking about a kid he didn't like because he was little, scrawny and always interrupted. Jeremiah thought his friends were his friends, and this kid was a bother.

Rather than saying, "Jeremiah, that's wrong," I said to him, "I once knew a little boy that was scrawny and got beat up in a parking lot, and other people would come out and watch. I once knew a little boy that was like that. And he grew up very angry and it took him a long time to get over that the hurt."

My son said, "Daddy, who was that?"

I said, "That was me, Jeremiah." I watched his eyes well up with tears. Soon he went to that little guy and pulled him in as part of their group.

That was a word picture. Anytime you can give a word picture — especially to guys — it is a very powerful communicator.

Asking questions is even more powerful. You know what you want to say, so give him the problem and let him solve it rather than telling all that is wrong with him. Guys were intended to protect, provide and problem solve. When you come to your husband and say, "This-and-that is wrong," you cross into a devastating proclamation that he is a failure. He sees you as criticizing him. But if you say, "Hey, we've got a problem that we need to solve; can we do this," you've formed a question and posed a problem to solve rather than another criticism for him to endure. This type of question doesn't polarize his thinking, so he jumps in because he sees a situation to fix.

A friend once said to her husband, "Remember when we were sailing? And we were stuck with no wind? Well, when you're not around, I feel like I'm out in an ocean and just feel lonely like you're not there." It was a great word picture for him. She painted a picture that helped him understand how isolated she felt.

One of my clients refused to enter into the verbal wrestling that couples do. Instead she said to her husband, "You know when you walk away or you answer me abruptly, you know what that feels like? You know how scared you are of heights? It feels like we're on a mountain-climbing expedition and we're up several hundred feet and you unclip your carabineer. I get really scared because my safety line just got disconnected. I feel like something is wrong and I'm no longer secure with you."

That picture grabbed her husband. He said, "Wow, I had no idea."

E Expectations and Assumptions

Ladies, a man comes to marriage thinking she will never change, and she does. She comes to marriage thinking he can be changed, and he doesn't.

Expectations can be a killer in relationships. We project expectations and agendas in our choice of words. And they can flow from a controlling heart. "You need to be better at what you do." "You need to be more spiritual." "Why can't you be like my dad?" "Why can't you bring in more income like so-and-so?" "Why can't you spend more time with me?" "Why won't you wash the car?"

Words of guilt and shame can be used by women in powerful ways. "I am just a little disappointed." Those are power words in a man's heart. One guy came back to me after four or five counseling sessions and said, "I had the greatest week ever."

"Really, what happened?"

He said, "You're not going to believe this, but around our house, everyone is told I can't fix anything. Everybody knows that I'm a loser when it comes to fixing stuff in the house. My wife always calls somebody before I'm given the chance to try. But this last week she said, 'Hey, the washing machine's broken. Can you fix it?'"

His eyes watered up with tears. I couldn't believe it. This man was an executive manager, but his eyes were filled with tears. I said, "What did you do?"

"I went in there and saw the hose was twisted and leaking. So I fixed the kink and turned the washer on and it didn't leak. With a smile of accomplishment, I turned around, and she said, 'My hero.'"

And women think guys are less sensitive. Ladies, don't assume. Honor him in his accomplishments.

We Don't Read Minds

One other note, ladies — we guys don't read minds. I've heard wives say, "How could anybody be so dense as to not understand what I'm feeling or thinking?" Most of the time, we need to be reminded what you're thinking. Take the time; you're dealing with a brain that thinks and feels differently than yours. Guys can read your eyes and body language, because they can see those, but they can't read what's hidden in your mind.

Our minds are accessed through our eyes. The mind of a woman is more complicated than merely what she sees with her eyes. The way she follows someone with her eyes reveals a complexity beneath the surface. We can see that our wife respects us, but we can't read her emotions and feelings. Most of our emotions and feelings are fear that we blew it somehow. But when we can see that honor in her eyes then we know that she's OK.

You ladies can show respect with your eyes. You can honor with your hearts. You can honor by posing questions. You can honor by being shoulder-to-shoulder. You can honor each other by lowering your expectations and assumptions. You can accept your husband for who he is — the man you chose to marry for good times and bad.

In the next chapter, we'll complete our RESPECT acrostic with respecting your husband's **(C)** Competitive nature and **(T)** Touching on the sexual side.

Prayer:

Father God, You've shown us wives that we have the authority to speak into our husbands' hearts. You've given us the gift to influence, help, and encourage our husbands. Restore and strengthen our relationship as we discover the strength of wives who have learned that their heart and their behavior can touch their men. We ask in Your name. Amen.

CHAPTER 10: NEW CAR SMELL

"It is possible to discover what is on the mind and in the heart of the woman a man married if he is indwelt by the Holy Spirit and begins displaying Christ-like attitudes toward his wife. You and I have to make the choice every day to minister in Christ-like ways to our wives. When we do that, we'll gradually discover that they are no longer mysterious and incomprehensible. After all, they never were mysterious to the Holy Spirit who is living in us."

—Ken Nair[61]

ONE thing we all seem to enjoy the first time we drive a brand new car is that "new car smell." Getting into crisp new seats behind a clean steering wheel, fresh carpeting, no dust in the vents, no scratches on the radio — all the things a new car brings. Wouldn't it be awesome if you could keep that "new marriage smell" in your marriage relationship? This chapter will address the things that vitalize marriages and cause us to stay on course and keep that new car smell.

Let's continue with our acrostics from Ephesians 5:31-33, the biblical hallmark God gave husbands and wives.

For this reason a man shall leave his father and mother and shall be joined to his wife. And the two shall become one flesh. The mystery is great but I am speaking with reference to Christ and the church. Nevertheless, each individual among you also is to love his own wife even as himself and the wife must see to it that she respects her husband.

I have two more letters for guys and two more for ladies.

In chapter 8, we started the acrostic CLEAVE for guys:

C Connect and Engage with Her

L Lead by Example

E Encourage and Affirm Her

---

[61] Ken Nair with Leslie H. Stobbe, *Discovering the Mind of a Woman*, Thomas Nelson, Inc., (Nashville, 1995).

A Appreciate with Affection

V Vows, Virtue, Live with Integrity

E Excitement and Mystery

V Vows, Virtue, Live with Integrity

Remember, boy babies are brain washed with testosterone. This chemical wash carries with it the inability for us guys to 1) understand our emotions, 2) communicate them to others, and 3) multitask like our female counterparts. It does give us the ability to be focused, to quickly gravitate to plotting sequential solutions, and, bottom line, to enjoy fixing things. So, guys, we need to use God's given ability to focus on the right things. We need to become men of our vows.

In Eden, Ish and his Isha had a deep, inborn sense of integrity. Honesty with each other was natural because they had nothing to hide. Then came the Fall. His integrity crumbled like an over-baked cookie. Ish 1) hid because he was afraid, 2) covered himself by sewing fig leaves together, and 3) blamed God and Isha for his sin. Hiding and more hiding. Gentlemen, integrity doesn't hide; it takes great joy in telling the truth even to one's own hurt.

Early in life I struggled with a very compromising character. No out-and-out lies, but white lies, truth shaping and positive spinning. (I would have made a good politician.) God broke me of that. I developed a passion for telling the truth without caring what it cost me. I learned character.

Character is a statement of what one loves more than what one wants. If a person loves truthfulness more than achieving some end, then that person will hold truth even to his own demise. Character — it's why a man jumps on a grenade to save his buddies. He loves others more than his own skin.

For Adam integrity was gone. Sin became blaming. Blaming became betrayal: "The woman YOU gave me." Integrity was lost. Replaced by hiding, covering, blaming and betrayal. Man up, Adam. You did the deed; take it straight on. Be a man of integrity.

Being a man of your vows starts with your eyes, how you look at other women. You need to affirm for your wife that she is the only one for you. Wives live in a very competitive market. They frequently compare themselves with how other women dress, accessorize, and do makeup and hair because they have to measure up.

Guys, we don't need size-3 girls. By not looking, we show our wives that they have our hearts. We will notice other women naturally. Yet it's not the first look but the second that hurts our wives and causes insecurity. Wives need to hear from their husbands they are secure, and it is our character that stops the second look.

"The end justifies the means." That's the way I was raised. I would justify a lot of truth shaping. Eventually, God brought me a tremendous sense of conviction over this rationalizing. Typically we guys will do or say anything to keep the peace. But that can be lying.

Have you considered that making a promise you don't keep is an integrity issue? Your wife may say, "I want to talk to you about something," or "I want to share this with you," or "I want to work with you on this." And you may respond with "I don't want to talk about it right now," but then never bring it up and resolve it later. When you ask for a time out, your integrity is on the line to bring it up later and resolve the issue with her.

Character or integrity is all about who you are inside, not about a spouse's approval. You are your own competition.

And don't walk away. When I get into a disagreement with my wife, I don't walk away, I don't drive off, I don't go someplace else, because I'm a man of my vows. I stand into that conversation. I may not have a lot to say and I may feel like I'm getting over-talked or overrun, but I don't leave; I stand firm. Being a man of my vows means that I'm standing in the discomfort. I may go to the garage for a time out, but I'll come back to it.

Once I figured this out, I liked being valued for my integrity. I may say to Cheryl, "I can't deal with this right now. We've discussed five issues; my mind is exhausted; I can't take anymore. Can we come back to this?" Being a man of my vows means that in an hour or two or the next day, I will go back to her and say, "Can we finish our discussion? Thanks for being patient."

If I tell her that I'm going to do something, I follow through and do what I said I would do. That's what it means to be a man of my vows. That works in my words and my actions. If I tell her we are going to do such-and-such, then I make sure we do it. Being a man of my word means I say what I'm going to do and then do what I said.

Virtue also means looking at your wife and giving her your full attention during conversations. Look her in the eyes, not just in her general direction because the strength of your character says, "I'm not going to give up." Being a man of your vows builds a stable marriage and family. You're dependable.

When my daughter was going through her early teen years, I took her aside and invited her to go for a walk. We talked and I drew big lines in the air. "You're going to experience lots of feelings — extreme highs and extreme lows. Life will discourage you and hurt you. Friends will move away, let you down. Peer pressure intensifies.

"And then there are boys. You'll be thinking, *My life is a mess; I can't go on.* But I want you to know with confidence where I'm going to be." And I drew a level line right through the center. "I will be right here. You'll see me on the way up; we'll talk, I'll hug you, and we'll laugh. And then you'll come down again, and you'll pass me again right in the center." That's being a man of strength and virtue for your family.

Part of your responsibility is to be the stable mind in your home. That is also a reflection of your character. A wife will see her husband as her burden bearer, someone to call when things go wrong.

When Cheryl tells me, "The softener quit. Water's all over the floor," instead of getting upset, I just deal with it. Being there. Holding things down. Having the stability that people can rely on — that's character.

I asked a few friends to give me examples of how they display character and integrity in their marriage. One guy said the following:

"It was my first time coming to church. We hadn't really found a church where we felt welcomed or that God was saying, 'This is where I want you.' I felt in my heart that we had to keep looking and attending church, and there

were times when I wasn't feeling good, and I would still go to church fighting against Satan's attack.

"My wife told me, 'I really respect your leadership, that you didn't quit or stay home making excuses. And I know that you are praying for me and our family.'

"I try to be a man of my word, sharing the things that I see in the Bible with my wife, praying together, doing what God is leading me to do as the accountable one for my family.

"Last night, my wife and I were getting ready for a big meal that we were hosting and it was getting late. She was getting tired; she wanted to postpone the meal or go out to eat instead. I said, 'I'm here to help you.' So we jumped in together to make the deadline. We were shoulder-to-shoulder because I had eyes of honor and could see in my wife's eyes that she was tired, frustrated and crying for help."

In another example of integrity, a father was at the park with his young sons. He noticed some teens had left baseball equipment behind. He jokingly yelled to them as they walked away, "Hey grab your bag, or we'll take it with us." It was a lot of expensive baseball equipment. His boys were watching.

The teens didn't hear the father's suggestion and kept walking. So this dad told one of his boys to catch up with the teens while the other son ran to fetch the bag.

A lot of people think its OK to walk off with someone else's personal property — "Finders Keepers," so to speak. But this father taught his sons the value of virtue and doing the right thing. Even when no one else is watching, Father God is watching.

Guys, this is how we were intended to operate. God wants us to be passionate.

Who may ascend into the hill of the LORD? And who may stand in His holy place? He who has clean hands and a pure heart, who has not lifted up his soul to falsehood, and has not sworn deceitfully. He shall receive a blessing from the LORD and righteousness from the God of his salvation.[62]

---

[62] Psalm 24:3-5.

E Excitement and Mystery

The "E" in CLEAVE refers to learning to be a man of excitement. Be a man of mystery. What does it mean to be a man of excitement and mystery? It's part of keeping the new car smell. But human nature is to get used to a person and start taking him or her for granted.

Remember the husband's diminishing concern in the "coughing wife" illustration from the "Marriage 911" chapter? That is not how God intended us guys to be. He intended us to keep the newness of our marriage. Part of that is accomplished by changing it up. Excitement and mystery do that. "You know, you really are the most important person in my life. And know what? Thirty years from now, when all my friends and my health are gone, it will be you bending over my hospital bed to wish me a good journey goodbye."

Guys, we're all about destinations. *Let's get to Sea World and get the family vacation done!* Our wives tend to be all about the journey. She looks forward to the journey together, spending time together. The mystery and the adventure. And we gotta get this. Which of us has not rolled in laughter at *National Lampoon's Vacation* and the Clark Griswold family's mishaps? Who would care about that movie if the Griswolds left the house then arrived at Walley World without incident the next day? *Big deal!* Ahhhh, but the fun is in the adventure. A station-wagon-full-family adventure.

That is what excitement and mystery are all about. Now I confess, I can make (and have made) any trip an absolute horror story. Some people have the gift of criticism; I have the gift of making a wonderful trip a nightmare. We're driving along and a little stand with some blankets and souvenirs pops us. I think, *What a tourist trap.* Someone (Cheryl) says, "Let's stop."

I retort, "Well, you know, we only have this much time; we gotta keep moving. Hurry! C'mon, get back in the car! Let's go."

Someone says, "I've gotta go to the bathroom."

"Well, hold it! We only have about 10 more minutes."

"I really gotta go."

"You just went to the bathroom 20 minutes ago."

I'm all about the destination and all about getting there and getting the job done without stopping to enjoy the trip. But pretty soon everyone is mad at me. It's OK if we get to the destination an hour later than I planned. Nobody's mad at me. Nobody's opening the car door and throwing me out.

Another way to bring excitement and mystery — giving gifts. Find a little something to bless your spouse's day. And here's another secret: Do things so that your wife or husband can tell others. Guys, we want to do things right. So we buy a dozen roses. But how about buying one rose every month for 12 months? And then, if you really want to multiply the surprise, get it to her at work so her friends can see it.

Be discerning, though. One time, wanting to give my wife a rose, I walked into a gas station shop. I saw flowers and got her one. Should have known something was up because the price was $5.98 … for one rose. I took it home and I handed it to her. She looked at it and I thought, *How come she didn't smell it and say it was pretty?* That's when I realized it was a fake flower.

And don't diminish the value of date nights. Guys, if you haven't scheduled date nights, start. I suggest this with all my clients. My wife and I have dates as often as we can. It doesn't have to be a huge event, but date her; keep the new car smell. Sit down and watch a chick flick. Watch these kinds of movies with her because excitement begins right there in her world.

Did you know that sex begins in the kitchen? It doesn't begin in the bedroom. Your wife's sexual desire begins in her mind. You connect with her first thing in the morning, which is when you usually connect with a cup of coffee. She feels appreciated that you take the time with her in the morning. She needs to feel the connection and that sense of attachment to you. Her emotional response becomes reflexive; she wants to embrace you and give you the affirmation you're looking for to start your day.

Ladies, let's look at your list:

C Competitive Nature of Men

When you're working with your guy, ladies, remember that he comes with some interesting wiring. Part of that is a competitive nature. He loves to see things as a challenge, to problem solve, to see the problem and fix it. It's part of his mother tongue. So in your communication, stop trying to change him from the outside in. Learn to change him from the inside out. Build within him a desire to see a problem and solve it rather than talking at him, cajoling him, nagging him, reminding him, or any of the hundred other ways you try to figure out how to change him.

He needs a problem to solve; he does NOT need to be shown what a problem he is. Motivating him from the inside out means that he WANTS to do it rather than that he HAS to do it.

Help him to see your marriage as a way to honor God. Encourage him to pursue Christ. Pray for him to take the challenge to be the spiritual man he was designed to be. Let the words he hears be from the Holy Spirit, not your words of disappointment or criticism. Help him hear, "The solution to our marriage is written in your heart."

Don't tell him, "Man, you need to get counseling. Your problem is you're not spiritually strong." Instead help him see the value of growing in Christ by letting him see it as a challenge he can take up. Then encourage him in his efforts to grow. If you have something you want him to see or understand, first, take it to the Lord in prayer. Then remember guys need massive encouragement. (They are super sensitive.) Next provide insight to see growth in terms of goals and challenges (which guys need more than they need criticism). And top it off by providing appreciation or affirmation.

Remember that guys see criticism as acid to the soul. Emmerson Eggerichs aptly illustrates this in his *Love and Respect* material when he describes a wife who wanted to change her husband's thinking about reading a marriage book. She purchased the suitable book with a typical feminine touchy-feely cover and set it by the remote. Nothing happened. She placed it by the toilet and nothing happened. She was speaking to blue sunglasses through her pink world.

To understand how this feels to a man, let's say he purchases a *Sports Illustrated* swimsuit edition and a diet book and places them by her favorite chair. Then by the toilet ... and finally at the bedside. Can you see the toxicity that your man might feel?

Remember, ladies, guys need to change from the inside out — because they want to, not because they have to. Let's say you're driving in the car, and he's busy telling all the other drivers how they should be driving. He's got a little bit of rage building in his competitive mind. At that moment, he doesn't need to hear you say, "Stop yelling at the other drivers! They can't hear you. Why do you drive that way? Why don't you slow down? Why don't you grow up, act your age, be mature?" And so on.

Instead, challenge him with that sense of competitiveness. Say things like "I'm glad you don't drive like those other maniacs and you keep us safe. Thank you." Or "One of the things I would love is for you to help us be more positive. Help us enjoy this trip."

See the difference? Instead of forcing from the outside in, give him encouragement and a problem to solve.

When I was working on my commercial license with a senior pilot, he concluded a session saying, "Jim, you are an amazing natural pilot but you lack something — finesse. Don't force the aircraft to the ground. You need to finesse to a beautiful landing. And do it in such a way that your passengers enjoy the ride. Right now I'm not enjoying the ride. I know you can do this because you are just that quality pilot."

I was encouraged. The words "great pilot" presented a challenge/ problem to solve. "Finesse the aircraft" added to the challenge. Then he affirmed me with "I know you can do this." Ever since, I set that goal of finesse when I'm flying.

Ladies, when you're in the process of helping your guy, you want him to learn how to do things God's way. You need to understand that he needs the challenge of being competitive with himself. Pray for him, encourage him, challenge him and then affirm him. Talk to your guy about this. After he gets over his defensiveness and the shock that you aren't going to entrap him, he will open his heart and talk.

T Touching the Sexual Side

Let's touch on the sexual side. During a marriage enrichment conference, I was counseling a couple, both 65 years old. They were delightful people, a pastoral couple for many years.

I asked them to write a list of three things they would like to fix in their marriage. For 35 years she had a specific list of things that she would love to see change in their marriage. I looked at his list, and he'd written two significant items: "I'd like to be a lot less stressed about the way I handle myself," and "I'd like to have a better sexual relationship with my wife." I about fell off my chair. Thirty-five years of marriage and 65 years old, and yes, ladies he was still thinking that like that! The average male's sex drive doesn't diminish all that much. Yes, 92 percent of the time, this is what guys are wishing for.

I wanted to understand this distinctively male need, so I studied various research findings from the dissection of men's brains. Deep in the center of male brains, scientists found a mechanism called their "pleasure center," and it has one switch, which is either on or off. That is the way God made guys. It's not that your husband is a pervert. There's not something wrong with him. That's the way God made him.

Researchers also dissected the female brain and discovered that women have lots of different "switches." Those are women's "control boxes," and men need directions to discover how they work. Comparing the male brain and the female brain reveals that we need to understand as much as we can about the two.

> **SEX IS A GIFT GIVEN FROM GOD TO A WOMAN TO BE GIVEN TO A MAN.**
>
> **GOD PLACED IN MAN THE SEXUAL DESIRE FOR A WOMAN.**

Let's see if we can understand the difference between a man's brain and a woman's brain. In the center of their brains, men have a cell called a *nucleus accumbens*. It's that "pleasure center." Guys associate sexual intimacy to that center. When something negative happens to a guy, like receiving a discouraging phone call, or hitting a pothole with his tire in the middle of the highway, or something positive like walking a woodsy trail, he has a familiar reinforcement sense. It's located in the pleasure center and will come on and off based on his experience. For a guy, that pleasure center is connected to sexual intimacy. His nucleus accumbens will glow like a light bulb when he is in a sexually intimate situation.

Beneath that is his sensory information, where he keeps visual files. He sees something and remembers it, especially the shape of a girl, her hair and eyes. During a favorable pleasure experience, he remembers the sight, and his brain immediately pictures enjoyment.

Cheryl and I were talking about *The Avengers* movie after we saw it. I was asking about the Incredible Hulk. "Does this stuff ever affect you?"

She said, "No, it doesn't."

I said, "But when you saw Mark Ruffalo, the Incredible Hulk, not wearing a shirt and showing off his muscular six pack, didn't you like that at all?"

She said, "No, it didn't impact me."

I kept questioning because I didn't understand her mind. "Really?"

You know, if Scarlett Johansson, the Black Widow in that movie, had taken off her shirt, I'll tell you right now it would take me years to get that out of my head. My visual file would have downloaded that image and locked it in like you can't believe. Let me see if I can demonstrate for you how this works.

Guys experience events very visually, and store the images for years. Women have certain physical parts that men see very clearly. They associate those files to that pleasure center. This is how drug addiction works, and this is how porn works in the mind of a man. It can be very addictive.

The man's mind also contains two *amygdalae*. We have the pleasure center, we have the visual sensors and then we have two almond-shaped groups of nuclei, each called an amygdala. That little piece of equipment builds up all of our experiences so when this visual image starts coming down our mental pipeline, and it hits that spot, we reflexively send it over to action because this is the way our brains are trained. This is the part that we need to change; it's the shortcut across the brain. We think, *I've seen this before, I will react the same way.* Our emotional response becomes reflexive. This is how strongholds form, and we build out a pattern or habit of thinking. Sex for guys in the fireplace — it's OK. In the curtains — it's OK. That's how we remember pleasure.

Lets talk about character. Brain research reveals two sides to our brains, right and left. The right side is the seat of our emotions and pulses at six times a second. The left side — our analytical, organized, and controlling side — pulses at five times each second. Obviously we sense our world far faster than we analyze it.

Both sides contain white and grey matter. White matter oversees both sides, making instantaneous decisions on what is acceptable behavior and what is not. Here habits and reflexive behaviors are formed and locked into place. Making decisions repeatedly forms character. Repeated actions become habits and core beliefs.

Now, get this: White matter pulses at 200 TIMES PER SECOND. That is why character building is so important. Our character — built over days, months, and years — determines our INSTANTANEOUS RESPONSE.

Character is built in white matter over time. The decisions of integrity are not made on the spot. They reflect our past thoughts that formed habits. Character failures such as affairs are not mainly impulsive decisions. They are mostly a reflection of past weak decisions.

This is where guys become men of integrity. Just like with recreational drugs, we need to say no. Ladies, you need to understand that's the way that your guy thinks. That shortcut across his brain, that's his physical pleasure that he feels in that part of who he is. His body actually feels a sense of pressure — it's been described to women like breast feeding — and he feels that physically in relationship to sexual intimacy. He looks at sexual intimacy as an emotional need for connection; it's a high.

Sex for a guy is very highly emotional, and he is sharing his vulnerability, which carries a deep risk of rejection. It plays a large role in his self-affirmation and his confidence. When guys are engaged sexually, they feel wanted, embraced and accepted. They are expressing themselves in a way that God designed them.

You are the only woman that he, as a Christian can look at. Did you know that? You are the one girl that he can freely, biblically, allow his eyes to caress. When a man has a sexual relationship, a cuddling hormone called *oxytocin* is released in him; it is designed to draw him near and be close to his sexual partner. It's his connection and it's extremely important to a man. Sex is a gift given from God given to a woman to be given in turn to a man. God placed in man the desire for a woman.

A woman's greatest sexual desire is found in her mind. Children, schedules, sleep, unresolved conflict, sickness and multitasking can switch a woman to the off position. Ladies, I encourage you to work on the sexual excitement and mystery in your marriage; it's an extremely important area. I strongly recommend to women whom I coach to invest some time in blogs that explore the subject, such as intimacy expert Allana Pratt's. Other useful blogs are *The Forgiven Wife: Learning to Dance with Desire* (http://forgivenwife.com) and The Marriage Bed: Sex and Intimacy for Married Christians (http://site.themarriagebed.com/frontpage).

There is no better work than *Pursuit of Passion: Discovering True Intimacy in Your Marriage* by Jeff & Glynis Murphy and Randall & Julie Sibert.[63] Knowing Julie Sibert personally, I could not recommend her book more highly. I also recommend *31 Days to Great Sex* and *The Good Girl's Guide to Great Sex* by Sheila Wray Gregoire.[64] These authors also maintain helpful blogs.

One final word: Couples use sex as a weapon. This is absolutely not God's plan; it is so hard on marriage relationships. Be careful. God warns us of this in 1 Corinthians 7:3-4: "The husband must fulfill his duty to his wife, and likewise also the wife to her husband. The wife does not have authority over her own body, but the husband does; and likewise also the husband does not have authority over his own body, but the wife does."

Be impacted by God's grace. Be a man of integrity, learning to enjoy intimacy as it was intended. Get a coach to help with larger concerns.

Remember: Winners use good coaches!

---

[63] http://www.pursuitofpassionbook.com.

[64] https://www.amazon.com/Days-Great-Sheila-Wray-Gregoire-ebook/dp/B00A7KRKHO.

Prayer:

Father, help us understand our marriage and keep that new car smell in our relationship. We want to keep that brightness and not allow our relationship to become ho-hum or take it for granted. Give us the courage to stay true to our values and integrity. Train and teach us to keep the excitement and mystery alive in our marriage and remind us to plan our date nights. Please take care of all the details because it is for Your glory. We ask that our hearts might be humble before you. Station Your angels around us, guard our thinking, fill our hearts with your Spirit and Your love. Thank you, Lord. It's in Your name we pray. Amen.

CHAPTER 11: DETOX YOUR TALK

"You can be hurt by love or healed by the same; timing is everything."
— Natalie Hemby and Troy Jones[65]

CHERYL and I had a pickup with bench seats, which were cool, especially when we were dating. While driving we would slide close together, she'd put her hand behind my head and play with my hair and I would put my hand on her knee. Or we would just hold hands. I like the concept of the old cars.

But bucket seats arrived on the car scene and with them yet another reminder of our communal drift towards independent comfort and isolated non-communication. Built for community, our lifestyles speak of our continued efforts to be superficial and self-consumed. Like the silent couple we may witness in a coffee shop and remark, "They must be married," our chummy bench-seat positions testified of a couple dating and in love. The longer a couple was married, the harder they were pinned against their own doors.

Reversing the process doesn't mean we exchange buckets for benches. Good communication involves a set of skills we develop. Communication involves hearing skills and sharing skills. And usually it is done very poorly. The devil is in the details. Here is an example:

One icy winter, a northern states couple decided to head south and stay at the same hotel where they'd lodged 29 years earlier. The husband flew in early to coordinate their plans. Upon arrival, he checked in and emailed his wife. But he left out one small detail in her address.

Meanwhile in Houston, a widow had just returned home from her husband's funeral, a minister called home to glory. As she checked her emails from relatives and friends, she screamed and fell to the floor. Her son ran over and found the following:

---

[65] https://en.wikipedia.org/wiki/Country_Strong_(soundtrack), lyrics by Natalie Hemby, Troy Jones.

Subject: To my loving wife, I have arrived.

I know you're surprised to hear from me. They have computers down here now and you're allowed to send emails to your loved ones. I've just arrived and have checked in; everything has been prepared for your arrival tomorrow. Looking forward to seeing you then, dear. I hope your journey is as uneventful as mine was.

P.S. It sure is hot down here.

This illustration shows the humor of details gone wrong, but much of our communication can become highly toxic and hurtful.

In this chapter and the next, you'll learn some principles of communication to help detoxify your relationship. Here are five important foundations:

D Don't Quit Trying

E Environment of Trust and Safety

T Take Ownership of Your Stuff

O Other People Are More Important

X Exchange Your Strength

> **GOOD NEWS AND BAD NEWS:**
> **WE CAN GET BETTER**
> **BUT IT WILL HURT A LITTLE.**
> **SPEAK THE TRUTH IN LOVE.**

These principles are not just for marriage; they are universal. I developed many of them negotiating high-end insurance claims. Learn these skills, and I promise you, they will change all your relationships.

D Don't Quit Trying

Never lose hope. All relationships have their ups and downs. In the down times, the temptation is to isolate and reject. The core value is to not fall apart. Maintain hope that God (not you) will bring His change. From that base of hope, instead of falling apart, you can fall together. Under pressure and feeling hurt, you can choose not to hurt the other.

Our natural, human tendency is to polarize and use critical, isolating, rejecting statements to control others. We criticize our partner using statements like "My family thinks you're an idiot;" "Talk to the hand, cuz the face ain't listening;" "I'm outta here;" "I'm leaving." Don't stop trying, because communicating through conflict has the potential of greater connectedness and joy.

Conquer Fear. One thing we can do to improve our communication is to conquer our own fears. We don't have to be aggressive but we can stay engaged. We often enter conflict feeling pressured, anxious, scared to face what may happen. Sometimes people say, "I can't really talk during conflict because I get so emotionally overwhelmed, and even cry."

Breathe. Bring a sense of calm. Instead of waiting to champion your point, breathe, listen, and hear ... until you really understand the other person's point of view. Detoxify communication by refusing to be afraid or walk away. Learn to stand, hear and wait, then speak truthfully. Then let things land where they land. If the other person gets upset and leaves, then you spoke the truth.[66] Let your voice bring calm and clarity of thought. I repeat, breathe.

Givers and Takers. I don't like conflict. In the past, as soon as I felt things getting tense, I backed away. I would tell others anything they wanted to hear so that I wouldn't have to deal with their emotions. But that is not speaking truth. Typically there are givers and takers in relationships. Givers are constantly trying to keep the peace. Those who take in relationships feed off the givers. They never give the extra effort to make peace. They intimidate or manipulate to get their way. By backing away from conflict, the givers let the takers win.

So in communicating, don't back away. Don't quit. Don't leave. Keep trying to figure it out. Tell yourself, "I'm going to stand into this; I'm not

---

[66] As a disclaimer, there are some relationships that are emotionally, spiritually, and/or physically abusive. You should not remain in situations that are unhealthy for you or your children. Use a trained counselor to help you discern when to engage and when to seek safety.

just going to sit back and give in. I will be assertive and will speak the truth with confidence." Don't stop trying. Keep hoping, knowing that God uses situations to better our relationships. He allows those kinds of things to come into your life because God is in the process of transforming you and teaching you or the other person, so don't run away from it.

Learning the Value of Commitment. The Bible clearly portrays that committed hope: "Love bears all things, believes all things, hopes all things and endures all things."[67]

On the other side of conflict is the potential for great connection. If you back away in the midst of conflict, you often lose the connection in marriage. You hang up the phone. Intimacy suffers because you don't stand up.

Not quitting is also important because issues you don't resolve stack up like cards of resentment. Resentment is emotional stacking, and as it mounts up, even the smallest irritations can set you off. When you stick with communication through hard issues and don't quit every time something negative arises, resentments don't pile up.

Parent-Adult-Child. Couples often relate to one another using a model of "parent-adult-child." One person assumes the role of a parent, the other assumes the child's role. This results in poor communication. One calls the shots; the other complies. Strive to communicate adult-to-adult. Adults say what they mean and then they do what they say. No matter how the other person behaves, learn to speak as an adult.

E Environment of Trust and Safety

A safe environment means you and another are working to keep each other protected in your openness and vulnerability. You build a safe place when you work to allow the other to be heard, to be encouraged and to be vulnerable with his or her emotions. Sadly I have known couples to go 30 years without talking deeper than level two because they don't feel safe with each other.

Right Time and Right Place. Work to find the right time and place to discuss your concerns and listen to your spouse. You may need to say,

---

[67] 1 Corinthians 13:8.

"Can we talk about that later?" or "Is this a good time to talk?" and then, if not, be willing to wait.

For instance, when your spouse first walks through the door is not usually a good time to talk. Check to see if they've had a bad day; don't dump on them everything that's gone wrong in the past week. "Right time, right place" is all about timing. Not being willing to wait communicates control by demanding attention according to your timetable.

Right Words. Safety also means carefully choosing the words you use. In most situations, it's not what you say, it's how you say it. It's not the product, it's the delivery. Cheryl and I have a cat that will kill a mouse then leave it at the door for us to find — it's all about the delivery.

Listening. The key to success is found more in how well you listen than in how eloquently you get your point across. In the next chapter I'll teach you Alpha-Omega communicating. The first step is "Be quick to hear, slow to speak and slow to anger" (James 1:9). In an environment of trust, you seek not to be understood, but you try to understand.

To build an environment of trust, drain your emotions, drain your assumptions and drain your judgments. Learn to stop trying to be understood. Learn to drop your agenda. Don't try to force your opinion; don't try to get your partner to think what you're thinking. Try to hear and understand where the other person is coming from. Try to understand what he or she is thinking. Try to place yourself in the other person's circumstance, his or her position.

Safety means you don't treat your spouse as an enemy. Do you trust him with your child? Is she a good person? Then believe in him or her. When your spouse comes to you to start a conversation, even if you know it will be frustrating, don't try so much to be understood; try to understand. Drain out the emotions and the assumptions and the judgments.

It only took me 35 years to figure this one out. I used to talk a lot as a kid, and my grandfather would quote me a nursery rhyme:

A wise old owl sat in an oak

The more he saw the less he spoke

The less he spoke the more he heard.

Why can't we all be like that wise old bird?

Emotional Hooking. When people can get you to respond in anger or sadness, they have emotionally hooked you to them or their argument. Learn to see your own emotions building and return to that sense of calm. When someone uses this manipulative technique, your angry or emotional response validates their control. In an environment of trust, drain down emotions, assumptions and judgments.

Laughter. If possible, use humor, especially at your own expense. In the middle of an argument, some of the things people say are so extreme, they're hilarious. If you can defuse the emotional tension with humor, your partner can stop worrying about the conversation and can realize, "This isn't a bad thing; this is safe; we're OK; we're gonna make it through this."

I mentioned before that our friend John drove Cheryl and me to the airport as we were trying to resolve some of the many details ahead in our travels. Some were fairly significant obstacles. We were laughing through the problems by poking fun at each other, lightening the environment. When we told John that he had just witnessed us arguing, he said, "Wow! That's how it's supposed to be done."

Body Language. Sometimes during counseling, I'll see the guy turned sideways with folded arms, and suddenly I'll make a deprecating remark toward him, because that's one way guys demonstrate love to each other. I'm trying to lighten the environment.

One guy showed up for counseling wearing a purple T-shirt with kittens on it. I stared, thinking I could never wear a shirt like that in my entire life. This guy is all guy; his image defines masculine — hunter, knife, Thor, that sort of thing. Right in the middle of a conflicting discussion between him and his wife, I said, "Hey, are those kittens real?"

He looked down at his shirt. "What?"

"Are those kittens real? Is that like a picture of your family or something?"

"No, they're not a picture of my family." And he looked at me and smiled. See, it's not that big a deal. So next time you're in the middle of an uncomfortable conversation, drain your emotions, drain your assumptions, drain your judgment, stop right there. Clear the tension by saying something nice and create a safe environment.

I like to think of communication like watching for trains — Stop, look, listen. It works.

T Take Ownership of Your Stuff

Take ownership of your own shortcomings before you start pointing the finger or blaming others. I like to think of finger pointing as one pointing out and three pointing back at one's self. Live your life vertically with God; walk with God. Take out your own garbage. Jesus said,

> Why do you look at the speck in your brother's eye, but do not consider the plank in your own eye? Or how can you say to your brother, 'Let me remove the speck from your eye' and look, a plank is in your own eye? Hypocrite! First remove the plank from your own eye, and then you will see clearly to remove the speck from your brother's eye. [68]

I challenge you to always check your own issues first. Start evaluating your conversations by the number of times you use the word "I." Jesus talked about the "eye" problem; I think a powerful way to observe the "eye" problem is to count the "I's" you use in your speech. It's pretty indicative of how much your focus is on you and your agendas.

If you really want to see the heart of Christ in your marriage, don't play the tit-for-tat game. Shut that off immediately. If you can see 5 percent of your contribution to the problem, own it. Especially you guys. If you want respect, then lead in humility. Humility says, "Percentage doesn't matter; integrity does. I own what I did." You will absolutely neutralize the intensity by simply owning what you did.

And don't say, "Well, I was a little wrong, but you were mostly wrong." Stop that! Own your own stuff. Capturing trust through humility builds safety.

Truthfully search your heart and ask God if your attitude reflects one of Dr. John Gottman's four horsemen: criticism, contempt, defensiveness and stonewalling.[69] First check yourself for those things that you may be doing. Take ownership of your own things. When you take ownership of your own stuff, you drop your guard.

---

[68] Matthew 7:3-5.

[69] https://www.gottman.com/blog/the-four-horsemen-the-antidotes/.

When people communicate with you, they want to see if you're vulnerable. As soon as you start sticking up your walls, they start constructing their own.

You need to take ownership of your defensive emotions. When I say "drain the emotions," I'm not saying deny them or pretend that they don't exist, but take the steam out of them. Take away their power. One way to do that is to simply name them and verbalize them. Say, "I feel angry," or "I'm feeling put down."

Verbalize instead of acting out. For example, instead of scowling and stomping around the room and raising the intensity of your voice, say, "Right now, I am so ticked off!" Speak the truth in love and say, "You know, I'm feeling angry; I'm feeling frustrated; I'm really hoping that we can change the tenor of this conversation," or whatever, but get on the same side as your partner emotionally, so you're not pushing the other person away by your emotions. Instead, take ownership of your feelings. When you don't have anything to prove (like your pride), you don't have anything to lose.

> **BUILD AN ENVIRONMENT OF SAFE CONVERSATIONS.**
>
> **TAKE OWNERSHIP OF YOUR OWN "STUFF."**
>
> **DRAIN EMOTIONAL ENERGY.**
>
> **LISTEN 10 TIMES MORE THAN YOU TALK.**

O Other People Are More Important

Let's just cut to the chase. Almost every marriage problem begins with selfishness. "What is the source of quarrels and conflicts among you? Is not the source your pleasures that wage war in your members?"[70]

---

[70] James 4:1.

Unseat your four horsemen of criticism, contempt, defensiveness and stonewalling. Take ownership and drop your guard; become vulnerable. Most conflict has fear and distrust at the core. When you offer an olive branch of trust, you diffuse tension. You don't have to win every point of every argument.

The greatest gift I can give to people working on communication in their marriages, is to say, "Check your selfishness. Check your agenda, your desire to control." Read and reread the words Paul wrote to the Philippian church:

> *Do nothing from selfishness or empty conceit but with humility of mind regard one another as more important than yourselves; do not merely look out for your own personal interests, but also for the interests of others. Have this attitude in yourselves which was also in Christ Jesus, Who ... emptied Himself ... humbled Himself by becoming obedient to the point of death....*[71]

Jesus Himself spoke of that attitude on nine different occasions. "For the Son of Man did not come to be served but to serve and to give His life as a ransom for many."[72]

I must confess, often, once I back away and identify selfishness in myself, the Lord begins to show me that my percentage was more than 5 percent. It was actually 50 ... 70 ... 90 percent. In fact, many times I see that 95 percent of the problem is me. ME!

So let God talk to your heart first. "Brethren, even if anyone is caught in any trespass, you who are spiritual, restore such a one in a spirit of gentleness; each one looking to yourself, so that you too will not be tempted."[73] Change starts within your own heart — you seeing yourself as the Holy Spirit sees you. Take the time to let Him reprove you. Man up (or woman up) and try it.

Being Right. We'll discuss this further, but when I began identifying my own selfish agendas and attitudes, and calling myself out on them, I received some deep insight. I stopped needing to be right and started

---

[71] Philippians 2:3-8.

[72] Matthew 20:28.

[73] Galatians 6:1.

asking my adversary to help me find right. Don't be right; find right together.

This attitude shift absolutely changed the way I communicate. I stopped needing to be right. In fact, I started looking for ways to get shoulder-to-shoulder (S2S) and find right together.

There's great beauty in portraying that other people are important too. Garrett Hedlund sang about the value of timing in the movie *Country Strong*: "You can be hurt by love and you can be healed by the same, timing is everything."[74] I love that lyric.

Win-Win. You have four options in any conversation: (1) I lose, you lose; (2) I win, you lose; (3) I lose, you win; or (4) WE BOTH WIN!

When you lean S2S (shoulder-to-shoulder) with your spouse, you'll find the win. When you think, *I have to win; this is all about me winning*, your partner can sense the tension. If your partner is competitive, too, then he or she starts to push back — not because it's that important, but because they have to win, too. Your push for a win activates their push back to win. The potential outcome is now lose-lose.

But what's best for your relationship is win-win. You don't win unless your spouse wins. In any conflict, you need to remember that the relationship is more important to you than the issue at hand. You don't need to win. It's not a competition. When you win that relationship with your wife, that's when you both win. That's called win-win.

Apply Philippians 2:3-4 to your communication and choose to "do nothing from selfish ambition or conceit, but in humility count [your spouse] as more significant than yourself." Don't just look out for Number One, but also for your Number One Partner.

X EXchange Your Strength

The last part of DETOX is to exchange your strength. The best preparation for an argument occurs during the two weeks before it happens. If you're walking with the Lord with intentionality and living your life with the Lord, you're prepared for whatever may be coming. Trying to

---

[74] https://en.wikipedia.org/wiki/Country_Strong_(soundtrack), lyrics by Natalie Hemby, Troy Jones.

prepare for an argument the moment you face off is futile. Build God's gentle heart and loving perspective into your life. Then when conflict arises, you can immediately rely on the filled cup from the previous two weeks. Charge your battery; keep it charged. Your daily time with God is your trickle charger. Captain Picard would never beam in with an uncharged phaser. You shouldn't either.

Thermostat or Thermometer. In conflict resolution you need to learn to be a thermostat instead of a thermometer. A thermometer does what? Reads the environment. Temperature gets hotter; thermometer goes up. Colder; it goes down. A thermometer is controlled by its environment.

A thermostat, on the other hand, does what? It controls the environment. That's what you do when you exchange your weakness for God's strength. So if the conversation is hot, and you see your spouse starting to emotionally heat up, then you need to start doing things to cool it down. Control the environment.

Act like a thermostat — it's what Jesus called us to do. She goes up, we're bringing the temperature down. She talks louder; we talk softer. She talks more aggressively, we talk less aggressively. She presses in; we step back. Someone told me that using this principle is like being out of his own body watching like a bystander.

Exchanging your weakness for His Strength involves allowing God to control and not worrying about what you can't change. Twentieth-century theologian Reinhold Niebuhr composed the well-known "Serenity Prayer" that summarizes this concept:

God grant me the serenity to accept the things I cannot change,

Courage to change the things I can,

and wisdom to know the difference. [75]

Satan, the enemy of God and all that is good, loves a fight because he wants to discourage, divide, disrupt and destroy. Whether it's in your business or your marriage, he enjoys people getting angry with each other. The Apostle Paul wrote:

---

[75] https://en.wikipedia.org/wiki/Serenity_Prayer.

Finally, be strong in the Lord and in the strength of His might. Put on the whole armor of God that you may be able to stand against the schemes of the devil. For we do not wrestle against flesh and blood, but against the rulers, against the authorities, against the cosmic powers over this present darkness, against the spiritual forces of evil in the heavenly places.[76]

When conflict begins, I start praying, "God, please take over. Please bring your peace. Please give me wisdom to see and keep me from trying to make it all about me." I like to ask myself this simple question: "Is it a hill to die on?"

Choose your battles. If someone wants to go off about it, you don't have to participate. God often comes back to me and says, "Did you pray about it?"

Learn to wait on God. "Those who wait upon the Lord shall renew their strength; they shall mount up with wings as eagles; they shall run and not be weary, and they shall walk and not faint."[77]

Exchanging your life for His power in you happens in the same way as flight comes to an eagle. An eagle knows (or, in spiritual terms, believes by faith) in its ability to fly. God meant us to "fly" in relationships, not to fail.

So believe in your ability to live your life in the power of God's Spirit. Then, like the eagle, move from faith to trust by stepping back and WAITING on the Lord.

Depend on Him, watch for Him, yield to His power, as we discussed in chapters 2 and 3. Use this progression in your life daily. In the Bible, the word for "wait" was used of a servant whose eyes were trained on his master's eyes. The servant would wait for just the right signal and then move forward with the next course for the meal. This is the same concept Father God wants us to apply when He says, "Wait."

Prayer:

Father, thank You for teaching us how to detox our communication. Help us understand how we can be better communicators, how we can

---

[76] Ephesians 6:10-12.
[77] Isaiah 40:31.

touch each other heart-to-heart in love rather than face-to-face in anger. Father, I pray that we would be willing to let others drain out some of their emotions, and to exchange our emotion with Your strength, Your heart. Help us apply these principles to all our relationships, not just marriage. I pray that we will learn how to communicate well. Let Your Holy Spirit show us the areas we need to change. Show us Your wisdom; help us learn how we can share and hear what the other person is saying. Change the horsemen in us, so we can learn to drop our selfishness. Help us see that it's not about us. Help us be grace-filled in our conflict and in our communication, so that we can glorify You. Jesus, we pray in Your name. Amen.

Chapter 12: Couple(d) Talk

"Let your speech always be with grace, as though seasoned with salt, so that you will know how you should respond to each person."
— Colossians 4:6

LEARNING good communication skills is like learning to talk and listen all over again. While it doesn't change our human core problem of selfishness, good communication allows us to prevent unnecessary irritation and hurts along the way.

I call this practice "Couple(d) Talk." It's what people do when they sit in a car together. They talk about their trip, they share their excitement, they engage in the adventure of traveling together. It's a way of connecting. It's Couple(d) Talk.

Typically, hurts come when a disagreement affects our desires or needs or wants. When we're happy or having fun, our misunderstandings usually don't result in relational problems. We're excited, joyful, engaged. Hurdles come when we deal with issues that have emotional pressure behind them.

Think of an ice cream sandwich: chocolate wafer on top and chocolate wafer on the bottom. Whenever you approach a conflict of any kind, I want you to think of that sandwich. I call it "the positive-negative-positive approach" (PNP).

Let's say I need to work through a problem. I will start with a positive statement, such as "I just want to tell you what a good job you are doing."

Then I will state my concern: "I think we need to do things in a more timely manner."

And when I voice the negative, I will return to an affirming statement: "Thank you for hearing me. I really appreciate you."

No matter how long the center negative portion is, I start and end with a positive. Practice this approach with intentionality.

Now let's work on the middle part of that PNP. Let's learn how to talk and listen through the negative. The word OMEGA gives us the acrostic for the "how to talk" side:

O Observations   (PAUSE)

M My Thoughts   (PAUSE)

E Emotions I felt   (PAUSE)

G Goals, Hopes, Desires   (PAUSE)

A Action Plan   (PAUSE)

This process seems incredibly cumbersome at first, but just like learning to ride a bike, after a while you will do it naturally, reflexively, without having to think it through.

By the way, these principles have been developed by many different independent sources and used in many global international venues. So they work in the marketplace and they work with your kids.

O Observations

In order to discuss any issue, you and your partner must first be aware of the facts. For your partner to know what is going on with you, you must first get in touch with your sensory observations. This is what *I saw*; this is what *I heard*; this is what *I smelled*; this is what *I tasted*; this is what *I touched*. Like Joe Friday in *Dragnet*, you're looking for "just the facts, ma'am, just the facts."

Reporting the simple facts of what you saw and the words or sounds you heard and other sensory perceptions (taste, touch, smell) stops the need the other person may feel to put up defensive posturing or positions.

You may say, "This is what *I saw* .... Is my perception correct?" Then you PAUSE. This space of time allows the other person to correct misperceptions of things you may think you saw or heard and just assumed were correct. *Notice the pause.*

Sometimes, a couple will come in for counseling and start blaming and condemning each other: "You did this and you did that." "You make me so mad." "You make me so frustrated." "I'm so upset." "I can't believe ...."

So I have them start by saying, "This is what I saw. These were the actions I saw you do. These were the facial expressions, the gestures, the postures, the silence, the pitch, the pace or the tone used."

M My Thoughts

Next I will say, "This is what I *thought*" or "This is how I *interpreted* what I saw." Now I know you are thinking this may be cumbersome, but give this process a chance. You will be surprised at the different outcomes.

So here's what I may have thought: "When I saw you do that, I thought you were mad at me, impatient with me, abandoning me, criticizing me and so forth." These are thought (or interpretation) statements only. Then again, pause.

The story is told of a man who was driving his fairly new car when suddenly a young boy threw a rock and hit the car door. WHAM! He slammed on the brakes. He was mad. He was about to scream at this kid, when the boy said, "I'm sorry to hit your car, mister, but my little sister was just hit by a car. Please help us!" In an instant, the irate driver's assumption was corrected.

"Next time, throw a bigger one. It's OK. Let's get your little sister to the hospital."

The man had judged the boy's motives before he had all the facts. This sort of judging happens in marriage constantly. "When I saw you were mad, I thought I was the problem." PAUSE. Allow the other person to say, "No it's not you."

Emotions I Felt

Now I can use a word picture that says this is how *I felt*. "This is what I saw when you ... . PAUSE. This was my thought ... . PAUSE. This is how that made me feel."

I want to try to say these things without the use of rejection or condemnation. Rejection means I will say something like, "This incident made me feel angry, and I'm out of here." Rejection has a threat clause in it.

Condemnation will use language such as "You made me angry." Condemnation usually includes a "you" statement. "You did this, you did that, you made me feel" ... rather than "I felt this way ..." Watch for rejection and condemnation in your communication, especially you ladies. Guys do it, too, but women tend to resort to finger pointing more often.

Use word pictures. Learn to communicate emotion without explosion. If possible, I like to use a word picture to describe how I feel. Guys especially do not do well with feeling, emotive words. Basically they have three: sad, mad, hungry. So try to find a word picture, such as "Do you remember when you were out with our friends and they made fun of you? That's how I felt when this happened."

When I'm discussing an issue with Cheryl, I'm actually sending messages of what I am feeling spirit-to-spirit with her. Emotions are the language of the spirit of another person. Words are how we package those feelings. All the power in relationships is in the emotions.

Say, "This is how I felt: ... ."

Then what do you do? PAUSE.

> **THE GREATER THE CONFLICT INTENSITY,**
>
> **THE LONGER THE PAUSE.**

G Goals, Hopes, Desires

The next thing I do in OMEGA talking is share what I would like to see happen in the future. These are my goals, hopes, or desires. One way to do that is to say, "This is what we have done *in the past*," (good and bad). Or, secondly, "This is what we are doing *in the present*," (again the good and the bad). Thirdly, I might say, "Here is what I would like to do *in the future*." You need to verbalize, "This is what I want," in terms of actions and emotions (for instance, "I want us to be able to voice disagreement yet still keep the peace between us.") These statements set solid expectations. When all these elements are stated clearly, you are able to work on compromise as a team.

This allows you to make sure the other party has agreed to what you have projected. If not, then you can find out their desires and goals and wants before you move forward. Listen to their reasons. Enlisting the help of another is a productive way to engage or connect. Setting future goals "S2S" together brings mutual ownership.

I never want to be in conflict where I don't provide that sense of my hope for the future. Often after a conflict, people leave their partner feeling empty because they don't say how much their hope for the future lies in working together. Don't mistake this sharing of goals, hopes and objectives for your opportunity to unload more issues or overload the other person with illustrations. Keep it simple, and stick to one issue at a time. Win-win and step back. You can return at another time to discuss other issues not related to this particular incident.

Action Plan

I meet many people with different strengths and weaknesses. Some set a task and get it done. Others talk about it but never do it. One for the money, two for the show, three to get ready and four to get ready, and five to get ready ... THEY NEVER GO.

You need to specifically plan how to change the situation causing the conflict. Describe what it looks like to you. Explain how you can start first. Announce what you are going to do and plan how you are going to do it. THEN DO IT.

Again, enlist each other's help. Lean shoulder to shoulder. Develop clear expectations together and always end with providing hope for the future. Take the challenge — make a goal to avoid the conflict the next time it arises.

> **I CHALLENGE YOU TO GET INVOLVED AND GROW IN THE AREA OF OMEGA TALKING AND ALPHA LISTENING.**

Listening skills provide a powerful leg-up in any relational arena. I have found that listening is more powerful than talking. This is why I call these skills ALPHA (first) listening and OMEGA (last) talking. Here are the five principles of ALPHA listening:

A Attend and Acknowledge

L Lean in and Listen

P Participate

H Hear the Heart

A Affirm and Appreciate

Let's say a conflict occurs in my business. I go to my employee and say, "I think you're a valuable worker; I love teaming up with you, but I have a concern." Those words, "I have a concern," are code words that we develop in relationships.

My wife has a way of telling me that she wants to discuss an issue. She says, "Can we go upstairs and talk?" Now I know that we've got something specific we're going to talk about and it doesn't mean we're going upstairs for another reason. It means we are going upstairs to have a serious talk. The first thing I do is remember to look her in the eye and listen.

A Attend and Acknowledge

I was brought up on a farm right by a train track. We went over railroad tracks 10 times a day. Once my grandfather drove through the crossing without looking and we nearly got hit by a train. We learned very loudly when the horn blasted how valuable it was to obey "Stop, Look, and Listen." It's more than a catchy little safety rule kids learn at school. It's a lifesaving technique. Relational conflicts can be train wrecks in our lives. Learn to stop, look, and listen.

I used to get anxious, like "I can't breathe!" I really struggled. I immediately thought I'd done something wrong and was about to get into trouble. My mind started thinking a million thoughts of what I may have done and what excuses I was going to use.

I used to find that in conflict I'd be looking at the floor, looking to the side, looking at their lips, looking at their chin.

But once I recognized what I was doing, I stopped being distracted and started focusing on the other person. Instead of thinking how I needed to defend myself, I started listening to understand.

People are not objects. Open up your heart. Don't look off to the distance. Listen with interest and acknowledge the other person's concerns. When you look him or her in the eyes, you can realize that behind those eyes is a person whom God loves immensely.

As soon as I start looking at Cheryl and I see those beautiful blue eyes, she starts to melt my heart where it needs to be melted, and I start to listen. When I look at those eyes, I realize how much I love her and that I may have hurt her. As my heart begins to soften, we start communicating with truth and love.

Attend to the moment and acknowledge the other person's thoughts and feelings, watching for nonverbal questions. Allow him or her to vent their concern then show them you've heard them by bouncing back their ideas without changing them. Pump up the person.

The process is like a sonar submarine signal. She pings me, I ping it back. I'm allowing that process to start occurring. She might start by saying, "When you said this …."

I need to develop an appropriate response. I am sending both verbal and nonverbal signals — I'm nodding, I'm responding, I'm smiling, I'm agreeing, I'm listening. I'm letting her ping me and I am pinging back. I'm not tapping my fingers or looking to the side and biting my nails; I'm listening and I'm letting her know I'm listening. I attend and acknowledge.

> **YOU'RE NOT THE PROBLEM;
> THE PROBLEM IS WHAT'S COME
> BETWEEN US.**

Lean In and Listen

Learn the art of moving toward your partner just a bit. Set aside whatever you've been doing (laptop, tablet, phone, book, magazine). Open your posture. Get just a little closer without infringing on their personal space if you can. Let down your defensiveness. Your body language — folded arms, pushing back — is easily read or misread as cold, unyielding, uncompromising, harsh.

All these speak loud and clear that you don't care and aren't going to listen. Drop your shields. Let down your defenses. Lean and assume a relaxed position. Lean sideways, lean backwards, and lean shoulder to shoulder. So what if your spouse says, "Your eye makeup isn't right," or "You burp after meals"? If it's not a fire in the curtains, let it go; it's not that big a deal. You might even say, "You know, it's hard for me to hear this, but I know I need to."

Sometimes I do that with Cheryl. "It's hard, honey, but I know I need it." Now that's not a signal for her to pour it on; it's a signal to let her know that I am listening.

Shoulder-to-shoulder not face-to-face — I keep bringing this up because it's so important that you communicate back and forth, that you're S2S. You are telling the other person, "You're not the problem; the problem is between us." I'm making sure that I'm leaning in and letting down my defenses. We have a problem; I got that, but we can solve this together. How can we do that? Through ALPHA listening, leaning in.

Thermostat and thermometer — I want to remind you again to lower the emotional pressure when you're listening. When they're getting upset, let them be upset. As I saw in Turkey, yelling at non-English-speaking people does not help them understand your words any better. We often raise the pressure and raise our voices trying to make our spouse understand. But we need to lower the pressure and remember to find humor, especially laughing at ourselves.

Participate

The third principle in ALPHA listening is to participate and not polarize. "I'm good and you're bad;" "I'm right, you're wrong;" "I'm on top of this and you're not." "You" statements typically polarize. "We" and "us" statements connect. Don't polarize. While you're listening, don't be thinking of how you're going to argue your point.

Emphasize what you agree with and find common ground. To further participate, you might ask questions to help your spouse share more, like, "What else did you see?" "What else did you think?" "What else did you feel?" "I can see that you're hurt, I get that. What did you feel? Is there anything more?"

Reflective Listening. I loved the results I saw learning this principle. I frequently use it in counseling. It works like this: As a couple talks in my office, I can tell that one or both are not listening. So I will have him repeat what she said. Then I will turn to her and ask her, "Is that what you said?" Not even close. She will repeat it three or four times before he finally starts to hear what she's saying.

Reflective listening occurs when you listen to what your partner said to you and then you say, "Let me see if I have this straight. I heard you say ...." And you repeat your partner's message. And you allow them to clarify what they meant then repeat it again until your partner is satisfied that you got it. Reflective listening. I "reflect" back what I think I heard you say. Again the key to success is engaging with your spouse. You do this by actively participating in the relationship.

Hear the Heart

The goal of communication is to hear another's heart, not just the words they use. Watch for non-verbal cues and body language. Try to place yourself in a reverse role; this will help affirm the other person. You are showing that you care for them, care about what they have to say, affirming and validating their concerns.

Hear his or her heart, not just the words. Listen and ask yourself, "Is this someone God loves?" How would you feel if you were in their situation? I believe one of the greatest secrets of communication in deeper relationships like marriage is to hear the emotion behind the words.

"How did that make you feel?" "What were you sensing at the time?" "Did that make you feel angry, mad, discouraged, frustrated, exasperated, down, happy?" The goal of listening is to speak the language of the spirit. Emotions are the vocabulary of the spirit or soul of another person. As you work through issues with your spouse, get past all the other stuff and give them time to share their heart.

A Affirm and Appreciate

As I study the life of Jesus, I am always amazed at how He guards people's dignity. Jesus was very concerned about other people even above His own interests. Matthew records Jesus telling His followers how to confront someone: "If you see your brother sinning, go to your brother in private."[78]

Why does Jesus say to approach your brother one-on-one, away from other people? Because Jesus was teaching us to be concerned about another person's dignity. Embarrassment, shaming, denigrating, talking down to someone, condescending, mocking, making fun of — these were never part of His daily discourse. Jesus protected others' dignity. Conflict can tear someone's self-worth deeply. Love doesn't do that.

Remember the "ice cream sandwich." The last thing I do in my ice cream sandwich approach is return to the positive. Affirm and appreciate. Proverbs 28:13 says, "He who conceals his transgressions will not prosper, but he who confesses and forsakes them will find compassion." God wants us to acknowledge our sin, our weakness, before we start retaliating with defensive stone throwing. Acknowledge and affirm the other person's concern and examine your own heart in truth and love.

A mother shared with me a technique she uses at home and encourages her children to use with each other. The person who is speaking (the "message sender") holds a simple, lightweight object such as a tissue, a pencil, a sponge ball, etc. As long as the sender is holding the object, he or she "has the floor" to speak without interruption. When that sender is done with his or her statement, he or she asks the listener, "What did you hear me say?"

Once assured that the listener received the message, the sender pauses, affirms, shows appreciation for the attentive listening, and hands the small object to the listener. It is now the listener's turn to be the sender.

---

[78] Matthew 18:15.

They take turns holding the object and using reflective listening skills until they are both satisfied that the concern has been resolved. They use the ice cream sandwich idea — positive, issue, and positive. This skill has become a rule in their household so they don't interrupt and argue. Instead they are taught to participate, respect and listen.

This is how to approach a potential conflict by coming to a conversation with a win-win perspective. It's tempting to unload too many issues or overload your spouse with illustrations, so during the conversation stick to one issue at a time. That ice cream sandwich is a good thing unless you eat too much too fast and you get a headache.

Prayer:

Father, thank You for these principles of communication. You are the Alpha and Omega, the first to listen to our heart and the last to speak Your words of truth. In the end, we will prosper if we acknowledge and examine our own hearts first. Help us to start slowly and steadily and to keep trying to figure out how we can communicate better. Help us, Father, to understand the skill of OMEGA speaking and ALPHA listening. Help us figure out how to use them in our daily lives. Please administer communication to us so we can use it not only in our marriages, but also in our relationships with others. Father God, I pray that Your Spirit will guide us to be people whose speech and conversations are seasoned with grace. I ask You to bless us, Jesus, in Your precious name. Amen.

CHAPTER 13: ROAD RAGE — MANAGING ANGER

"A time to love, and a time to hate; a time for war, and a time for peace."
—Ecclesiastes 3:8

"This you know, my beloved brethren. But everyone must be quick to hear, slow to speak and slow to anger; for the anger of man does not achieve the righteousness of God."

— James 1:19-21

How could you go wrong with Jack Nicholson and Adam Sandler starring in *Anger Management*? What a great movie! We all have favorite parts but mine is the bridge scene with Sandler singing, "I feel pretty." And wouldn't it be convenient if saying the word "Goosfraba" — which Nicholson's character defines as a "derivation of an old Eskimo word that mothers use to calm their children" — would melt away anger? But, alas, Hollywood and real life seldom match.

Anger is defined as a response to a threat, real or perceived. It may be loud or suppressed. It demonstrates as aggressive or passive. Research shows that an angry response occurs within three seconds of a perceived threat. Startled, our heart rate jumps up and our breathing rate increases. We get a hormonal surge that will last up to 30 minutes from the time the anger was triggered. This response can be used for good or for bad. Anger is a basic emotion common to all of us. It's the emotion that motivates us to fight or to flee. We all have this God-given emotion, but it raises many questions.

Is Anger Good or Bad?

What does God say about anger in His Kingdom? Is anger good or bad? Is anger right or wrong? Am I wrong to get angry?

Jesus responded with anger when He came into the temple in Jerusalem and saw the religious leaders taking advantage of families who had traveled for days to worship there. He was upset about the way people were being treated. By charging an unfair exchange rate for temple money and requiring worshipers to purchase temple-approved sacrifices at exorbitant prices, the priests were merchandising God.

Jesus was incensed. A bystander would have heard an angry Jesus. Jesus shows us that God gave us anger to be used as a tool when circumstances mandate disobedience. Anger is neither good nor bad; the difference is in the way we use or misuse the emotion. Anger itself isn't the problem. The problem comes in how we manage it.

Anger that achieves God's purpose is motivated by a godly unselfishness. But when it is focused on self, the anger of man does not achieve the righteousness of God.

Anger Is OK; Wrath Is Not

To help us understand the difference between good anger and bad, let's examine another passage: "Be angry and yet do not sin, do not let the sun go down on your anger and do not give the devil an opportunity."[79] You see, we can be angry, but not sin. Realistically, sometimes you need to be angry, when you have to rise up and correct something because it is wrong. "This is not going to happen again," you may say. That's the kind of anger God honors.

I need to measure anger by asking myself, "Am I seeking my own agenda or the best interest of another?"

I've also learned to ask myself, "Did it feel good to be angry?" When it feels good to give someone a piece of my mind, my motivation probably wasn't from God. God says, "Be angry but do not sin."

Anger needs to be monitored. Am I on a quest for my own agenda? Am I offending God? Am I seeking another person's best interest? Am I protecting others from hurt?

Ephesians 4:26 continues, "… and don't let the sun go down on your anger." The Greek word used for anger means "wrath," and wrath is anger out of control. It is seeking revenge, to harm and bring retribution. Wrath is more about self-agenda and revenge, harboring a grudge, taking into account a wrong suffered. God doesn't want simmering followers,

---

[79] Ephesians 4:26-27.

He wants clean slates. God asks us to resolve our conflicts daily, with Him and others.

Envision four canvas paintings on a wall:

- A Flowing River
- A Concrete Dam
- Gates in the Dam
- Floods Downstream

The Source: A River Runs Through Me

You might think anger begins when something bad happens. But you need to understand that anger starts way upstream, where the river runs into the dam. This is the river of life. Life happens. It flows with things you can control and things you can't. I love (and often quote) the *Serenity Prayer.*[80] Here is the common version I use:

> *God grant me*
> *The serenity to accept the things I cannot change,*
> *The strength to change the things I can, and*
> *The wisdom to know the difference.*

Don't pooh-pooh this. Dealing with life on life's terms is all about learning to be calm in the storm. We all need to accept things we can't change, such as friends rejecting us, a marriage that falls apart, decisions others make and we can't control, and yes, other drivers! We also should recognize what we can change and have the courage to take the necessary steps toward action.

Now take a look upstream at things that cause you to feel angry. Make a list of stuff that bothers you, big or little. Little things such as people cutting you off in traffic, or larger things like not getting your way, being mistreated, experiencing injustice, financial shortfalls, time pressures, people being late, dealing with willful stupidity, the death or injury of a loved one. Each of these situations can cause an emotional response called anger — the emotion used to conceal pain (or other

---

[80] https://en.wikipedia.org/wiki/Serenity_Prayer.

emotions people, especially men, typically feel ashamed to reveal) and to control our lives.

The pressure in the dam can be lowered by learning to take control of the stream feeding into your life. One way is to insist on balance. Use the word "No" or "Next" more often. Balance the demands being placed on you and allowed to control your life. You may not know how to say no to the demands that keep pouring in. Or you might not feel able to move on (from someone who's sucking the life out of you) to someone else by saying "Next." Or you may have failed to set proper boundaries or to agree with your partner on your expectations.

These pressures in our lives pour into the dam from upstream. There they build up as disappointments and frustrations then anger and aggressiveness or hostility. Learn to control the upstream pressure by saying no or next. This process of setting upstream boundaries and expectations is so crucial that I have dedicated the next chapter to putting up "stoplights."

The Dam: Holding Back as Pressure Builds

The concrete dam illustrates the screaming, raging emotions held back as a dam stops a running river. We hold our anger (and our tongue) so we don't hurt the people downstream. Many scriptural proverbs are dedicated to the power of holding the tongue when one is angry. "The one who guards his mouth preserves his life; the one who opens wide his lips comes to ruin."[81]

The dam represents your ability to exercise common social grace. You learn not to pop off or wear your emotions on your sleeve. While you may be angry within, you hold it, control it, monitor it, manage it until you know the appropriate time to act. To some degree this self-control has merit, but it can also carry a burdensome price if controlled with your own agenda.

Blowing the Dam

Here's the problem. When a person stuffs and doesn't resolve issues, the buildup of emotions rises behind the dam. The pressure mounts in the

---

[81] Proverbs 13:3.

back of one's thinking. Lights are blinking alarms all over the dashboard. Suddenly, the pressure against the dam hits its limit. This person can't take any more disappointment or frustration, or add another task to their plate. They begin to nurse it, curse it, rehearse it and before long they're ready to blow.

Imagine an old-fashioned telephone board with multiple lines. A call comes in and the new receptionist hears, "I need to speak to Ms. Jones right now."

Triggered by a rush of anxiety, the receptionist stutters, "Oh, OK, one moment please." She doesn't know where Ms. Jones is, so she puts the caller on hold.

Another call arrives: "I need to speak with, Mrs. Stone right away."

"Let me see if I can get her."

The receptionist can't locate Mrs. Stone either. Two lights are blinking. It's a busy day and soon there are eight or ten flashing lights. She is overwhelmed.

In walks the UPS guy with a package. He cheerfully says, "Hey I have a package for you!" What do you think happens? Bam! The dam blows! This harried receptionist doesn't have time to stop and sign for a package!

Was her explosion the delivery guy's fault? No. The pressure built up behind the dam with no release. Just as a dam requires energy to hold back water pressure, so do we with our mounting frustrations. Like water rising behind the dam, we use anger to hold back frustrations. More and more emotional pressure results in more and more anger.

Refuse to Let the Dam Blow

Looking back on some of my blowups, I realize they were senseless. I didn't benefit from the explosion, nor did anyone else. I learned to recognize the signs that would disappoint me. Instead of ignoring them or running away and allowing them to build to the point of eruption, I began to teach myself to step back and take a deep breath. *Settle down Jim. What is it that makes me angry about this situation? Can I deal with it tomorrow? Think it through and pray about it.*

Ask God to reveal the truth and give you strength to refuse to let the dam blow.

Don't Dishonor Yourself

Angry people create drama and see every circumstance as a problem. A person can get stressed just being next to them. Proverbs 12:16 says, "A fool's anger is known at once, but a prudent man conceals dishonor." This proverb says an angry person is recognized immediately as "a fool." "But a prudent (wise) man conceals (hides) dishonor (disgrace)." When the angry person blows the dam, it not only reveals his foolishness, but it also brings dishonor and shame to him, and humiliation to others around him.

Holding back anger is honorable, especially in marriage, especially with children, especially when knowing it will hurt someone. Back up and conceal the dishonor before you make a fool of yourself.

Don't Let Yourself Get So Worked Up

Stop and think. Learn to stop thinking everything rises or falls on something someone does to you. Breathe. Maybe your expectations are too high; reset them. Maybe you need to revisit the situation later after you've thought about it. Stop living life in such drama. Give it a day.

Evaluate. What's really going on inside? Where's your heart? What's your motive? James 4:3 also says you have not received because you ask with wrong motives for your own pleasures. Often people's motives, especially in anger, are completely self-centered.

Identify Yourself as Responsible. I'm the one who got mad. It wasn't somebody else who got me mad. I'm the one who let them get to me. I let them pull my trigger. I made the choice. I made the decision.

Yield Control. One of the fruits of the spirit is self-control. When you see that you're out of control, what does that say to you? "Well I'm just struggling; I'm angry; I'm just worried; I'm just ... you know."

Yes, I know. You're not walking with God. Your anger is splashing downstream and over the dam. The fruit of the spirit is self-control. Confess your anger, get back into God's presence, and evaluate what this anger is about. Yield self-control and let God push you back into His Spirit and to His presence.

Learn to see the pressure rising and start resolving the issues in your life. Learn to set boundaries and start managing them before the dam blows. Before you let the trigger go, remember "Safety on, finger off." Control your emotions and let the pressure out slowly.

As you look at your own anger issues, I want you to see how God's grace impacts your life and marriage. Learn to be anxious for nothing but in everything by prayer and supplication, give your heart to God and let His peace rule your heart. I know that's a lofty goal, but as Paul told the Philippian church, "I press on to the high mark of the calling of Christ."[82] Make it your first goal to work on godly responses.

ANGER IS NOT THE PROBLEM; IT'S THE SYMPTOM.

Manage the Gates in the Dam

Imagine the gates in the dam that are used to control the water flow. Release the water flow slowly, gradually allowing the pressure back into the river of life as you start resolving the built-up issues from behind the concrete wall.

If I get bumped while I'm carrying a cup of coffee, what splashes out? If my cup is filled with coffee, orange juice doesn't splash out — coffee does. Whatever fills my cup is what comes out. Jesus puts it powerfully in Mark 7:20-23:

> That which proceeds out of the man is what defiles the man. For from within, out of the heart of men, proceed the evil thoughts, fornications, thefts, murders, and adulteries, deeds of coveting and wickedness, as well as deceit, sensuality, envy, slander, pride and foolishness. All these evil things proceed from within and defile the man.

But we excuse our overflowing anger and develop the "they" syndrome: "They made me do it!" "They make me so mad!" "They are so

---

[82] Philippians 3:14.

irritating!" "They make me so frustrated!" "They just got to me!" "They shouldn't have done that!" We use the "they" syndrome as an excuse. We rationalize our anger by blaming someone else. We need to realize no one has the power to make us mad; anger is a choice. We choose it.

We also rationalize with "Don't take it out on me"; "You're too sensitive"; "Just accept me for who I am"; or "I can't help myself." If you don't agree that anger is a choice, visualize yourself in the thick of a heated argument when the phone rings. As you answer the phone, your emotional explosion suddenly subsides. "Oh, hi there! How are you?" You can see that your expression of anger is a choice. You can choose not to blow the dam, to not dishonor yourself or your spouse. I'm not suggesting that you deny your emotions. I'm simply stating that you can learn to manage your emotions. It's your choice.

When you start managing your anger, you learn to count to ten and take a time out. Cheryl and I do this in our marriage when we have conflict. One of us will say to the other, "I need some time alone." When Cheryl first said this to me, I felt rejected and isolated, but then I learned that it's okay for us to ask for and respect each other with a time out. We're able to let some water out of the dam. Then we can see the issue is not as important as we thought it was. It's not a hill to die on. We don't deny the emotion; we manage it by identifying, evaluating and counting to ten.

In chapter 14 we'll explore the concept of an "action line," and you will learn how to see the pressure and release it.

Downstream Flood Damage

As water pressure rises and builds against the concrete wall, the dam has a good chance of blowing, causing flooding and taking out everything downstream. Similarly, a triggering event causes pressure to mount in life, and our emotions may explode, wiping out our loved ones on the receiving end of the eruption. This is the emotional anger we want to learn to control as we see it building upstream. "The beginning of strife is like letting out water, so abandon the quarrel before it breaks out."[83]

---

[83] Proverbs 17:4.

I learned a lesson about consequences when I was framing a house. I purchased a heavier framing hammer instead of a lightweight one. Translation: Hit your thumb, multiply pain by 100. Then a professional framer showed me if you hit the nail hard enough, you could drive it in with one stroke. I kept trying and missing, and my words were getting louder and stronger. My thumb was so sore I could barely hold a nail.

One. More. Time. BAM! Missed.

This time, after a few more choice words, I heaved the hammer against the floor. By the way, framing hammers are very springy. So it bounced and ricocheted off the floor, then off a wall stud, then up to a ceiling truss and literally came roaring at my forehead. If I hadn't ducked, it would have been death by framing hammer.

This is how anger works. When I let frustration build, I pull the trigger, the dam blows, and I have consequences to face.

Proverbs 12:18 gives us these words of wisdom: "There's one who speaks rashly like the thrust of a sword, but the tongue of the wise brings healing." When I get to that place where I'm thinking about hurting somebody or hurling a hammer at a wall, I need to remember that there are downstream damages. Remember, you're a thermostat not a thermometer. Take action, not merely reaction. Learn to exercise emotional control.

Further Downstream

Motivational speaker Zig Ziglar was fond of the following illustration:

> *On his way to work a CEO is ticketed for speeding. He is upset. Fuming at the office, he calls in the VP of sales.*

> *"You need to get your sales up! If you don't, you're not going to have a job." Now the VP is upset. He calls in his account manager.*

> *"You have a job to do. You're not getting it done, and we need sales right now!" The manager is really upset.*

> *She calls in her sales guy. "You better start selling more. Our jobs are on the line." He is really upset. As he pulls in at home, he is still fuming. Bikes in the drive; toys on the porch; he bangs through the door, yells at his wife. She is really upset.*

*She yells at the kids, "You better clean up or you're grounded for a week!"
They are really upset.*

*Out the back door they storm, and there, lying in the sun, is the family cat.
BAM! One of those kids kicks the cat over the back fence.*

*Now wouldn't it have been far easier if the CEO had just gone to the back
porch and kicked the cat himself?*

This boss's anger caused a ripple effect, capsizing many others downstream, including a cat.

> **ANGER OVERFLOWS AND GIVES BIRTH
> TO MORE ANGER.**
>
> **IT CAUSES A RIPPLE EFFECT AND INJURES
> OTHERS AND OURSELVES.**

Our anger injures others and ourselves. When I realize I have hurt
someone I need to go back to apologize — first, to heal their wound and
second, to avoid a hardened heart (being a jerk). Going back and apologizing for things I've said is humiliating, especially when the other person was also wrong.

Unfortunately, when we survey downstream damages, we realize that
some words can never be taken back. Restoring trust takes a long time.
In my counseling practice, I have helped couples walk through the healing process for wounds they've stored up for years. Injuries are hard to
heal because of hurt feelings. Some injuries never heal because of things
that were spoken in anger. Go back to James 1:20 "... for the anger of
man does not achieve the righteousness of God."

Downstream: The Demonic Side of Anger

The exercise of anger comes with a warning. When anger originates
from your core of control, you open yourself to give Satan a "beachhead" in your life. This military term means to gain a foothold while
invading a country. Your mind and heart are a country, and Satan will

do anything he can to get inside. As soon as you open yourself to anger from selfish motives, he begins construction on a foothold. As if you have a runway inside your mind, Satan can land incoming thoughts. When you're in the midst of anger responses and giving in to bitterness, wrath, anger, clamor, and slander, along with malice, you can recognize that you are under attack by Satan.

Have you ever noticed each successive time you get angry it's a little bit easier? That's because Satan is establishing a stronghold in you. A stronghold is a habit or reaction that requires no rational thought on your part. Once it's constructed, you start acting by reflex.

Anger Gives Birth to More Anger

Anger produces visible long-term results in two additional ways; first, visibly in our faces and secondly, anger in others.

Sadly, as a counselor, I often see people who have been angry for many years and it shows on their faces. Frowns and wrinkles pattern their face. I challenge people to live their lives in a way that leaves laugh lines rather than frown creases. As anger builds in them, anger also builds in others affected by them — family, friends and those in their circles of influence.

I confess, sadly, that I'm one of those drivers who believes I can sit in my car and talk to drivers in other cars and help them see the foolishness of their ways. One day, to my amazement, my sweetheart started saying some of my oft-used phrases while driving. I'm thinking, *Where in the world did you learn that?* Talk about leading by example — right, guys?

Then I began to notice my children doing it also. One day while traveling together, we had to abruptly stop. I heard all five voices in the car shouting things like, "What an idiot!" "If stupid could fly, you'd be a jet!" It was funny, sort of, but I thought to myself, *These members of my family have ALL taken on my bad habit of driver talking.* We can chuckle at this, and correct it, but it's not funny in other arenas.

Anger begets anger in children, families and other relationships. Oftentimes, if I see anger demonstrated in little children, I'll watch the parents. Quite consistently, the apple lands mighty close to the tree.

Use this downstream consequence to check your reactions. Anger begets anger.

Prayer:

Father God, thank You for moving our hearts and minds to understand who You really are rather than ignoring Your words and wisdom. Give us the strength to break the chains in our minds and families. Teach us to take a breath and relax. Help us to want to live with the discipline of self-control. In Christ's name we pray. Amen.

CHAPTER 14: DESTINATIONS AND STOPLIGHTS

"God's plan of responsibility has not changed. We are not at the mercy of our spouse's behavior or problems. Each spouse can act both to avoid being a victim of the other spouse's problems and, better yet, to change the marriage relationship itself. The process always begins with taking responsibility for your own part in the problem."
— Dr. Henry Cloud & Dr. John Townsend[84]

As noted earlier, drivers are responsible to abide by certain rules of the road to avoid hitting other cars or hurting pedestrians. We don't cross certain lines and don't run red lights. We respect the rules and expect others to do the same. These lines and lights define specific boundaries of dos and don'ts.

Boundaries are designed to protect us from injuring each other. "I will not do such-and-such" and "I will not accept if you do such-and-such." Boundaries are designed to protect us.

We agree upon certain expectations prior to marriage and speak to the mutual goals we have set for our relationship.

Comparing driving to marriage, when people back the car out of the driveway, they have a destination in mind. In marriage, they expect integrity, openness, hopes and dreams they work on together.

Women typically set boundaries in the form of house rules, like "Lower the toilet seat when you finish." Breaking that boundary rule is not worth the price you pay when you hear that scream at 2:30 in the morning when your wife sits down on the cold porcelain rim. She expects the courtesy of a lowered seat. It's a boundary for her.

Guys' boundaries are more about not touching their stuff. Leave the garage alone; "That's my man cave"; don't interrupt or talk during the game on TV.

---

[84] Dr. Henry Cloud & Dr. John Townsend, *Boundaries in Marriage*, Zondervan, (Grand Rapids, 2009).

The bigger challenges to setting boundaries in marriages are over finances, childrearing, and how free time should be spent.

> **BOUNDARIES ARE THE LINES WE SET THAT SAY,**
>
> **"I NEED YOUR RESPECT IN THIS AREA."**

When we understand the value of setting boundaries, we will build deep mutual respect. Respect is the foundation of a strong and solid marriage (or any relationship).

Boundaries can also test your spouse's commitment. If a specific boundary is set, such as working a job for financial stability, and your spouse follows through with that commitment, your expectation is met, establishing respect and trust. If your spouse doesn't honor that boundary, it indicates that your spouse is not invested in the marriage. Boundaries are lines that test respect.

In relationships, people can be givers or takers. Therefore, boundaries need to be created and enforced. Givers will give and give without expecting any return. Takers will hold out their hand to receive as if entitled but never step forward to initiate or sacrifice. Boundaries help givers identify the stoplights for takers by saying, "I won't put up with this."

Without boundaries, behavior patterns continue until takers suffocate and givers are exhausted. People need to set healthy boundaries to provide balance between giving and taking. Givers need to learn to respect themselves enough to say no. Takers need to show their commitment by respecting others' decisions to say yes or no.

Boundaries also help define accountability. One spouse's responsibility is not the other spouse's burden to bear, though they often must bear the penalty of their husband's or wife's problems. An alcoholic, for instance, may be protected from public disclosure by the excuses of the non-alcoholic spouse. This pattern will continue until the overly apologetic spouse is exhausted and drained. Setting boundaries and drawing a line will force the one with the problem to bear the repercussions of the problem.

Takers may view a giver's boundaries as statements of rejection. When a taker hears a habitual giver say, "I won't be treated this way," a sinister monster raises its head. The taker doesn't want to respect the normally giving spouse's boundary and may threaten to leave. In this case, the giver needs to stand firm and enforce his or her boundary line. By no means am I condoning divorce, but sometimes separation is necessary for a time of reconciliation.

Typically fear of rejection causes givers to not follow through with a boundary. People pleasers want others to be happy and like them. The danger in this is sacrificing their healthy boundary so another will stay happy with them. In essence, the people pleaser sacrifices his or her self-identity on the altar of another's ego.

I've had clients report years and years of not being able to say no. They live unhappy lives with alcoholics, sex addicts, workaholics, drug addicts, gamblers, status seekers, and dozens of other manifestations of addictive behavior. Like the 110-pound wife who gets knocked around by her 300-pound football-player husband, they passively continue in the relationship because they don't respect themselves, have no self-worth, and can't say no. The wife compromises, afraid her husband may get angry and leave.

Boundaries are necessary. But they're also complicated. A good mentor or coach can help you set them correctly.

Expectations are different from boundaries. Expectations involve setting goals you mutually agree to strive for. These goals can be about life in general: "Let's plant a garden together and grow a crop of corn." Expectations may involve setting goals for finances or use of time, agreeing on certain manners or household decorum, how children should dress for church or school, or where to go for vacations.

Like a fence around a garden, boundaries are designed to protect us. Your boundary says, "You cannot drive your truck through my garden. You are welcome here, but please use the gate." See the difference?

PRE-AGREE BEFORE YOU DISAGREE.

The Law of Mutual Agreement is the key to setting healthy boundaries and expectations. You can accomplish great goals in your marriage if you and your spouse learn to set expectations together.

Set Boundaries and Expectations CLEARLY

Whether setting a boundary or an expectation, learning to communicate it clearly will keep others from assumptions and trying to read your mind. If you speak with kindness and patience, the one receiving your message will appreciate the calm, clear communication and be more likely to respond positively.

To understand boundaries and expectations, I use the acronym CLEARLY.

C Check your spirit for self-motives. A boundary is set to build respect for each other, not to use for selfish manipulation. If you set an "if-or" boundary, your motive may be to manipulate for your personal agenda. "If you don't take the trash out, then don't expect me to fix dinner tonight." That is a manipulative boundary.

L List specifically your boundary or expectation. Be specific so your partner can comprehend the value of your boundary. Don't be overly concerned about the other person's feelings. Instead concern yourself with stating the boundary or expectation precisely. Use words only, give examples of what you expect, and specifically list what you intend to result from the boundary.

Here's an example of an *expectation*: "Son, when you borrow the car, I think it's reasonable to expect gas in it when you return it." Here's an example of a *boundary*: "Son, if you take the car and don't put gas in it before you return it, I won't allow you to use it the next time you ask."

Often relationships break down because boundaries or expectations are not fair or are not communicated specifically. Before reacting to any frustration, ask yourself if you were pursuing your own agenda. And did you specifically list and/or show the other person what was expected? If you didn't speak it clearly then you can't complain.

E Engage others in ownership. This is what I call the "buy-in." If the other person doesn't buy in, then they have no commitment to hold to their part of the agreement. Look at each other eye-to-eye, and ask, "Do you agree?" This is called mutual agreement. "Do you feel this is fair?" "Am I respecting your wishes?" "What would prevent you from doing this?" This way, you both pre-agree before you disagree. It's the *law of mutual agreement* in a relationship.

Many couples I work with have failed to set mutual agreement. I'll hear exchanges like this:

"We said we'd do this before we got married."

"No we didn't. You told me this is what we'd do but I never agreed to that."

Children can be a huge point of conflict:

"We have to take care of the children."

"Well, I never wanted kids in the first place."

Mutual agreement and getting ownership before you act are crucial.

A Action lines. Most people have no idea what an action line is. This is where you set a boundary then move from hearing and seeing to action. The action line factors in two elements: time and emotion. Let me illustrate:

Little Johnny is playing in the sand box. He hears mom's voice: "Johnny, it's time to come in now." He ignores her and continues to play. Mom gets frustrated and begins to go up an emotional level.

Now her tone is more firm: "Johnny, it is time to come in." Still no response.

Mom jumps another emotional level: "John Alexander Smith, you need to get in here." No response.

She rises to another level: **"Listen, buster, get in here now! If you don't start moving, I'm telling your father."** The dam has busted through, and here comes the flood downstream — Mom makes her move.

The door slams, "JOHN ALEXANDER SMITH, GET IN HERE RIGHT NOW OR YOU ARE DEAD MEAT!" Whoa! Now Mom's actions are speaking loud and clear.

Little Johnny gets up, dusts himself off and says to himself, "Well, guess I gotta go now." What's going on here?

As time moved forward, Mom kept raising her emotional level until she hit the point where she acted. Her action line was at emotional level 7. The door slammed and she was on the warpath. Action! And guess who knew her action line? Johnny has her number on speed dial.

Mom needed boundaries and should have clearly set her action line before they disagreed.

1. Checks her motives. "Johnny, I'm starting supper so we can eat."

2. Engages ownership. "When you're outside playing, I will call your name, and blink the lights twice."

3. The third warning. "I'll expect you to be walking in. If you are not, we will eat without you, and you will go to bed without supper. Do you understand?"

Johnny responds with an understanding "Yes, Mom." Now he's engaged in ownership, and Johnny and Mom have a mutual agreement. It only takes once for Johnny to learn the consequence of crossing Mom's boundary line if he's denied a hot meal. It's important to his tummy. Johnny learns to respect his mother and discovers the rule isn't so bad.

An action line often occurs when we get mad enough to make a move. Picture an "x-y" axis. Time is along the bottom. Emotional level runs down the side. The point is, we have to lower the emotional level at which we act.

R Real Time Value. If you say, "Johnny the table needs to be set by 5:30," at 5:15 you give warning one, 5:20 warning two, 5:25, ACT.

Here's another example: You might say to the family, "On Sundays, I would like to go as a family to the 9 o'clock service at church. Then we can have the rest of the day to have family time together. Is this acceptable to the rest of you?"

If the family agrees, the expectations are specified clearly by mutual agreement. "We'll leave the house at 8:30 a.m., go for lunch afterwards and then do an activity we planned together." Eye-to-eye they commit and engage. The boundary is relative to a specific mutual agreement for the family to spend quality time together on Sunday.

A clock and calendar are "real time" tools that can be used. Use the clock and calendar for good visuals and timetables when setting expectations or boundaries.

L Look for ways to encourage. When I set an expectation, I don't just tell someone, "Do this," then walk away. Find small ways you can share and encourage. One of the challenges of setting boundaries is that they can create negative emotional responses, like "You don't want me" or "I let you down." These occur especially in marriage relationships because spouses carry a certain burden to not disappoint the other.

Y You have to watch for motives. Accountability is a good thing. Remember, the person who lacks respect for others needs to bear the penalty of the consequences. In Mom and Johnny's case, Mom's escalating emotions reveal that she is bearing the weight of Johnny's disrespect. The person who has the problem needs to wear the problem.

Let's say Priscilla has decided to leave after 20 years of marriage. The children are gone, she has a good job, and she wants her independence. Priscilla kicks Mike out of the house. A month later, the sink backs up and she needs Mike to fix it. Is this Mike's problem, or does Priscilla need to bear the problem and call a plumber that will cost her $400 out of pocket? He may still be married to her in his promise to God, but she made the choice to not live together as husband and wife.

Don't become emotionally hooked with excuses. Don't be worn down by words. And don't relax and agree to something that's unacceptable to you when you set a boundary. Don't get talked into renegotiating expectations until you have sufficiently resolved the broken one.

Prayerfully seek God's expectations, read His Word, walk with Him, talk with Him, understand His boundaries. Getting advice or professional counsel can help you see clearly, set healthy boundaries and hold people accountable to the action line.

From my Nebraska farm days there's an old adage: "You can lead a horse to water but you can't make him drink." Build out the power of change by developing a vertical walk with God and then let Him affect others. Get a coach or a counselor or other trusted, mature Christian people involved in your life so you can clearly recognize your destination stop.

And always remember to speak the truth in love, as Ephesians commands us.

Prayer:

Father, thank You so much for Your grace and compassion, for the impact of Your Word, and the way You change us. God, I pray that You build all marriages into relationships that reflect grace, love and respect. Help us set clear expectations and boundaries that show mutual respect.

Help us to know when to say no, when it's on our agenda for accountability. Thank You for applying Your truth to our marriages, Father. We pray in Jesus' name. Amen.

CHAPTER 15: MAPPING COMPROMISE

"Marriage is built on compromises and a great deal of give and take on both sides. When you fall in love with a person, appreciate their unique- ness, and adjust to each other's habits, instead of trying to change each other to fit your requirements."

— Aarti Khurana

"It's not always rainbows and butterflies / It's compromise that moves us along."

— Adam Levine and James Valentine[85]

LEARNING the value of compromise is an art. Sometimes a request may sound like a demand when this was not the intent. Compromise is not agreeing to relinquish your core values. It is not sacrificing your identity on the altar of another person's ego to keep the peace. It is not doing whatever someone wants because you're afraid they will leave (which is the foundation of co-dependency). Compromise is not a deci- sion you make when you run out of alternatives. Compromise is not giving in to avoid turmoil in the relationship. And compromise is not being weak. In fact, the best compromises come from a position of strength.

Compromise Does

- Work together to accomplish a mutual goal
- Involve finding common ground and meeting in the middle
- Willingly adjust to reach the same destination
- Involve a sense of give and receive

Relationships are challenging. Without compromise, over the course of one's lifetime relationships become inflexible and break. People who don't compromise say things like "What a jerk," or "That guy has the

---

[85] Adam Levine and James Valentine, "She Will Be Loved," *Songs About Jane,* (2002).

personality of a raw sunburn," or "We tried to talk, but he just thumps on the Bible and we lose," or "He's like a porcupine — lots of great points, but you can't get near him." I know, because people have said these things about me. Compromise is not only hard and challenging to learn, but also humbling.

Couples need compromise to resolve disagreements about finances, use of time, sex, kids, friends, and hobbies. When two sinners get married, changes must occur or they'll kill each other. Learning to give in over non-life-threatening issues changes the landscape of marriage. Working toward resolving differences can be laborious. The key to mutual agreement is learning to compromise.

I relate these principles to taking a road trip. Cheryl and I don't go to the same destination every year; we learn to compromise. Cheryl likes to go to the cool mountains. She loves to drive great distances and enjoys the journey until she arrives at her destination among the tall pine trees. I like traveling by air, being served, resting and reading while I enjoy the peace before reaching my vacation spot. We've learned to take turns and meet in the middle for our choice of destinations.

Learning to compromise and map our relationship together has allowed us to explore new places, experience new things, and respect and appreciate each other's unique qualities.

The word "compromise" comes from the Latin word, PACTUM, meaning an agreement, a bargain. The word is formed from two words, COM "to be with or together" and PROMISE "to make a commitment to future action." You and your spouse can learn to see the value at the center of the bridge and work together to strengthen the walkway. Together you can commit to walk hand-in-hand to the center of the bridge without fearing wobbles because you've mapped the road for the future.

Calm Down ... It's Not About You

As God's grace works in our hearts, we realize who we are in Christ and develop an attitude of gratitude, willingly meeting each other halfway or even further. Compromise involves a mindset that the priority of our marriage is more important than the priority of self.

Prioritize your marriage first in your life and in making decisions. God places value on serving rather than on being served. This attitude also works in childrearing and in the workplace. I formerly worked in a job that was extremely litigious. There was a lot of fighting and arguing over big dollars. I learned there to compromise and have a servant's heart, which resulted in win-win outcomes. We reached an agreement in which each person gave up something they wanted in order to end an argument.

Use ALPHA-OMEGA Communicating

Learning to use a skill in communicating takes work and practice so don't shortcut the techniques outlined earlier in chapter 12, ALPHA Listening and OMEGA Talking. Learning to communicate with another person is crucial to approaching mutual agreement anytime you have issues between you and are not on the same page.

We learned to listen by A) attending to the conversation and acknowledging the problem, L) leaning in, letting down our defenses, and looking eye-to–eye, P) participating actively with reflective listening, H) hearing the heart, not the words, and A) asking further questions.

We learned to talk using the OMEGA system: O) Observations — this is what I saw, M) My Thoughts — this is how I interpreted what I saw and heard, E) Emotions I felt — this is what I felt, G) Goals, Hopes, Objectives — this is what I would like to do, and A) Action Plan — this is my goal and this is how I would like to proceed. The skills of compromise are found in ALPHA-OMEGA communication.

Watch for Giver and Taker Mentality

When compromising, be aware of givers and takers. Takers are bossy, pushy and domineering; they are on the high side of winning the conflict. Givers are on the low side of the conflict. They may have no conviction, or they may want to do something other than what the taker suggests, but they remain easygoing and give from the heart. Giving in is easy for them.

God wants us to work together, to meet in the middle, be willing to give and take, to collaborate and not just settle for any compromise.

Givers tend to be compliant and takers tend to be controlling. Givers tend to be unwilling to confront, usually because of fear.

Takers tend to be aggressive and not cautious.

Givers tend to be too soft; takers tend to be too hard.

Givers will accept poor treatment and assume things will get better; takers may yell, get angry and intimidating.

Givers tend to believe God doesn't honor arguments in relationships; takers will follow their partner around the room nagging.

Learn to see these characteristics in you and your relationships. Once you recognize if you're a giver or a taker in your marriage, you can learn to collaborate and plan ahead for the future.

For insight, ask yourself, "Do I HAVE to win?" If the answer is yes, consider the danger to your relationships. Maybe you are not "right," but just intimidating.

BE WILLING TO GIVE AND TAKE.
COLLABORATE, DON'T JUST COMPROMISE.

The giver may need to graciously remind the taker, "We did it your way on such-and-such an occasion, so I think this time we should try it this way." Cheryl loves to make our home very clean and orderly. I, on the other hand, need some freedom to make a mess sometimes. I often will say, "The garage is mine." (But I'm willing to share.)

Make an Offer

Another effective tool in compromising is making an offer to do something to help the other person. Let's say one spouse wants to move closer to work and the other wants to move out to the suburbs. Perhaps one might say, "I would be willing to move if we can find property near a park or a biking path or some other outdoor recreation."

Making an offer places you halfway toward the middle.

Find Common Ground

Find the things you agree on. You agree you both need a vacation. You want to take it together. You would like to be gone a week. And you have to stay within a budget. To find common ground, come with an attitude of honesty, and willingness to look at all aspects, listen to both opinions and work to find a compromise. Usually this works best when you don't have to win every point. Let little issues slide and focus on arriving at your major destination.

Compromise involves giving up items on both sides to find agreement in the middle. By finding common ground to agree on, each side relaxes their hold on "my way or the highway" and finds some middle win for both parties.

Understand the Relational Banking System

In relationships, both parties make deposits and withdrawals. I call this Relationship Banking. Certain behaviors, like not respecting one's partner, make withdrawals from the relational bank. Let's say Rosetta has dinner on the table for Joe at 5:30 p.m., their usual supper time. One evening, Joe forgets to call Rosetta to let her know he has a late meeting then doesn't get home until 6:45 p.m. They have a mutual agreement, and Joe overstepped the boundary by not respecting their plan. Joe has just pulled a relational withdrawal from Rosetta's account.

Or, putting the shoe on the other foot, maybe Joe arrives home on time, and Rosetta has failed to make dinner because she stayed late after school and was too tired. Despite her apology, "I'm sorry, honey, I didn't make dinner tonight," she has made a withdrawal from Joe's account.

Other withdrawals come from sarcasm, irony or laughing in the middle of a serious conversation because you're nervous. I tend to do this to Cheryl. When I get nervous, I make jokes because I'm trying to lighten things up. A husband may fail to follow through on a "Honey Do" task he told his wife he would finish. A wife might criticize a job her husband tried to do as a surprise. Spouses may be unaware of the withdrawals adding up.

Recently as Cheryl and I talked with a couple, I went to find a picture of Jaxon to show them. When I returned with it, I interrupted Cheryl. I felt her foot on my leg, and knew what I had done. I immediately said, "Oops! I interrupted. Sorry about that."

Later, when we were alone, I addressed the issue with Cheryl. "I'm sorry, sweetie," I said, "I spoke and interrupted you. That was wrong." That was making a deposit in the relationship bank.

The mindset is not one of "minus one" or "plus one." In reality, marriage is a mutual debit card. I want to be on the plus side for her. I want to be making lots of deposits. Why? Because there will be withdrawals. If I don't make deposits, the withdrawals keep subtracting, and I end up in the hole.

I need to build dividends to avoid having insufficient funds. If I keep taking withdrawals, I'm pulling from the account. Then when I need her to compromise on a mutual agreement, her attitude could be, "Forget it, buster." But if I'm building into our relationship and making deposits in our account, she's more likely to be willing to make the compromise.

Regarding relational banking, Dr. John Gottman says, "Stable marriages have a 5:1 ratio of positivity to negativity during conflict, whereas in unstable marriages the ratio is 8:1."[86] Studies conducted by Dr. John Cacioppo and his colleagues have shown what he calls "the negativity bias" of the brain.[87] Our brains are actually more sensitive and responsive to unpleasant news. That's why personal insults or criticism hit us harder and stay with us longer. It's why negative ads are more effective than positive ones — political or otherwise.

Following the logic, it takes ten compliments to make up for one criticism. You could say that complimenting your spouse about his or her identity, who they are, is worth 10 points, while criticizing him or her strikes at a deeper level, about 100 points of negative withdrawals. That's why so many marriages are like a desert where the rivers dried up long ago.

If I give Cheryl a compliment that builds her self-image, such as, "You're special to me because you take the time to listen to me every day when I come home from work. You act interested." That's a 10-

---

[86] https://www.gottman.com/blog/the-four-horsemen-the-antidotes/.

[87] http://www.wisebrain.org/media/Papers/NegativeBiasInEaluativeCategories.pdf, Cacioppo & Berntson,1994; Cacioppo, Gardner, & Berntson, 1997; Ito & Cacioppo.

point deposit. In the spirit of compromising and understanding our relationship, I want to be ahead of the game in relational banking.

In this relational banking system, you cannot do a big "One Time Deposit" to offset several withdrawals. Rather, what counts is the sheer number of deposits, not the size of one. The husband who buys his wife a diamond ring as a deposit to make up for the hurtful things he said during an argument the night before doesn't earn a refund. Nor the wife who thinks one week of showing respect, keeping the house clean, making dinner every night and giving sex for dessert will counterbalance her overdraft of disrespectful stonewalling.

Being Responsive to Each Other

Building the relational bank account comes from learning to be responsive to each other. Pay attention to one another like you did when you were dating. Sit and listen with curiosity. Hold hands. Try a new restaurant. Bring home a "Thinking of You" gift. Send a "Thinking of You" text.

Remember to keep flirting, bat those eyelashes, and rub your knee against her leg in the dark theater. Run errands and do jobs around the house together. Laughing and going for walks reduce stress.

I give my clients homework assignments in which they can talk about serious issues between them for only 10 percent of their time. The other 90 percent must be fun, loving, and incorporate laughing while getting things done. They can address issues with me in their counseling sessions, but while they're at home, I want these couples to learn to be responsive again and beef up their relational bank account.

Mapping Your Relationship

Through extensive research, Drs. John and Julie Gottman have found that emotionally intelligent couples are "intimately familiar with each other's worlds." They call this having a richly detailed "Love Map."[88] The principle of building this sort of relational map is to help couples know their spouse's inner psychological world.

---

[88] https://www.gottman.com/about/the-gottman-method/, *The Gottman Method for Healthy Relationships*, "The Sound Relationship House."

As couples map their relationship, they "remember the major events in each other's histories, and they keep updating their information as the facts and feelings of their spouse's world change. They know each other's goals in life, each other's worries, each other's hopes and dreams."[89] These couples take the time to know each other well. What's her/his favorite color? Favorite food? Favorite activity? Favorite way to spend an evening? Greatest fear? Childhood pet's name?

Sharing your inner self is an ongoing process. Creating this sort of relational map as the foundation of your marriage will make you and your spouse better friends and make it easier to compromise during conflicts. You'll know each other's inner secrets and build a reserve you can use for the future when you need to compromise. Without creating a detailed couple map, your relationship will lose its way when your lives shift with challenges and stress. By mapping your relationship, you earn trust and commitment to put into your relational bank.

Separate Rights from Responsibilities

In order to compromise, people need to understand the difference between rights and responsibilities. "The Pineapple Story," which I heard from missionary Otto Koning, illustrates this concept. Koning and his wife went to Papua New Guinea as a doctor and nurse to help the poor tribal people there.

> **IT'S NOT OUR FIGHT;**
> **THAT'S GOD'S RESPONSIBILITY.**

Koning was irritated with the natives because they were chronic thieves who stole pineapples from his garden. Ballpoint pens went missing from his clinic. One day he saw a native wearing his ballpoint pen through his nose. Another was using baby diaper pins as earrings. Another wore Koning's can opener around his neck as a piece of jewelry.

---

[89] Gottman, ibid.

Koning had been looking for that opener for a week and was using a machete to open his canned goods. His irritation was growing into anger. "I'm here to serve these people, and all they do is rob from me and my family," he said.

The natives didn't understand this angry missionary. They believed you eat what you plant.

Since they got their hands dirty planting the pineapples in Koning's garden, those pineapples were theirs to eat. It didn't matter that the missionary bought the pineapple seed, soil, and tools then paid the natives to work the garden. With mounting anger, Koning decided to bring in a German shepherd to guard his possessions. This big scary dog actually forced the natives to leave the area.

Then Koning left for a sabbatical during which he attended a seminar. There God spoke to him about fighting for his rights rather than leaving the responsibility with God. If he gave with the right motives, he would never lack in that area. God was the true owner of Koning's possessions. As a missionary representing the ultimate self-sacrificing Lord of the universe, he would never be able to win these people for Christ if he kept fighting against them.

Here's what God was teaching Koning: Never make it your goal to be right. FIND RIGHT together and stand on it. If we keep fighting for our own rights, we'll lose our health; we'll lose sleep. As believers we need to learn that God is the owner of everything and we're just managers of the gifts He's given us.

God has called us to John 12:24-26:

Truly, truly, I say to you, unless a grain of wheat falls into the earth and dies, it remains alone; but if it dies, it bears much fruit. He who loves his life loses it, and he who hates his life in this world will keep it to eternal life. If anyone serves me, he must follow me; and where I am, there my servant will also be. Anyone who serves me, the Father will also honor him.

Who's the grain of wheat? We are.

What is Jesus trying to teach us here? Die to self.

Give of yourself. It's a concept of the surrendered life. God wants us to surrender our garden, our battle. Give our battle away and watch Him compromise.

It's not our fight; it's God's responsibility.

> ## THE POWER OF GRACE IN OUR LIVES IS LEARNING TO LIVE THE SURRENDERED LIFE.

The power of grace in our lives is learning to live the surrendered life, not on the sacrifice of someone's else's surrendered life but by surrendering our own life before the Lord. Therein lies the essence of compromise.

According to Galatians 2:20, "I am crucified with Christ; it is not I who live but Christ who lives in me and the life I now live, I live by faith. The Son loved me and delivered himself up for me."

A person crucified on a cross doesn't have a whole lot of dreams, doesn't have lots of things he's worried about. That's who we are in Christ. We live by faith in the Son of God who loved us and delivered Himself up for us.

If this is true of us, then we should be easy to work with, willing to compromise.

This crucified life is not easy in marriage. It's about yielding because our marriage is a reflection of Christ. It's supernatural. We are following in the footsteps of the Master who bought us.

That's what John 12:26 says: "If anyone serves Me, he must follow me; where I am there my servant will also be. Anyone who serves me, the Father will honor him."

So when we give our life, what is the promise? We bring forth fruit. As we learn to follow Christ, we will be what? Honored by our Father.

The key to compromising is to develop an eternal perspective. How important will your argument be five years from now?

Compromise to Collaborate

In compromise, both parties win some things and both lose some things. It is an exercise that balances competing interests and a tool that develops cooperation.

Ultimately, you should both aim for a collaborative relationship. Your common activities, pursuits, shared living arrangements, etc. result from your collaboration. Both of your input bears equal weight, considers the other, builds on all the positive aspects of your contributions and creates an environment in which each of you thrives as a distinct, important individual who is totally supportive of the other.

Collaboration carries no sense of either partner having to give up anything for or feel subsumed or outshone by the other person. Instead, each individual makes choices with love, respect, and care for the other uppermost in the decisions. This wonderful journey can take years to perfect.

Compromise: Getting a Good Coach

The question always arises: "What happens when we can't agree? What do we do?"

Every marriage struggles at times. That's why I believe God raised up pastors and coaches who can help partners listen, communicate and resolve conflicts together.

Guys often say, "I don't want to go to a counselor. I'm embarrassed to tell someone else our problems." Or "I don't want to be told that I'm the one who's wrong." Have you ever felt this way?

In every sport, winners use winning coaches. The most important fix I know for a marriage, beyond a solid vertical walk with God, is investing in a mentor. I coach as a ministry, and I know that couples need to evaluate what's working when their marriage is thriving as well as when their marriage needs a 911 call.

Temporary Separation Leading to Compromise

When conflict over a disagreement continues, consider Jesus' guidance in Matthew 18:16 where He advises bringing in another person or two to help restore broken relationships.

Or see Paul's counsel in 1 Corinthians 7:1-11, in which he recommends separation for a short time while a couple prays and works through their issues toward compromise. Ultimately, seeking God's will results in His blessing.

God is able to move in your life when you're willing to back up and say, "Maybe I can compromise on this." That's the impact of grace — learning to deal with the trouble, because "it's not about 'me.'"

When you get to eternity, you'll remember with tears that you did what was right; you compromised in your marriage and left the responsibility with God.

Don't underestimate the importance of celebrating, respecting, loving, and prioritizing your spouse every day. Work together to make your marriage golden.

Prayer:

Father God, thank You for the blessing of Your presence, and for instruction on compromising and mapping our relationship to strengthen the basis of our marriage. Your principles are foundations to Your desires and the way You created our marriage to be. You train and teach us Your ways if we have willing hearts. Father, press it into our hearts, help us learn these skills. Give us willing hearts to be open to Your Spirit. Jesus, thank You for taking such good care of us. We're in Your hands, Lord. Teach us to follow You as our Master. That was good enough for You; it's very good for us. In Your name we pray. Amen.

CHAPTER 16: REARVIEW MIRRORS — FORGIVING

We have to remember, when we forgive we're not doing it just for the other person, we're doing it for our own good. When we hold on to un-forgiveness and we live with grudges in our hearts, all we're doing is building walls of separation.

— Joel Osteen

Do not grieve the Holy Spirit of God, by whom you were sealed for the day of redemption. Let all bitterness and wrath and anger and clamor and slander be put away from you, along with all malice. Be kind to one another, tender-hearted, forgiving each other, just as God in Christ also has forgiven you."

— Ephesians 4:30-32

AS WE come to the final chapter of *Marriage Made Simple*, I want to highlight a crucial skill I've learned from my life experience — forgiveness.

Sharing this with you, my reader, comes not from my academic study but from hard lessons learned, sometimes on skinned knees. Whether by my own stupidity, ignorance and foolishness or by being pushed down, I've frequently found myself before the headstones of damaged dreams, the graves of lost hope. Things didn't go as I'd thought or planned they would. People didn't do what I expected or what they said they would. Time and again, dead visions needed to be left behind. Life taught me I could not scan the horizons of God's future by digging in the graveyard of the past. I had to learn (and continue to learn) to forgive.

God is always faithful. While I may find myself lonely, I am never alone. He never abandons me, never forsakes me.

We don't drive in an empty-minded state, staring at the rearview mirror. We drive in anticipation of getting to a destination. We have an expectancy, a hope of arrival. But those who cannot forgive cannot look forward. They drive looking to the rear, finding their identity in their woundedness rather than in the hope of what is to come.

A rearview mirror focuses on what is behind us, what has happened to us and what we have done to ourselves. It's always in the past tense. Those who drive by rearview mirror are always looking back, bringing up the past, unable to "get over it" or "leave it behind." None of us would ride in a car driven by someone who continually stares into the rearview mirror instead of watching the road ahead. Yet we frequently try to navigate life by focusing on the past.

Let's look at the serious impact of not forgiving, the cycle of resentment, the meaning of forgiveness, and the damaging effects of unforgiveness. Then we'll look at some practical ways to forgive.

The Impact of Not Forgiving

The impact of not forgiving has been studied for years. Some estimate about 75 percent of mental health issues are directly related to the inability to forgive. Stop and think about this: Three out of four mental health issues trace back to the inability to forgive.

- A study at the University of Tennessee in Knoxville, conducted by Kathleen Lawler, a professor of psychology, found a direct link between forgiveness and physical well-being. She found that people who had forgiven their betrayer had decreased blood pressure, muscle tension, and heart rates when compared to those who had not. The forgivers also reported less stress in their lives and fewer physical symptoms of illness. Dr. Lawler, surprised at the results, said, "These effects were so strong and so robust. I did not expect it would be such a clear mapping of the whole body response."[90]

- At Stanford University, Frederick Luskin, a senior fellow at the Center on Conflict and Negotiation is quoted as saying, "All forgiveness studies have shown positive outcomes. People who went through our forgiveness training had lower

---

[90] Karen Rowinsky, "Forgiveness is good for the heart and soul," http:// www.cmu.edu/CSR/case_studies/forgiveness.html.

levels of anger, hurt, stress, and reported better physical health."[91]

• In Harvard Medical Studies on incest survivors, severely depressed, schizophrenic personalities showed remarkable improvement after forgiveness training.

• Recent studies on sex offenders who could comprehend the impact of their actions on others showed they were significantly changed after they spent a year in forgiveness training.

• Herbert Benson, the president of Harvard's Mind and Body Medical Institute states, "Hatred is a banquet until you recognize you are the main course. Forgiveness reduces anger and stress ... and 60 to 90 percent of all the business that comes to physicians is stress-related."

THE PROBLEM IS NOT WHAT YOU'RE EATING;
THE PROBLEM IS WHAT'S EATING YOU.

Dealing with hatred, bitterness, resentment and unforgiveness reduces anger and stress, a huge component in our physical health. Literally, not forgiving can eat you alive. As numerous health experts from dietitians to psychologists have noted, "When dealing with unforgiveness, the problem is not what you're eating; the problem is what's eating you."

Unforgiving attitudes deeply affect marriages. Unforgiveness can be a poison that affects what we say and do. We think about it, rehearse it over and over, get upset and curse it, or we nurse it by feeling sorry for ourselves. I've heard it said that unforgiveness is like trying to get revenge on someone by drinking poison and waiting for the other person to die.

---

[91] ibid.

Understanding the Cycle of Resentment

Unforgiveness creates an environment in which a cycle of resentment builds. When an initial offense occurs, the offended party tends to excuse it at first. Their trust and commitment extend additional chances toward the offending party. But with repeated offenses, a sense of hurt forms. This is followed by loss of trust and hope. Anger then becomes a beachhead, and the enemy of Christ, Satan, begins suggesting thoughts to the injured spirit. As resentment mounts, the hurt person starts reacting, rejecting the offender by walking away. The hurt, resentful person reinforces rejection by talking to friends and retaliates in other areas. Anger builds when offenses and hurts unresolved on a daily basis morph into resentment.

Remember the dam from chapter 13? The river flows downstream into the reservoir, which gets higher and deeper. Pressure builds and gets stronger. Resentment holds that dam erect. If you don't deal with it ... then BAM! Here comes the BLOW OUT!

"I said this; she said that; I said this; she said that." That's the cycle of resentment. But forgiveness will wipe the slate clean and stop the cycle. Here's the key: Begin each and every day of your life with prayer, asking God for forgiveness both for yourself and to extend to others.

When you don't forgive others, resentment — like a cat with a dead mouse — drags the negatives into your marriage. Picture that cat dragging in Dr. Gottman's four horsemen of criticism, contempt, stonewalling and defensiveness. Resentment drops them enticingly at your feet.

If I'm struggling with unforgiveness, my wife may approach me with a simple request and I'll turn around, irritated or angry with her. "What?"

I've let resentment build and the cycle continues between us. I've left the door open to allow the enemy of our souls to influence me with the power to injure again.

I believe that unforgiveness is a demonic stronghold. When we allow its presence in our life, we offer Satan a beachhead. Like an army invading our marriage by sea, Satan and his forces land on the shifting sands of our relationship and begin building a fortress from which they can send out forays to "steal, kill and destroy"[92] our marriage.

Matthew 6:12-15 says:

> *Forgive us our debts, as we also have forgiven our debtors. And do not lead us into temptation, but deliver us from evil. For Yours is the kingdom and the power and the glory forever. For if you forgive others for their transgressions, your heavenly Father will also forgive you. But if you do not forgive others, then your Father will not forgive your transgressions.*

STOP! Jesus warns us here to deal with unforgiveness before resentment gets out of control. If we don't, we give the offender the power to injure us, and all our resentment doesn't affect him or her one bit.

"Do not grieve the Holy Spirit of God, by whom you were sealed for the day of redemption" (Ephesians 4:30).

> ## FORGIVE EACH OTHER, JUST AS GOD IN CHRIST HAS FORGIVEN YOU.

Unforgiveness Grieves God's Spirit

In Ephesians 4:30, the Apostle Paul used "the day of redemption" as a reminder that we are to forgive because we were first forgiven. Most unforgiveness stems from not understanding our own need of forgiveness.

In essence, when we do not or cannot or choose not to forgive, we are saying that each warm drop of divine blood shed on our behalf is not sufficient to cover the sin of another. With this belief, we diminish the value of Christ's death.

Forgiveness Defined

The spirit of forgiveness is described in the Greek word APHIMEI. It means "to let go of one's power, to free, to pardon, to cut someone

---

[92] John 10:10.

loose." When you forgive someone, you let go of your power to hold something against them. You release your hold on them. You set them free, pardon them, and cut them loose, even when you've been deeply hurt and the thought of setting the offender free is like acid on your heart. Because you participate in Christ's forgiveness, the fact is, Christ says His blood is sufficient, and the offender is also set free.

Additionally, to not forgive the one who hurt you is even more harmful to you, because the word translated "not forgive" means to be bound to or roped to the back of another. Through unforgiveness, you bind yourself to that which you hate the most. Biblically, you're called to extend forgiveness to those who hurt you because God has extended forgiveness to you. "We love, because He first loved us."[93]

Your basis for forgiveness has nothing to do with the other person and everything to do with what you've received. You cannot give away what you don't own.

Ephesians 4:31-32 tells us to put away bitterness, wrath, anger, clamor, slander, and all malice. We're called to be kind to one another, tenderhearted, forgiving each other, just as we've been forgiven by God in Christ. The value of the forgiveness we extend to others comes from what we received in Christ when He died on the cross.

I've come to understand that when I refuse to forgive someone, I am saying the value of Christ's sacrifice is insufficient. Who am I to devalue Christ's atoning death and say it is not sufficient to forgive me or anyone else? In Colossians 3:13-14 Paul presents this idea:

> So as those who have been chosen of God, holy and beloved, put on a heart of compassion, kindness, humility, gentleness and patience, bearing with one another and forgiving each other, whoever has a complaint against anyone; just as the Lord forgave you, so also should you. Beyond all these things put on love which is the perfect bond of unity.

Forgiving is not a suggestion; it is a command from God. Forgiving someone doesn't mean you deny what they did and excuse it or let someone off free. It's not minimizing; it's not justifying; it's not approving or rationalizing or pretending it didn't happen.

---

[93] 1 John 4:19.

Forgiveness is not a one-time event. It's not easy and it's never taken lightly. It's not a feeling — "I'll forgive them when I feel like it." Forgiveness is a choice. You can't push it, you can't force it, and you can't fake it.

In counseling, I tell my clients who are hurting and in bondage to resentment, "You must understand the value of forgiveness. And you make the decision to forgive. So let's not paint clouds on the prison wall. Call it what it is: You're in prison. When you're ready to get out, you will. It's not about someone else."

For me, forgiving **was** all about **someone else**. I needed to help them see they should ask for my forgiveness. Then I learned, **No, it's not about someone else; it's about my freedom.** That was a lightbulb moment.

Some people think that the person who's forgiven them now should trust them. But forgiveness and trust are separate processes. Trust is earned over time; the wound still needs to heal.

Forgiving is a **legal decision** that I make with God: "I'm not going to be the judge, jury and jailer here. I am trusting this to you." I am not going to seek my own revenge. I'm not going to hold that person accountable. I'm not going to be their police force, and I'm not going to drive by their house and throw rotten eggs at the window.

If I were a juror, I would yell, "Guilty!" If I were a judge, I'd decide what the appropriate sentence is — "Terminate him!" If I were a jailer, I'd use every opportunity to keep them in prison, "Make them pay every last cent."

But God is the Judge, not me. When I forgive, I choose to agree with God and say the blood of Christ is enough. Ultimately, when one person injures another, the crime is actually against God. And when Christ died on the cross, He served the perpetrator's sentence, whether years or life in prison or death.

When I understood from Scripture that Christ's sacrifice is sufficient for not only my sins but also for those who sin against me, it became so much easier for me to forgive.

Jesus had a conversation with Peter that's recorded in Matthew 18: 21-22:

> *Then Peter came and said to Him, "Lord, how often shall my brother sin against me and I forgive him? Up to seven times?"*
>
> *Jesus said to him, "I do not say to you, up to seven times, but up to seventy times seven."*

We should choose to forgive more than once or seventy times because Jesus has forgiven us far greater. We may not always feel like forgiving, but we need to make a choice — the blood of Christ is sufficient for us. It's not about our feelings; it's about faith in the Lord and His sovereignty.

We choose to pray for and love our enemy as we are commanded in Matthew 5:44. We humbly go before our Father and approach the throne of grace, asking Jesus, "How do You have mercy and compassion on me?" We then petition our case to God pouring out every act of pain and then we choose to leave space for His sovereignty:

> "Please forgive this person, Father, for they didn't know what they were doing when they sinned and caused me pain, just as I didn't know the agony I brought on You when You were hanging on the cross for my sins."

Now we can leave the pain behind and permit God to heal the wound stained deep in our heart.

How to Forgive

- **Don't Nurse It.** When we nurse an injury, we feel sorry for our self and go through the painful experience again and again. "Poor me. That was so wrong. They were so hurtful. How could they do something like that? That's so unfair. I can't believe it. I'm so sad." We continue to repeat self-pity messages and say we forgive the person, but inwardly hope God will judge and punish him. Really? God's forgiveness always restores.

- **Don't Curse It.** Even if we never curse or swear public, we all have those conversations in the shower or car when that person's face comes to mind. When we fully forgive the person, our anger will be replaced with pity for that person, leading us into praying for them and learning to love them.

- **Don't Rehearse It.** When we've been hurt, the act and pain keep going through our mind. It drives us nuts, like a song that gets stuck in our brain for a week; we sing the same song over and over again. We can't get it off our mind. We have trouble accepting God's love and forgiveness, so we stand in judgment of others.

- **Immerse in the Blood of Christ.** The magical part is that every day is new and amazing. Lamentations 3: 22-23 says, "The Lord's loving kindnesses indeed never cease, for His compassions never fail. They are new every morning; great is Your faithfulness." Go to His Word daily to immerse yourself in His mercy. He gives us freedom to walk with Him in the new day, which He gives us so we can rejoice.

God threw our sins into the depths of the sea and remembers them no more. That's His promise to us in Hebrews 8:12.

Forgiveness means when I forgive you, the deal is between you and God now. I'm not going to remember that sin against you when we're talking. I'm not going to be bitter in our conversations. If there is a consequence, that's between you and God. I won't rejoice in it, but I will pray for God's mercy on you.

> ## TO FORGIVE IS TO PRACTICE GRACE.
>
> ## THE ACT OF SEEKING SOMEONE'S BEST INTEREST IS NOT DEPENDENT ON THE ACTIONS OF THE ONE LOVED,
>
> ## BUT ON THE CHARACTER OF THE ONE LOVING.

Practical Application

Here's an excellent exercise that many counselors, including myself, use to help clients walk through the process of forgiving:

- Specifically list hurts or frustrations you feel.
- Go through the list and pray to forgive each one.
- Tear up your list just as God has torn up His.
- Destroy the list so you do not keep a record of wrongs.
- Ask others to list things you need to ask forgiveness for.

This is tough stuff, but it's biblical — read Matthew 5:24. You can go through the motions, but look at your heart and acknowledge the things that you are doing, the things that you're holding captive as resentment. Acknowledging your source of resentment is important for understanding the problem and releasing the other person. You may discover the resentment is foolish and Satan's way of triggering wounded memories.

Memory Triggers

An overactive conscience may continue to reopen a wound which God wants to heal. One day, one moment when you least expect it, someone makes a statement, you watch a movie, and some association will trigger that offensive memory and bring on the pain and resentment, and the cycle will begin again. You begin to question and doubt yourself — "Maybe I didn't forgive, or maybe I wasn't punished for this sin; maybe God is saying I still have consequences to pay!" "I can't shake the guilt and shame." "My road to forgiveness is obscured by condemnation." "This is the way I was brought up."

Identifying the foundation will aid you in your battle to victory over resentment, and understanding the root cause will help you identify when you are about to start the process of being offended again.

Demonic Stronghold

In Matthew 18:23-35, Jesus illustrates forgiveness with a story about a slave whose master forgave him a huge debt. Apparently the man had lost 10,000 talents. A "talent" was about 15 years' wages. Doing the math, we are talking 150,000 years to repay the debt.

This slave, though, didn't understand the master's generous, gracious heart. So he went out and beat on another slave who owed him one year's wages worth of debt. When the master learned what happened, he drove home his point:

> *Then summoning him, his lord said to him, "You wicked slave, I forgave you all that debt because you pleaded with me. Should you not also have had mercy on your fellow slave, in the same way that I had mercy on you?"*

> *And his lord, moved with anger, handed him over to the torturers until he should repay all that was owed him.*

> *My heavenly Father will also do the same to you, if each of you does not forgive his brother from your heart."*[94]

Without equivocation, I believe this passage warns that when we don't forgive, we will reap serious long-term consequences. Not only do we allow Satan a beachhead and a stronghold, but we also open ourselves to demonic tormentors (sent by God) until we figure out how to forgive.

> ## FORGIVING IS NOT SOME GAME. IT HAS SERIOUS, PROFOUND, LIFELONG CONSEQUENCES.

Forgiving Yourself

We often focus on the consequences of our past mistakes that keep us in bondage, rather than on God's grace that gives us freedom. The power of God's love overpowers any of our guilt, and He will restore our fellowship with Him. In Psalm 51:4, David cries out to the Lord in repentance, "Against You, You only, I have sinned and done what is evil in

---

[94] *New American Standard Bible*: 1995 update. (1995). (Mt 18:32–35). LaHabra, CA: The Lockman Foundation.

Your sight, so that You are justified when You speak and blameless when You judge."

Yes, David made mistakes, but he had a heart for God, and God knew his heart. If you love God and want to do what is right, He already knows your heart, and you're not surprising Him when you mess up. He still loves you. Ask for forgiveness; He'll throw your sins into the fire and move on. Remember to:

- Receive God's forgiveness (2 Corinthians 5:21)
- Love yourself as God loves you (John 13:34)
- Realize that God knows you and doesn't expect you to be perfect (Psalm 139)

Once you can comprehend His forgiveness for you, you can put on the armor of God (Ephesians 6:10-18). It will help you recognize a coming offense and forgive before you are offended. Your heart will be right with God and you will understand it's not about you; it's about Christ's forgiveness in you.

A counseling client shared with me a story that blew open the doors of forgiveness for her. As they concluded a class she had taken on forgiveness, each participant received a red paper heart on which they were instructed to write all they needed to ask forgiveness for. After completing their lists, they left the classroom to sit in the church sanctuary and pray about the hurt for the things they did and had failed to do. Next they would burn those hearts in an incinerator.

After completing her list, this person had folded her heart and brought it with her to the sanctuary. As she prayed, she unfolded the heart to make sure she didn't leave anything out of her prayer.

Because she happened to sit in direct sunlight, her body cast a shadow on the paper heart she held in front of her. She couldn't see anything she'd written on her heart. It appeared blank.

She felt an inner sense of peace that surpassed all understanding and heard Jesus say, "This is how I see you after you ask Me for forgiveness."

From that point on, she has never again questioned God's forgiveness.

Grace Impact

Father God wants you to incorporate His Shepherd's heart into your marriage and relationships. Your heart has to be right with God first.

Lamentations 3:22-23 says, "The Lord's loving kindness indeed never ceases, for His compassions never fail. They are new every morning; great is Your faithfulness."

To forgive is to practice grace, the act of seeking someone's best interest not dependent on the actions of the one loved, but on the character of the one loving.

Do you know that in the Old Testament, God commanded the Jewish people to yearly observe a holy day called the Day of Atonement (meaning "the day of forgiveness")? That's what grace is really all about. We start with grace and we end with grace. That's the Shepherd's Heart.

A Final Word

Even in the economy of God's love and sovereignty, you may think you can't forgive someone for the pain of your injury. You may think nothing and no one could ever take that scar away. And you're absolutely right, because ONLY our Father God's sovereign love can do this. He will heal and transform your heart if you ask for your heart to not be hardened.

Pray and ask Him to give you a heart of grace. He already has answered that prayer.

> ## GOD **NEVER** WASTES ONE OF OUR TEARS. NOT ONE.

A leader in our local ministry shared her personal story about the abuse she endured as a child and her painful years to recovery. She needed to forgive her abuser, her mother who didn't believe her, and God for allowing the abuse to happen. She says, "I learned to give thanks for what happened to me because now I can sit with others and understand their suffering."

Some of us may think we can never say that, but she did. She had me riveted on her grace-filled heart. I was blown away.

And then her husband turned and said something even more riveting: "It's about sovereignty."

Prayer:

Father God, thank You for teaching us about forgiveness in our marriage and relationships. Thank You that love is kind and love is patient, because it's what we receive from You. We begin with Your forgiveness and end with Your forgiveness. This is exactly the kind of people You call us to be. Lord, it's really all about Your Spirit. Jesus, may our walk glorify and honor You. We commit our marriage to you. Please help us keep it as simple as you created our love to be. In Your precious name, Jesus, we pray. Amen.

APPENDIX I: CHOOSING A GOOD COUNSELOR

PEOPLE seeking counsel have varied options in choosing a counselor or coach — Christian or secular, biblical or psychological. Many counselors and coaches bring health and wholeness through sound practices and wisdom. Others can do their clients much damage. It's a "buyer beware" market. Even a championship NFL coach lacks the qualifications to lead a women's Olympic gymnastics team to victory. Following that line of reasoning, you need wisdom in choosing a marriage counselor.

People need to interview prospective counselors and ask the following questions:

1. "What training have you had?" Get an idea of what they have done to learn, train, and improve themselves.

2. "What strategy will you use?" Determine if they even have a strategy, a plan, a format they follow. This tells you they are prepared.

3. "What courses have you taught?" Many counselors teach seminars. This is a good way to determine areas of competency.

4. "What biblical principles will you hold to?"

5. "What is your view on accountability?"

6. "What is your success rate with couples?" Ask others about their experience with a certain counselor. Get recommendations.

7. "Do you have confidence in yourself, your future and God's Spirit?"

8. "What do you do on a daily basis to walk with God?"

The first questions bear great weight if you are a Christian and believe in biblical guidance. The last question is the deal breaker. If a counselor doesn't have a walk with God then what and how will they teach you?

APPENDIX II: 1 CORINTHIANS 13

If I speak with the tongues of men and of angels, but do not have love, I have become a noisy gong or a clanging cymbal. If I have the gift of prophecy, and know all mysteries and all knowledge; and if I have all faith, so as to remove mountains, but do not have love, I am nothing. And if I give all my possessions to feed the poor, and if I surrender my body to be burned, but do not have love, it profits me nothing.

Love is patient, love is kind and is not jealous; love does not brag and is not arrogant, does not act unbecomingly; it does not seek its own, is not provoked, does not take into account a wrong suffered, does not rejoice in unrighteousness, but rejoices with the truth; bears all things, believes all things, hopes all things, endures all things.

Love never fails; but if there are gifts of prophecy, they will be done away; if there are tongues, they will cease; if there is knowledge, it will be done away. For we know in part and we prophesy in part; but when the perfect comes, the partial will be done away. When I was a child, I used to speak like a child, think like a child, reason like a child; when I became a man, I did away with childish things. For now we see in a mirror dimly, but then face to face; now I know in part, but then I will know fully just as I also have been fully known. But now faith, hope, love, abide these three; but the greatest of these is love."[95]

---

[95] *New American Standard Bible*: 1995 update. (1995), (1 Corinthians 13). La-Habra, CA: The Lockman Foundation.

APPENDIX III: HEARING THE VOICE OF GOD

Adapted from *4 Keys to Hearing God's Voice*
by Mark and Patti Virkler

CHRISTIANITY is unique among religions, alone offering a personal relationship with the Creator beginning here and now, and lasting throughout eternity. Jesus declared, "This is eternal life — that they may know God" (John 17:2). Unfortunately, many in the Church miss the great blessing of fellowship with our Lord, having lost the ability to recognize His voice within them. Despite the promise that "My sheep hear My voice," too many believers are starved for that intimate relationship that alone can satisfy the desire of their hearts.

I was one of those sheep who was deaf to his Shepherd until the Lord revealed four very simple keys (found in Habakkuk 2:1-2) that unlocked the treasure of His voice.

Key #1 God's voice in your heart often sounds like a flow of spontaneous thoughts.

Habakkuk knew the sound of God speaking to him (Habakkuk 2:2). Elijah described it as a still, small voice (I Kings 19:12). I had always listened for an inner audible voice, and God does speak that way at times. However, I have found that usually, God's voice comes as spontaneous thoughts, visions, feelings, or impressions.

For example, haven't you been driving down the road and had a thought come to you to pray for a certain person? Didn't you believe it was God telling you to pray? What did God's voice sound like? Was it an audible voice, or was it a spontaneous thought that lit upon your mind?

Experience indicates that we perceive spirit-level communication as spontaneous thoughts, impressions and visions, and Scripture confirms this in many ways. For example, one definition of PAGA, a Hebrew word for intercession, is "a chance encounter or an accidental intersecting." When God lays people on our hearts, He does it through PAGA, a chance-encounter thought "accidentally" intersecting our minds.

Therefore, when you want to hear from God, tune to chance-encounter or spontaneous thoughts.

Key #2 Become still so you can sense God's flow of thoughts and emotions within.

Habakkuk said, "I will stand on my guard post ..." (Habakkuk 2:1). Habakkuk knew that to hear God's quiet, inner, spontaneous thoughts, he had to first go to a quiet place and still his own thoughts and emotions. Psalm 46:10 encourages us to be still, and know that He is God. There is a deep inner knowing (spontaneous flow) in our spirits that each of us can experience when we quiet our flesh and our minds. If we are not still, we will sense only our own thoughts.

Loving God through a quiet worship song is one very effective way to become still. (Note 2 Kings 3:15.) After I worship and become silent within, I open myself for that spontaneous flow. If thoughts come of things I have forgotten to do, I write them down and dismiss them. If thoughts of guilt or unworthiness come, I repent thoroughly, receive the washing of the blood of the Lamb, putting on His robe of righteousness, seeing myself spotless before God (Isaiah 61:10; Colossians 1:22).

To receive the pure Word of God, it is very important that my heart be properly focused as I become still because my focus is the source of the intuitive flow. If I fix my eyes upon Jesus, the intuitive flow comes from Jesus. But if I fix my gaze upon some desire of my heart, the intuitive flow comes out of that desire. To have a pure flow I must become still and carefully fix my eyes upon Jesus. Again, quietly worshiping the King, and receiving out of the stillness that follows quite easily accomplishes this.

Fix your gaze upon Jesus (Hebrews 12:2), becoming quiet in His Presence and sharing with Him what is on your heart. Spontaneous thoughts will begin to flow from the throne of God to you, and you will actually be conversing with the King of Kings!

Key #3 As you pray, fix the eyes of your heart upon Jesus, seeing in the Spirit the dreams and visions of Almighty God.

Habakkuk said, "I will keep watch to see," and God said, "Record the vision" (Habakkuk 2:1-2). Habakkuk was actually looking for vision as he prayed. He opened the eyes of his heart, and looked into the spirit world to see what God wanted to show him. This is an intriguing idea.

God has always spoken through dreams and visions, and He specifically said that they would come to those upon whom the Holy Spirit is poured out (Acts 2:1-4, 17).

I had never thought of opening the eyes of my heart and looking for vision. However, I have come to believe that this is exactly what God wants me to do. He gave me eyes in my heart to see in the spirit the vision and movement of Almighty God. There is an active spirit world all around us, full of angels, demons, the Holy Spirit, the omnipresent Father, and His omnipresent Son, Jesus. The only reasons for me not to see this reality are unbelief or lack of knowledge.

In order to see, we must look. Daniel saw a vision in his mind and said, "I was looking ... I kept looking ... I kept looking" (Daniel 7:2, 9, 13). As I pray, I look for Jesus, and I watch as He speaks to me, doing and saying the things that are on His heart. Many Christians will find that if they will only look, they will see, in the same way they receive spontaneous thoughts. Jesus is Emmanuel, God with us (Matthew 1:23). It is as simple as that. You can see Christ present with you because Christ is present with you. In fact, the vision may come so easily that you will be tempted to reject it, thinking that it is just you. But if you persist in recording these visions, your doubt will soon be overcome by faith as you recognize that the content of them could only be birthed in Almighty God.

Jesus demonstrated the ability of living out of constant contact with God, declaring that He did nothing on His own initiative, but only what He saw the Father doing, and heard the Father saying (John 5:19, 20, 30). What an incredible way to live!

Is it possible for you to live out of divine initiative as Jesus did? Yes! Fix your eyes upon Jesus. The veil has been torn, giving access into the immediate Presence of God, and He calls you to draw near (Luke 23:45; Hebrews 10:19-22). "I pray that the eyes of your heart will be enlightened...."

Key #4 Journaling, the writing out of your prayers and God's answers, brings great freedom in hearing God's voice.

God told Habakkuk to record the vision (Habakkuk 2:2). This was not an isolated command. The Scriptures record many examples of individuals' prayers and God's replies (e.g. the Psalms, many of the prophets, Revelation).

I call the process "two-way journaling," and I have found it to be a fabulous catalyst for clearly discerning God's inner, spontaneous flow, because as I journal I am able to write in faith for long periods of time, simply believing it is God. I know that what I believe I have received from God must be tested. However, testing involves doubt, and doubt blocks divine communication, so I do not want to test while I am trying to receive. With journaling, I can receive in faith, knowing that when the flow has ended I can test and examine it carefully, making sure that it lines up with Scripture.

You will be amazed when you journal. Doubt may hinder you at first, but throw it off, reminding yourself that it is a Biblical concept, and that God is present, speaking to His children. Relax. When we cease our labors and enter His rest, God is free to flow (Hebrews 4:10). Sit back comfortably, take out your pen and paper, smile, and turn your attention toward the Lord in praise and worship, seeking His face. After you write your question to Him, become still, fixing your gaze on Jesus. You will suddenly have a very good thought. Don't doubt it; simply write it down. Later, as you read your journaling, you, too, will be blessed to discover that you are indeed dialoguing with God.

Some final notes: Knowing God through the Bible is a vital foundation to hearing His voice in your heart, so you must have a solid commitment to knowing and obeying the Scriptures. It is also very important for your growth and safety that you be related to solid, spiritual counselors. All major directional moves that come through journaling should be confirmed by your counselor before you act upon them.[96]

---

[96] For a complete teaching on this topic, order the book *4 Keys to Hearing God's Voice* at www.CWGministries.org or call 716-681-4896. An online catalog of 60 books by Mark & Patti Virkler as well as 100 college courses through external degree is available at www.cluonline.com.

APPENDIX IV: ADDITIONAL COUPLE(D) TALK

SINCE 2014, when *MMS* was first conceived and taught, many researchers have contributed to a greater understanding of relational brain circuits and human communication. Their results have quite honestly surprised me. Dr. Allen Store (the Einstein of brain research), Dr. Jim Friesen, Dr. Jim Wilder, and many others affirm the priority God's Word places on listening. According to their research, people can build stronger relational circuits with others by using certain specific methods.

These researchers have established the skills needed to build strong "Secure Attachment Relationships" (SAR) and have highlighted the impact of those relationships on **joy**. The five factors in a SAR are 1) Belonging, 2) Importance, 3) Value, 4) Appreciation, and 5) Protection/ Provision. These five needs should be included in any study of human relationships.

I believe that **joy** is the center of what Jesus came to give us. John 15:11 says, "These things I have spoken to you so that My **joy** may be in you, and that your **joy** may be made full." John 16:24 adds, "Until now you have asked for nothing in My name; ask and you will receive, so that your **joy** may be made full." And in John 17:13, Jesus declares to His Father, "But now I come to You; and these things I speak in the world so that they may have My **joy** made full in themselves." Jesus intended for us to have His **joy**.

Therefore, I have rewritten my ALPHA listening acronym to reflect these strategies.

A APPRECIATE rather than dismiss or take for granted.

L Lean in with KINDNESS rather than disparage.

P Participate with CURIOSITY rather than criticism.

H Hear for the HEART of the other, rather than excuse them.

A Affirm with ICE CREAM SANDWICH rather than discount.

ABOUT THE AUTHOR

DR. James G. Johnson is a licensed, ordained pastor of 39 years, a board-certified Christian counselor with American Association of Christian Counselors (AACC), and a certified master coach with International Christian Counseling Association (ICCA). He holds a Doctorate in Christian Counseling from Northwestern University and a Master of Divinity from Talbot School of Theology.

He holds a Ph.D. in Christian Counseling from Northwestern University, is finishing a second doctorate from Christian Leadership University, holds a Master of Divinity from Biola University, and a B.A. from University of Nebraska. He is a conference speaker, author, marriage consultant, mentor/coach and Christian counselor. Jim and Cheryl have four children and several grandchildren. They reside in Omaha, Nebraska.

Jim is the author of *Grace: Orphans No More* and *Marriage Made Simple*. Be on the lookout for his future projects: *Grace: From Orphan to Son, Marriage Made Sim-pl-er (From Tools to Skills), Couple(d) Talk,* and *The Mission-Driven Life*.

Marriage Made Simple is the overflow of a commitment Cheryl and Jim made to give back to the Christian Community. Rather than strive for an easy retirement, they decided to dedicate the rest of their lives to serving others in their faith through Strong Personal Identity and Healthy Marriages.

After experiencing his own pain and failures in life and marriage, Jim (or DrJ as he's known by many), poured all his attention into figuring out relationships. On a snow-packed road in 1996, he told God through many tears that he didn't understand relationships very well at all. He heard God distinctly say in that still, small voice, "Well, maybe we could build it My way." He looked at God (much like Helen Hunt in *As Good as it Gets*) and said, "Well ... okay."

Since then, as a recovering dysfunctional, obsessive-compulsive, type A perfectionist, Jim has pursued, read and studied every book he could find on a relationship as God's child (Identity) and on the priority of all human relationships (Marriage). Thousands of hours of research later, he remains current in "vertical" (with God) and "horizontal" (with others) relationships. He also studies the neurological social field called brain science that lies behind relational circuitry.

Jim's Marriage Statement of Beliefs:

* God-first hearts produce healthy marriages
* Less heavy content, presented with more frequency
* No-Bash Zone (man friendly)
* Value joy (interactive learning made interesting and fun)

Jim lives and teaches from four core values:

* God First
* Brutal Integrity
* Positive Gratitude Attitude
* Believe God — "He will make a way for you"

DrJ is a sought-after national counselor, mentor, author and speaker. He and Cheryl don't advertise because they work from their reputation by faith. He is the executive director of Keys4-Life Ministry, a faith-based, biblical, nonprofit Christian counseling and coaching service. They provide clinical Christian counseling through in-office appointments, phone, Google hangouts, and Skype.

Jim and Cheryl live by faith, supported by the donations of those who value what they are doing. If you would like to make a tax-deductible donation to their ministry, they appreciate your support in prayer and in finances. They may be contacted for your community or church group using the information below.

Dr. James Johnson, Ph.D.
Executive Director, Keys4-Life:
Faith-based Counseling and Coaching
Contact: james@Keys4.org
www.drjamesgjohnson.org/contact
Facebook: www.facebook.com/marrigemadesimple ("Like" us!)
Also on Twitter, LinkedIn, Instagram, Pinterest

CPSIA information can be obtained
at www.ICGtesting.com
Printed in the USA
BVOW08s1004040418
512448BV00004B/504/P